V&R unipress

Bonner Schriften zur Universitäts- und
Wissenschaftsgeschichte

Band 11

Herausgegeben von
Thomas Becker, Michael Rohrschneider, Mathias Schmoeckel,
Joachim Scholtyseck und Heinz Schott

Frederick Alexander Mann

*Life and Cases*

Manuscript of an Autobiography

Edited by
Wolfgang Ernst

With a preface by
Mathias Schmoeckel

V&R unipress

Bonn University Press

Bibliografische Information der Deutschen Nationalbibliothek
Die Deutsche Nationalbibliothek verzeichnet diese Publikation in der Deutschen
Nationalbibliografie; detaillierte bibliografische Daten sind im Internet über
https://dnb.de abrufbar.

**Veröffentlichungen der Bonn University Press
erscheinen bei V&R unipress.**

© 2021 V&R unipress, Theaterstraße 13, D-37073 Göttingen, ein Imprint der Brill-Gruppe
(Koninklijke Brill NV, Leiden, Niederlande; Brill USA Inc., Boston MA, USA; Brill Asia Pte Ltd,
Singapore; Brill Deutschland GmbH, Paderborn, Deutschland; Brill Österreich GmbH, Wien,
Österreich)
Koninklijke Brill NV umfasst die Imprints Brill, Brill Nijhoff, Brill Hotei, Brill Schöningh,
Brill Fink, Brill mentis, Vandenhoeck & Ruprecht, Böhlau, Verlag Antike und V&R unipress.
Alle Rechte vorbehalten. Das Werk und seine Teile sind urheberrechtlich geschützt.
Jede Verwertung in anderen als den gesetzlich zugelassenen Fällen bedarf der vorherigen
schriftlichen Einwilligung des Verlages.

Druck und Bindung: CPI books GmbH, Birkstraße 10, D-25917 Leck
Printed in the EU.

**Vandenhoeck & Ruprecht Verlage | www.vandenhoeck-ruprecht-verlage.com**

ISSN 2198-5383
ISBN 978-3-8471-1350-8

# Contents

Geleitwort . . . . . . . . . . . . . . . . . . . . . . . . . . . . . . . . 7

Editorial Remarks . . . . . . . . . . . . . . . . . . . . . . . . . . . 9

## F. A. Mann: Life and Cases

Introduction . . . . . . . . . . . . . . . . . . . . . . . . . . . . . . 13

## Part I: Life

Chapter 1 – Background . . . . . . . . . . . . . . . . . . . . . . . 19

Chapter 2 – My Father . . . . . . . . . . . . . . . . . . . . . . . . 23

Chapter 3 – Early Years . . . . . . . . . . . . . . . . . . . . . . . 29

Chapter 4 – University and After . . . . . . . . . . . . . . . . . 35

Chapter 5 – Martin Wolff . . . . . . . . . . . . . . . . . . . . . . 41

Chapter 6 – The End of an Era: Emigration . . . . . . . . . . . 45

Chapter 7 – The Beginning of a New Era . . . . . . . . . . . . 51

Chapter 8 – The War . . . . . . . . . . . . . . . . . . . . . . . . . 59

Chapter 9 – A Last beginning: Germany 1946 and After . . . . . . . . . 67

Chapter 10 – England 1946 and After . . . . . . . . . . . . . . . 77

## 6 Contents

Eleonore . . . . . . . . . . . . . . . . . . . . . . . . . . . . . . . . . . 93

## Part II: Cases

Chapter 11 – Expert . . . . . . . . . . . . . . . . . . . . . . . . . . . 101

Chapter 12 – Divorce . . . . . . . . . . . . . . . . . . . . . . . . . . 113

Chapter 13 – Advice and Negotiation . . . . . . . . . . . . . . . . . 119

Chapter 14 – War and Litigation . . . . . . . . . . . . . . . . . . . 127

Chapter 15 – Families . . . . . . . . . . . . . . . . . . . . . . . . . . 141

Chapter 16 – Arbitration and Litigation . . . . . . . . . . . . . . . 155

Chapter 17 – Passing-off . . . . . . . . . . . . . . . . . . . . . . . . 167

Chapter 18 – Commercial Cases . . . . . . . . . . . . . . . . . . . . 171

Chapter 19 – Conflicts about Conflicts of Law . . . . . . . . . . . . 183

Chapter 20 – International Advocay . . . . . . . . . . . . . . . . . . 201

## Part III: Paralegomena

Select Bibliography . . . . . . . . . . . . . . . . . . . . . . . . . . . 249

Mathias Schmoeckel

## Geleitwort

Frederick Alexander Mann war ein außergewöhnlicher Mensch und Gelehrter mit einem besonderen Lebenslauf längst vor der erzwungenen Emigration. Seine vorzügliche Erziehung und insbesondere die Kenntnis von Fremdsprachen schufen eine Weltläufigkeit, die ihn nach Genf und London führte, längst bevor er Berlin verlassen musste. Die perfekte Adaption einer anderen Nationalität mit ihrer ganz eigenen Art von Jurisprudenz war seine Leistung und nicht zuletzt auch das Ergebnis einer besonderen Ausbildung. Seine Leistung darf nicht dadurch relativiert werden, dass sein Schicksal ebenso wie das vieler anderer Zeitgenossen als das Erdulden eines Schicksals verstanden wird. Letztlich gab die Emigration Mann nur die Chance, sich zu einem einzigartigen Gelehrten zu entwickeln.

Es war eine der Leistungen der Bonner Fakultät nach dem Zweiten Weltkrieg, die verlorenen Verbindungen zu den Emigranten wieder zu suchen. Persönliche Verbundenheit früherer Kollegen waren die Grundlage, um die Gräben der fürchterlichen Zeit zu überbrücken. Vor allem Werner Flume, aber auch andere Kollegen, wirkten hier, um die wissenschaftlichen Kontakte zu den emigrierten Kollegen wiederherzustellen und durch Einladungen und Rufe Wiedergutmachung zu leisten. So selbstverständlich das heute erscheinen mag, so ungewöhnlich war dies zu seiner Zeit.

Das war auf der Seite von Bonn kein Altruismus, sondern einerseits Aufarbeiten einer allgemeinen Schuld, andererseits auch eine ungemeine Bereicherung für die Bonner Studierenden. Bis zum heutigen Zeitpunkt bekommen deutsche Studierende – trotz aller Anerkennung der deutschen Ausbildung im Allgemeinen – zu wenig Kenntnis von der internationalen Dimension der Rechtswissenschaft. Vor allem die andere Herangehensweise der englischen Jurisprudenz, die ungeheure Erfahrung in der praktischen Betreuung großer Wirtschaftssachen und der Einblick in Materien, die in Deutschland selten behandelt werden, mussten für die Bonner Hörer des Honorarprofessors Mann den Einblick in eine fremde, aber aufregende Welt darstellen. Die Bereicherung, die von Max Grünhut, Frederick Alexander Mann, Stephan Kuttner u. a. in der Bonner

Lehre der Nachkriegsjahrzehnte geleistet wurde, bedeutete eine Internationalisierung des Studiums, wie dies weder vor- noch nachher in Bonn erreicht wurde. Immer wieder wird deutlich, wie sehr auch Mann seine Studenten in dieser Internationalität und seinem Verständnis für Wirtschaft und juristische Argumentation beeindruckt haben muss.

Die kargen Andeutungen der bisherigen Literatur lassen die Vielseitigkeit seiner Lebensbedingungen und die Fülle seiner Fähigkeiten und Erfahrungen kaum erahnen. Umso wichtiger ist es, nun von ihm selbst so viel mehr aus seinem Leben zu erfahren. Es ist das Verdienst von Wolfgang Ernst, diese wichtige Quelle entdeckt und herausgegeben zu haben. Es ist gut, dass die Universität Bonn und ihr juristischer Fachbereich wieder an die Tradition anknüpfen und mitwirken, an das Unrecht der Vertreibung und die Bedeutung der Emigranten für die Ausbildung in Bonn zu erinnern. Gleichzeitig können wir immer noch so vieles von diesen vorbildlichen Gelehrten lernen.

Bonn, im April 2021

Wolfgang Ernst

## Editorial Remarks

> I write [an autobiography], because I am persuaded that it
> is my duty to tell the story of a world that has disappeared,
> but should not be forgotten, – the story of a highly cultured
> German Jewish bourgeois milieu which perished in Auschwitz,
> though my nearest and dearest succeeded in escaping.
> The history of the rise and fall of that social class merits to
> be preserved, but stands in danger of falling into oblivion
> on account of the lack of specific material, – no great novel
> describing its drama and tragedy has yet been written.
> F. A. Mann

When F. A. Mann died in 1991, he had been working on an autobiography for a couple of years. Such progress had been made with the text that he sent out a draft to a number of friends, asking for comments and criticism. This was when I first got to read the text, given to me by the closest of his German friends, Werner Flume (1908–2009). Mann had already made plans to also produce a German version since he hoped for a wide readership in Germany.

Although no great input would have been needed to get the manuscript ready for the press, Mann's family as well as his executor were reluctant to go ahead with a publication. This may have been for the best. If colleagues, friends, and family would have gotten their hands at the text, in all likelihood they would have taken off the edge here and there. Mann was highly judgmental and did not mince his words, and these qualities are mirrored in his text, not to speak of sensitive details of family life which are set out with great candour. The publisher's copy-editor might only have polished and mellowed the text further.

This volume is not the book which F. A. Mann might have published had he continued to finalise his text and guide it through the press. Who knows what changes he would have made, what additions he might have put in? This edition does not try to finish the work which Mann had to leave unfinished. It is but an edition of a typescript from his estate.

In the past thirty years, copies of the manuscript have been in circulation, and scholars working on Mann's life already have made use of it frequently, provided they could get hold of one of the copies. It seems proper that the manuscript becomes available unrestrictedly for the legal community at large, and historians of the 20th century. Writers of legal history for the second half of the 20th century will not want to miss this text, and practicing lawyers today may be interested to learn how some of Mann's contributions have left their mark on contemporary laws.

This book is the edition of a historical document from the early 1990s. It consists of 205 neatly typed and numbered pages. The original page numbers are retained here in [] brackets. The same signs are used for a few editorial remarks. There are minor gaps that Mann had obviously intended to fill in later, such as dates of birth or references to cases. No effort has been made to amend the manuscript in such instances. Mann was not a native speaker of English and, on occasion, the linguistically sensitive reader may detect constructions and phrases betraying Mann's mother tongue. Apart from obvious typos and lacking interpunctuation, which were remedied here without editorial notice, all has been left as it came from Mann's pen. The titles and functions of the *dramatis personae* have not been updated.

The copies of the original typoscript which were used for this edition, together with pertinent correspondence and earlier drafts, will go to the Humboldt University, Berlin, to supplement the ample archival material on F.A. Mann which is inventoried and digitised by a team led by Prof. Gerhard Dannemann, who is also in a position to fruitfully involve the University's Centre for British Studies. The masterfully curated archive has become the basis for ongoing research projects dealing with Mann's role in 20th-century legal developments, for which substantial financial support was provided by the German Research Foundation, the *Deutsche Forschungsgesellschaft (DFG)*.

There is no reason to prolong these introductory remarks with substantive comments on Mann's life or the content of the autobiography. The manuscript speaks for itself. The reader will also learn about Mann's relationship with the Law Department of the University of Bonn, which is the reason this publication comes out in the series of the *Bonner Schriften zur Universitäts- und Wissenschaftsgeschichte.*

Many contributions made it possible for this edition to materialize. This is the rollcall for sincere thanks: first and foremost to Anne Kriken Mann, who as the widow of F. A. Mann's late son David holds the copyright and has also covered the print costs; further, to the editors of the *Bonner Schriften zur Universitäts- und Wissenschaftsgeschichte*, among them Mathias Schmoeckel as the former Dean of the Faculty of Law and Political Science of the University of Bonn, who contributed the preface; and last but not least to Stephen Ryan and Angelika Okotokro, both assisting Prof. Reinhard Zimmermann at the Max Planck Institute for Comparative and International Private Law (Hamburg), for the careful production of a processable document.

Oxford, April 2021

**F. A. Mann: Life and Cases**

# Introduction

Why do I write an autobiography?

A lifetime has been devoted to writing which studiously avoided the first person, as academic usage requires. Writing about myself deviates from long established habit and, therefore, characterizes the oddity of the undertaking upon which I am about to embark.

There are so many reasons why I should desist. The art of writing will not pervade these pages; the lawyer's dryness will not fail to determine the style and to remove all literary merit. The story I have to tell lacks that excitement, that unusual complexion, those heights of greatness or adventure, those features of individuality, that general interest which alone justify authors to bore the public with their own story. And above all, the genuine humility, the diffidence, the scepticism with which, as my readers must believe me, I regard my own life, should preclude an enterprise that must appear presumptuous and indicative of a vanity such as deserves contempt.

Why, then, do I write an autobiography?

I write, because I am persuaded that it is my duty to tell the story of a world that has disappeared, but should not be forgotten, – the story of a highly cultured German Jewish bourgeois milieu which perished in Auschwitz, though my nearest and dearest succeeded in escaping. The history of the rise and fall of that social class merits to be preserved, but stands in danger of falling into oblivion on account of the lack of specific material, – no great novel describing its drama and tragedy has yet been written.

I write, because the survival of that social group in the countries of refuge, particularly in England is equally lacking in illustration. The German Jewish immigration of the 1930's is a phenomenon which in many fields has led to remarkable achievements. Mine has not been remarkable, is somewhere in the middle, it is average and, therefore, less untypical than he work of many famous men, yet more vivid than that of the majority. Hence it is a contribution to a history which, again, has not yet been written.

I write, because I have been fortunate in leading a double life in the law, a double life in a double sense. I have been a practising [2] and an academic lawyer and I have had the experience of two legal systems, the English and the German. There are a few others who have done the same. Again, I claim nothing that is special or singular. But few can have had a similarly intensive life in two careers and few, therefore, can have had a similar opportunity of observation. And this produced the urge of saying a few things which cannot find a place in a strictly academic work. They are not objective or capable of proof. They result from beliefs, impressions, instinct. They can be said as part of personal reminiscences and, as such, may attract the attention of some readers who care less for the author than for his personal reactions or judgments. Perhaps it would have been possible and also attractive to let them speak for themselves, to remove them from the framework provided by the description of a life, which inevitably is filled with many different strands of events. But an autobiography is the only convenient method which permits the combination of personal experience with lessons I have learned and wish to pass on.

This, then, is the explanation, the excuse for an undertaking which, as I start it, seems formidable and, the product of almost unforgivable vanity. But if readers come across at least a few paces which give them food for thought or which retain their interest, then one at least of my purposes will have been served. In one respect I can reassure them. My memory is curiously selective. I remember everything that strikes me as worth remembering. I remember nothing that would be a burden on my memory or that is trivial. If I read in autobiographs how authors remember what sort of conversation they had on a certain day, what the Menu of their dinner was, what dress Mrs. X was wearing, I can only marvel at the excellence of their recollection, at their sense of importance (or self-importance) and at their curious illusions about their readers' interest (or lack of interest). These are the things which I simply cannot remember even if I wanted to and about which, therefore, my readers will not hear.

When I was very young I came across the following passage from a letter written by Turgenjev to Tolstoi, a translation of which I have never been able to discover, but which has pursued me all my life been something like a private *leitmotif*:

> "Humanität ist kein leeres Wort. Lasst Euch nichts weismachen von den Maulaufreissern dieser trübseligen Epoche, von den Amokläufern, den Veitstänzern und heulenden Derwischen irgendwelcher Bekenntnisse. Wahr sein, einfach sein, milden Herzens sein, heiter und gelassen bleiben in Leiden und Gefahr, [3] das Leben lieben und den Tod nicht fürchten, dem Geist dienen und an Geister nicht glauben, – es ist doch nichts besseres gelehrt worden, seitdem die Erde sich dreht."

If these pages reflected a little of the spirit so beautifully expressed, if even some of my readers were to remember and live according to the words I would like to be a motto, my satisfaction and, indeed, my reward would be considerable.

**Part I: Life**

## Chapter 1 – Background

I seem to remember that among my father's papers there were some family trees, but I cannot find them. So I have to reconstruct my family's background from such papers as there are (and there are few) and from some slight research I have been able to carry out.

My recollection is that on my father's side the records reach back to the second half of the 18th Century, when Jews on the left bank of the Rhine in the Palatinate did not have proper surnames, but were known, in the Hebrew fashion, by their first names and as their father's son, – Isaac ben Abraham, for instance, a practice which changed only as a result of Napoleon's decree of 20 July 1808. The only available documents indicate, that Alexander Mann, was born at Wattenheim, a little village in the heart of the Palatinate, on 14 July 1809, the son of Jaques, then aged 32, and of Caroline nee Mayer. He married Franziska Loeb and they had two daughters and two sons, Jakob and Benjamin, the latter born on 27 January 1842. On the 5 February 1863 there was registered in the Commercial Register at Frankenthal the banking firm of Mann & Loeb of which Alexander Mann and Hermann Loeb (I presume, his brother-in-law) were partners. As from the 1st October 1867 Alexander's two sons were the sole partners, but the later fate of the firm is unknown to us except that in about 1915 Benjamin and his then partner, Ferdinand Loeb, sold the business to one of the predecessors of the Deutsche Bank.

Benjamin was my grandfather. He died in 1917. I remember him well. He was a kindly, dignified man who, when as a child I went for walks with him, was generally treated with respect and affection. He must have been a man of some intelligence, for it is him who is alleged to have said: "If you have the reputation of being an early riser, you may lie in bed until midday."

On 28 November 1866 Benjamin married Johanna Kahn who had been born on 1 March 1845, the youngest daughter of thirteen children of Simon and Charlotte Kahn[1] and who died in 1906.

---

1 Simon and Charlotte Kahn married on 4 July 1825 and died respectively on 17 September 1848

[5] A good deal is known about the family of Charlotte Kahn who died in 1869. She was a child of the marriage between Jesche Isaak (1774–1842) with Fromel Machol who must have died before 1808, for by October 1808 Jesche had married a second time, namely Elka, later Blandina Oppenheim (1783–1836) with whom between 1807 and 1829 he had twelve children. I have the following document:

> Extrait due Registre de Declaration faite en Exécution du Decrèt Impérial du 20 Juillet 1808. Sur le changement de Nom et de Prénom, parler Juif habitant la Mairie et Commune d'Edenkoben.

> feuillet 1

> "Pardevant Nous Maire de la Commune d'Edenkoben Canton du dit lieu, arrondissement de Spire, Département du Mont Tonnère, est comparu: Jesché Isaak, qui déclare vouloir conserver son nom de famille Isaak et son prénom de Jesché. De Vouloir donner à son épouse Elka née Uppenheim, le prénom de Blandina.

> De conserver à son fils ainé le nom et le prénom de Michel Isaak, à sa fille China Jeché, celle de Charlotte Isaak et à celle Kailé Jesche celle de Karoline Isaak.

> Et a Signe avec nous à la Maison Commune d'Edenkoben le dix neuf octobre dix huit cent et huit.

> Sigt: Jsche Isaak et Steinbrunn Maire
> > Pour Extrait conforme
> > certifie par nous Maire à Edenkoben
> > Steinbrunn Maire."

Jesche Isaak, described as "un notable et regisseur" (whatever this may mean) lived at Edenkoben, another small town in the Palatinate. His ancestry can be traced back to one Isaak ben Jitzchock ben Sechel who died at Edenkoben in 1689.

I possess the matrimonial contract concluded on the 19 November 1866 before a notary at Frankenthal. It is a long document which established a community of earnings within the meaning of articles 1498 and 1499 of the Code Civil, i.e. the French Code, and recorded that the bridegroom had a property of 22,867.15 guilders and the bride 7349. guilders, the property consisting largely of her clothes and personal belongings which were meticulously enumerated.

Benjamin and Johanna had two daughters and six sons of whom my father, Richard, was one. He was born on 22 January 1873.

My mother, Ida Oppenheim, came from a family which for long had been settled in Bonn and Cologne. On her father's side, as appears from Schulte's book

---

and 18 February 1869. On 22 August 1849 their daughter Fanny married Heinrich Marum and one of their descendents was Ludwig Marum, who in my time was a leading lawyer in Karlsruhe and a Socialist member of the Reichstag and who in 1934 committed suicide in a concentration camp. A son, Jacob Kahn, emigrated to the United States and the famous banker ? Kahn was one of his sons.

Background 21

on the history of the Jewish community in Bonn[2] the family tree can be traced back to Salomon Herz Oppenheim (1694–1757). His son Salomon Hertz Oppenheim (1752–1832) had three sons the oldest of whom was Salomon, the founder of the still-existing banking house Sal. Oppenheim Jr. & Cie. in Cologne, and the youngest of whom was Abraham (1777–1853) whose son Marcus (1812–1889) married Regina Ungar. They had six children, a daughter Julia and five sons of whom Nathaniel August was the youngest. He was born in Bonn in 1847 and on 24 December 1874 married Anna Cohen who was born in Cologne on 19 October 1849. Her origins are equally interesting.[3] She was a descendant of the Bonn Chief Rabbi Simcha Benjamin Cohen (1734–1816) and the daughter of his grandson Anselm Cohen (18..–[6]1874) and of Rahel called Regina Cohen née Heymann (who died on·29 December 1862). August and Anna had two children, my aunt Laura (1875-l959) and my mother Ida Anselmine Franziska (19 April 1877–12 April 1936). August died in Cologne on the 10 February 1892, his wife having predeceased him and the death certificate described him as "der Rechtsgelehrte Doktor juris", – it being totally mysterious how he had spent his time, where he obtained his doctorate and what he did to deserve the description "legal scholar".

Their children were brought up by their mother's brother Franz Cohen[4] until they went to a finishing school in Bonn.

It was there that Richard Mann, when reading law at the university, met Ida Oppenheim. I infer from a letter written by Karl Helfferich[5] on 29 December 1899 that shortly before this date they announced their engagement. They married on the 23 August 1900 in Cologne and had one child born on 11 August 1907, – guess whom.[7]

---

2 Klaus H.S. Schulte, Bonner Juden und ihre Nachkommen (Bonn, 1976).
3 See Schulte sub verbo Cohen.
4 Franz Cohen whom I still knew was an extraordinary man. His real interest in life was Mozart and Mozart's music. He was one of the founders, perhaps the principal inspirator of the Mozarteum in Salzburg where his name is displayed on a marble plate in the entrance hall.
5

## Chapter 2 – My Father

My father was the only child of Benjamin and Johanna whose life took a course which, as I shall relate, is worthy of some general interest, – if I ignore the fact that two brothers emigrated to the United states around the turn of the century and died there childless and that another brother and his wife were killed by the Nazis during the Second World War in a concentration camp. My father, so I always understood, did well at school and spent the last few school years in a boarding school at Neustadt where he made friends with Karl Helfferich, later the President of the German Reichsbank and the author of a famous treatise on Money, with whom he remained in intimate touch until Helfferich's death as a result of a railway accident in 1924. Between 1893 and 1896 my father read law at the Universities of Munich, Berlin, Bonn and Erlangen, where on 27 February 1896 he qualified as a Doctor of law by virtue of a thesis on "the peculiar reasons for terminating the mandate or power of attorney" (Die eigentümlichen Endigungsgründe des Mandats bzw. der Vollmacht). In 1898 in Munich he obtained his final qualification as the eleventh among 263 successful candidates.

At Bonn, as I have already said, he met Ida Oppenheim and fell violently in love with her, for she must have been a very beautiful and attrac girl. This made him wish to marry at the earliest possible moment. But he could not expect to establish a practice with the speed he needed to found a family at any place other than his home town and so in 1898 or so he opened his office at Frankenthal.

In many ways this did not prove a bad choice. Frankenthal was (and is) a small town of some 30,000 inhabitants, but it has world-famous industries such as Schnellpresenfabrik Albert; Klein Schanzlin und Becker; Kuhnle Kopp and Kausch; Süddeutsche Zucker, and (which was decisive) it had the District Court, i. e. the court of first instance, for one of the largest and richest parts of Southern Germany. It comprised, in particular, Ludwigshafen with its enormous chemical industries, Speyer, the centre of the provincial government, and the greater part of the renowned wine and agricultural district stretching from Neustadt in the South to Deidesheim, Forst, Wachenheim, Bad Dürkheim, Freinsheim and beyond, – all familiar names to the expert of German wines. So the field for a lawyer was large and in due course my father built up a very considerable, profitable and remarkably distinguished practice in commercial and civil litigation. He acted for many of the industrial undertakings, for all public authorities (Reich and Bavarian Government, Post Office, Railway Administration) and for many of the wine producers; in fact he acquired a reputation far beyond the Palatinate in [8] the law relating to wine production and frequently was called upon to assist in cases arising from it in other parts of Germany. All this work he carried on in an office consisting of two rooms, with one secretary and a filing clerk and with a most primitive library, – one of the many curious features of his practice. Another one was the leisurely pace at which it could be carried on and which allowed him not only to be a very active member of the Bar Council for the district of the Court of Appeal at Zweibrücken, i. e. the whole of the Palatinate, but also to travel a great deal and to pursue his cultural interests.

The special luck which invariably, professional men need for their success, came to my father in the oddest possible way. Before he opened his office there was at Frankenthal a lawyer of the same name who was still listed in some of the usual directories. One day at the beginning of the century Hamburg lawyers acting on behalf of the Hamburg export and import merchants Baring Brothers sent the papers in an intended action to the deceased lawyer called Mann. The Post Office delivered the letter to my father who, not noticing the error, opened the letter. He then informed the Hamburg lawyers about the mistake and asked for instructions. They replied asking him whether he would take the case on. It was a case against a certain Eugen Abresch, a financier, who lived in great style in a palatial home at Neustadt – a most colourful figure. One of his manifold activities was the sale of mining shares in Africa and South American countries to wealthy German investors. In due course they complained of having been defrauded by him and litigation followed, since his residence was within the district of the Frankenthal court, all of it had to be brought there. The Baring case was the first of a long series in the whole of which my father acted for the plaintiffs, which brought him into contact with numerous leading figures in German commercial life, continued for more than thirty years and led to many personal friendships. My father became an "Abresch expert". He knew all the tricks of his Opponent who was always represented by the leading German lawyers such as Max Hachenburg, and I remember how amused my father used to be if he could use against Abresch an opinion which Hachenburg or another authority had given for him some ten years earlier. (But the incident was also told to me as a warning which all my life I never have forgotten: a lawyer who gives opinions or who publishes academic work over a long period must always take the utmost care to guard against a contradiction with earlier work the mere existence of which is liable to slip from his mind.) But in so far as I am concerned two personal friendships incidental to the never-ending Abresch-cases stand out. The one was

Mr. Faber, the owner of the Faber pencil factory at Nuremberg who frequently came to our home and whom my father, accompanied by me, met for conferences at numerous places such as Baden-Baden. (A visit there taught me a lesson which is worth passing on: we had dinner in an elegant hotel. The [9] table was elaborately laid. The first dish was being served. I asked my father which spoon to use. Whereupon old Mr. Faber spoke to me words I have remembered and observed on innumerable occasions: "Young man, when you are in a situation like this, always wait and do what the others do.") Another was Rudolf Plochmann, a banker and a partner of Merck Finck & Co., today still one of the leading private booking houses in Germany. He had a large and most charming family and we often spent a week or so with them in the summer in their old, but beautifully modernized little castle of Hüttenbach, perhaps 50 kilometers east of Nurnberg in that part of Germany which is known as "Franconian Switzerland".

Altogether the concomitants of my father's practice played a considerable role in private life. At an early age I met famous lawyers coming to Frankenthal to argue cases with or against my father. I remember Karl Geile Rudolf Neukirch, and in particular criminal lawyers, Max Alsberg (a university friend of my father's) above all. But I also remember Saturdays when we used to go for long walks in the wine country, usually visiting a producer or an inn or a merchant whose business my father was at the time attending to and discussed in the course of the visit. And all this without a car, – there were no motorways nor did the ordinary private person own a car. I cannot remember anyone who did. One went by train. And one walked. And one drank wine, – moderately, but always, that is to say, a meal or any sort of hospitality without wine would be unthinkable. And what was regarded as a moderate quantity would for me be a substantial one. Wine was a matter of importance. One had a carefully selected cellar with hundreds of bottles, a book recording them and each one that was drunk. And in the autumn one decided with much tasting and deliberation on what should be added to the stock. Where people today drink spirits one drank wine, – at twelve o'clock for lunch, at six o'clock, for dinner, as a night cup. Sherry, Whisky, Gin, – such things may have existed, but they were not for those born and bred in the wine country.

But I must return to my father. I was till his death in Oxford in 1953 deeply attached to him. I respected him with an affection but also with awe such as I have felt for few others. And I owe him more than I can realise. I owe him the standards which have decisively influenced my own life and my attitude towards people and things. I owe him the unbending professional integrity which, frequently quite unconsciously and incidentally he taught and impressed upon me. It was the little things I learned from him, yet they are so great: thus I remember that frequently we used to go for walks with the local Director of Public Prosecution; the time came when we did not, and I asked why not; I was told: "He has to decide at present whether to prosecute a client of mine, so it would not be proper for me to meet him just now." Or: he was called as a witness in the case against a man accused of [10] perjury committed in a case of his·He told me: "I did my best to prevent it, for you should never stand by if a witness is about to commit perjury and you can stop him."

It was style that I learned from him, – the style of doing, saying, accepting things, and also the style of writing simply, clearly and carefully, the choice of the right word, the pleasure of saying something with precision. Certainly he was not an easy man, – he was moody, frequently depressed, sometimes sarcastic, demanding and on occasions even spoiled and selfish. But these were by-products of a life that in many ways was hard, and his family and his numerous friends put up with them as inevitable foibles.

What surprised me at an early age was his complete lack of ambition. Here was an unusually intelligent man with great qualities as a lawyer, a man of the world, a fascinating character, very much in the modern English style, appealing to the intellect without drama or shouting and with a quiet voice, good-looking, witty, highly cultured, a man with many abilities, in sum a distinguished personality. But he never sought a larger, more prominent field of activity than the relatively narrow sphere Frankenthal permitted. Nor did he have any legal ambitions, – legal research, legal writing was not for him. Not even legal literature. Nor did he aim at an active role in professional organisations. He regularly attended meetings of the German Bar Association and the German Lawyers Association. He formed many friendships. But he never spoke or sought office.

The free time available to him he devoted to his literary and artistic interests. He was a man of that classical education which younger generations cannot even imagine. The German classical writers were part of his life. He knew by heart much of Goethe, Schiller and others. The fitting quotation was readily at the tip of his tongue. He read the current literature, whether German or foreign (in translation). He spent a whole winter translating for fun the chapter "Indian Summer" of John Galsworthy's Forsyte Saga. He followed the cultural events in the large towns and subscribed to the *Frankfurter Allgemeine Zeitung* as well as the *Berliner Tagblatt* (as a result of which he became a great admirer of Alfred Kerr with whom he started a correspondence and to whom he used to send gifts of wine.) He would read the modern German literature and discuss, analyse and sometimes annotate it. He would travel to Berlin, Frankfurt, Munich to see the latest plays. He would go to concerts in Mannheim, a traditional centre of music at the time, and himself play the piano a little.

At the same time he was not a political animal. Politics interested him, but he was not a politician. During the first world war he believed in the righteousness of Germany's cause. He was exempt from military duty until the very end, when he was called up for a few weeks. During the Weimar [11] Republic he was a Democrat without belonging to a party, leaning towards the Socialists rather than the Right. Nor was he a religious man. But he never concealed his Jewishness and during the critical years demonstrated it by taking an interest in the affairs of the small local Jewish community.

It was in many ways an idyllic, a successful professional and a full intellectual life.

It came to an end with Hitler. On 22 January 1933 my father had his 60th birthday. In the German fashion it was a great occasion which he celebrated by inviting Lore and me to Arosa. The papers were full of congratulatory articles. His clients sent flowers or other presents. The authorities sent letters of appreciation, – some of them I still possess. Eight days later Hitler came to power. Ten weeks later, on 1 April 1933, there occurred the official boycott of all Jewish offices, shops, businesses and so forth. Life underwent a radical change. At this point I merely recount the end of the stage I have been describing.

At the end of 1932, my father had defended a Jewish malt manufacturer in Ludwigshafen, Bendheim, who was accused in the first few weeks after the introduction of exchange restrictions in 1931 to have committed an offence. It resulted from a complicated commercial transaction and although my father did not accept the normal type of criminal case, be defended the man and after a trial of a few days was acquitted. The prosecution appealed. The appeal was to be heard in the spring of 1934. A short time before the appointed day the presiding judge asked my father to see him. When my father called on him he said: "I have read the papers. There is no doubt that your client ought to be acquitted. But I cannot have him acquitted. Recently I acquitted a Jew. There was such an outburst in the Nazi press against me and my family that I cannot take cannot take the risks which a second acquittal of a Jew would involve." Whereupon my father said: "If this is the situation I have no alternative but to have my name deleted from the roll of practising advocates". And this he did at once. Bendheim was fortunately able to leave the country a few days later and survived in Italy. [12]

## Chapter 3 – Early Years

My childhood had two "deficiencies" which stand out. In the first place I have no recollection of my mother and, moreover, I know very little about her. The fact is that I did not see her from my early days until her death in 1936. She fell ill, when I was very young and spent the rest of her life, I believe subject to one or two interruptions, in a private institution. I do not know the precise nature of her illness, – it was a mental or nervous illness which I was once told was caused by something that went wrong when she stopped feeding me as a baby. Perhaps it was an illness which modern medicine could have cured. As it was, she was unable to maintain normal human contact, and living with her together became impossible: all that I carry in my mind is one single scene of outburst and violence. But it was a shadow, a great sorrow and tragedy which for many years lay over our house and, particularly, over my father's life, – and one that one tried to avoid mentioning or asking about. When the breakdown occurred – I do not know when, but I do not think it can have been later than about 1910 –, my mother's sister, aunt Laura, came to our rescue; she had been a teacher of German and Italian at Hamilton House School for girls at Tunbridge Wells (whence her many English friends) but gave up her career to devote herself to my father and, more particularly, to me, – she brought me up, and she lived with us throughout and uninterruptedly until her death in 1959. She was my father's housekeeper; she was his companion (was she more to him?) and my governess.

Secondly, I was an only child. Nor did I have many friends, – hardly anyone whose name even sticks in my mind. I made, however, as a small child one very great friend and constant companion, an imaginary person called Fleming, a boy of my own age with whom I used to play and, indeed, to live as if he were an existing brother. In due course, however, I grew out of this and went to school, at first the comprehensive school everyone started at, where Miss Roemer taught me to read and write and told us stories (so that one day I allegedly reported at home that she had spoken about God, and asked: "Could I see it in print"), later the High School (Gymnasium) which had only the first six forms, so that for the last three years I had to travel 20 kilometers to Ludwigshafen where at Easter 1926

I obtained my School Certificate. We normally travelled for 15 minutes or so by train every day, when school started at 8 and ended at 2 p.m. (including Saturdays) but in 1923 there were about six months when, as a result of the so-called passive resistance against French attempts at creating a separate state on the left bank of the Rhine, there were no trains and we went by bicycle. This was the time when it was possible to cross the bridge to Mannheim on the right bank only by special permission of the French occupation army. Such permission was rarely given. My father did not obtain it. I received it in the summer of 1923 in order to spend a holiday with my father's [13] cousin Mrs. Emilie Mayer in Zurich who was one of our dearest relatives.

The occupation came to an end only in 1930 as a result of the Pact of Locarno. It had begun in November 1918 and throughout that period we had first American, then French soldiers billetted in the second floor of our maisonette. For years we had Monsieur le Comte Gary de la Garenne. He was a French royalist who served in the Republican Army, but refused to become an officer. My principal memory of him is the daily visit which during a period of many years he paid punctually at 6 p.m. to my aunt. He had himself announced, entered the room, bowed deeply and with an unforgettable movement of his arms used the standard formula: "Je vous présente mes compliments, Madame". He made polite conversation for a few minutes and retired.

1923 was, of course, the year of the raging inflation. Thinking back to that period it seems to me wholly incomprehensible how one managed to live when prices increased hourly by millions of marks until one U.S. dollar became 4,000,000,000 marks. This was the period, when municipalities and large industrial undertakings issued "emergency money" and somewhere I still have a collection of such curious marks which later would trouble me on account of the definition of their legal character. I remember one day in the autumn of 1923, when my father came home and told us triumphantly: "Today I earned a dollar!" The odd thing was that until a late stage people simply failed to realise or to understand what was happening. They were misled by the figures and counted themselves rich. They sold their belongings at what they believed to be "good" prices and did not realise that the best thing they could do was to hold on to their belongings, to keep "Sachwerte" which in any circumstances would retain their "real" value. (Hence during the English inflation I always acted on the principle that cash was the worst investment and that actual asset including the ordinary shares of first-class companies, were the safest hedge. And in November 1923, from one day to the other, the whole adventure was over. One began to count again in terms of real money. The period of readjustment (including revalorisation with its flood of litigation) began and soon normal conditions returned. By Whitsun 1924 stability had been reached to such an extent that my father could afford to take me to Bonn and Cologne and show me the places where he spent much of his youth. We stayed at the (old) Königshof in Bonn with its unique view of the Rhine, where in later years I was to spend so much of my time. I always remember the great impression the view from the hall of the hotel made upon me. Bonn at that time was a delightful, small, sleepy University town, quite different from what it is now. For the first time I saw the Rhine in its most beautiful parts and the Cathedral in Cologne which I was to see again some 23 years later when it was badly damaged.

At school I was, I believe, always top or near the top of my form. We were very hardworked, studying not only German, but also French, Latin, Greek and old-fashioned mathematics, also some chemistry and physics. My knowledge [14] of French and Latin lasted me a life-time, Greek and mathematics I have completely forgotten. The standard of the form was not only high, but I believe that the teaching was excellent, – intensive, liberal and broad-minded. I have no recollection of any political or antisemitic unpleasantness; indeed I must say that in so far as I personally am concerned I did not ever or anywhere have any experience of antisemitism directed against myself – a qualification by which I intend to exclude discussions of a general character which, of course, in later years were inevitable. We worked very hard, when I take into account the homework that was to be done after school. And there was much extra work. Thus we had to give from time to time a sort of lecture for which we had to prepare at home. On one occasion I gave a lecture about Frederick the Great based on the most remarkable book by Franz Mehring *Die Lessinglegende.* On another occasion I spoke about the reception of Roman law in Germany, – a topic that resulted from my talks with my father. I had, of course, no legal knowledge at all, but I read a good deal of general literature for the purpose, though I seem to remember that I also looked into my father's original edition of Jhering's System of Roman law which I still possess.

At 6 p.m. I used to collect my father from his office to go for a walk, either alone or with some legal friend of his. Inevitably and naturally I learned a lot about law and its practice in this way. As I grew up and my decision to become a lawyer began to form more and more firmly, I started to work in my father's office. In my university life nothing else proved equally useful and important. I was given some files to read, – I had seen what a writ looked like long before it was mentioned by the professor. I was taught how to take simple steps in proceedings, or why a case was handled in a particular way. I learned something about courts. I saw drafts of pleadings and was told about the problem whether a certain point should be taken or how it should be put. And I learned much about professional standards. The result was that in matters relating to the practice of law I had a good deal of practical knowledge when I reached the university and thus a considerable advantage over those for whom law was nothing but theory.

While I write these lines, I begin to marvel at the fullness of the life I was taught to lead. Sport outside school hours, it is true, was entirely missing, – I did not play ball games such as tennis; riding was unknown, mountaineering and skiing came much later. Swimming and skating was the only sport in which I engaged to a certain extent. But how much did I read! I think most of the great novelists, German, English, Russian and some of the French became known to me during school years. And then there was the occasional theatre and, more particularly, there were concerts in Mannheim, at the time no mean cultural centre, where the great Furtwängler started while I was a boy. And on top of it all I had piano lessons, – in Heidelberg, if·you please: after school I went by tram from Ludwigshafen to Mannheim, then by train to Heidelberg and back home. So I also practised the piano at home and I really do not know [15] now how all this was possible. But it was. It did occur as I have described it. And it has done me no harm. On the contrary, it did me a world of good. It prepared and equipped me for what lay ahead.

There is another oddity which strikes me while I am writing. Much that I have been describing, certainly all travelling and everything involving expense, occurred in the course of the 2 ½ years between the end of the great inflation in November 1923 and the beginning of my university life at Easter 1926, when I left Frankenthal for all practical purposes. The inflation destroyed the whole of the German bourgeoisie's financial basis. In November 1923 a fresh start had to be made. Up to that time one lived from hand to mouth, frequently on the basis of barter, – my father was paid in wine or potatoes or vegetables. After that time one could begin to earn real money, to save and to spend on things other than bare necessities. Life made a fresh start. It was still in progress, when in 1930 Germany was hit by the world economic crisis, and in 1933, all within less than ten years, when the world, as civilised beings knew it collapsed and hell set in.

Another indelible lesson I carried away from those early years is that the inflation in Germany and its simply phantastic proportions, exceeded only by what occurred later in such countries as Hungary and Greece, happened because money was printed. Once they stopped printing, the inflation came to an end. I never forgot the lesson. I remembered it throughout the English inflation. Stop printing, – it is as simple as that. Call it monetarism, if you please. But no great words are needed for so simple a recipe. But, of course, if you print so that you can fulfill new and increasing demands of trade unions, unaccompanied by increase in production, i.e. undeserved, then inflation is bound to happen, is in fact being created. There will be many readers, particularly socialists, who will consider me naive. I maintain that I am stating the simple truth supported by experience and observation in two countries.

In the light of subsequent events the other indelible impression I carried away was the prime importance to a civilised society of securing and maintaining a stable, reasonably content and broad middle class (which should not and need not mean that other classes have to be discontent). The Federal Republic of Germany adopted throughout its existence and under whatever party regime it was governed policies in the field of taxation, social services and so forth, which gave effect to that experience learned in the course of the inflation and deeply impressed upon the German mind.

The English Labour party learned nothing, the English Conservative party before 1974 learned little from that German experience. Inflation of more than 100 % in the short period of five years of Socialist government between February 1974 and February 1979 with taxation at a rate reaching 98 % is bound to undermine a society. Anyone earning more than £20,000 (or a mere DM 80,000) [16] being liable to tax at a rate of 83 % or, if he has investment income, 98 %. A University professor whose salary during the same period of five years does not reach more than £12,500 (or DM 40,000),– this is what in the end produces such violent reactions as in Germany's case took the form of Hitler. [17]

# Chapter 4 – University and After

At Easter 1926 I started my first term at the University of Geneva. It was my father's idea: He wanted me to acquire a complete command of French. Little did he know that in that particular year Geneva was the "fashionable" place for first term German students of law and that I was to meet some of the young men who were to make a name for themselves in later life and with whom I established life-long friendships.

I found a room with board in the house of Mme. Gentet, the widow of a professor of law, in old Champel, a part of Geneva which now is filled with apartment houses. She used to take two or three paying guests who at meal times had to converse with the charming and highly educated old lady in French and were mercilessly corrected when they made a mistake. We learned a lot in this very happy and congenial atmosphere.

The professor for French and Phonetics was Monsieur Thudichum, and since most foreign students came to Geneva to learn French, almost all freshmen met at the beginning of the term at his first lecture to be divided into groups according to their knowledge of French. The man was a genius, for he made every student read two or three lines of French text and then told him where he came from and what the state of his French pronunciation was. In my case he said: "from the eastern part of the Palatinate". In the case of a fellow boarder of Mme. Gentet's he said: "You trouble me, because I hear some Berne dialect mixed with a Breslau accent". She was the daughter of a professor of medicine and had lived as a child in Berne and then moved to Breslau, where her father was appointed to a Chair.

Geneva in 1926 was an entirely different town from the present one. In fact, I believe I do not know any other town which in the course of fifty years has so much changed. Everyone went about on a bicycle. A bicycle was so common an item that you could leave it unlocked at a particular place and pick it up again weeks later. The League of Nations and the International Labour Office were relatively young and exciting institutions which began to make Geneva an important centre. We watched the statesmen, we listened to their debates, we swam in the lake, we went mountaineering, we had French lessons, we participated in courses in history, philosophy and economics, we talked, debated, met hundreds of people of all nationalities, – but we learned no law. It did not matter. It was a first term, and a glorious summer. We were happy and saw no clouds on the horizon. After the end of term I made a trip through central France (Lyon, Vichy, Limoges), and ended up in a little village near Blois where I stayed for two months in the house of a retired headmaster of a Versailles High School for an intensive course of French conversation and literature. I saw all the Loire country, the castles, Tours, Orleans, and ended up for three weeks in Paris where I met [18] again many of my Geneva friends.

Many of them had come from Berlin and so I decided to spend the winter term 1926/7 in Berlin. In the summer term of 1927 (at the conclusion of which I went to England for three months much of which I spent in the very agreeable and instructive company of J.W. Robertson Scott, the founder of the *Countryman*, at Idbury, Oxon), and in the winter term 1927/8, together with a group of friends including, in particular, Edgar Bodenheimer, I attended the University of Munich, but I returned to Berlin in the summer of 1928 and stayed there until I had passed my first State examination in May 1930.

The difference between the two Universities was striking. Munich had same excellent men: Wilhelm Kisch for civil law and civil procedure, Frank for criminal law, Beyerle for history of German law, Karl Neumeyer for private international law, who was a very learned man, but whose lectures were unbelievably boring and as uninspired and uninspiring as his books (the principal one of which, Internationales Verwaltungsrecht, would and ought to have been forgotten long ago, were German lawyers not so embarrassed by his terrible death: he and his wife committed suicide when the Gestapo called to transport them to a death camp.) And there were the economists Lotz and Zwiedeneck-Üdenhorst. Kisch was an outstanding teacher and a most interesting man who took a great interest in me. The general standard, however, was low: the professor did not expect much of his students, nor would the average student have been able to achieve more than the minimum. Both in summer and winter the attractions of the town – the wonderful country around it, its theatres, concerts, its arts, its festivals – were such as to tend to deflect the student's attention and the professors knew and surrendered to it. So the competition was in a low key and the educational benefits were limited. It was during this period in Munich hat I made one of the great mistakes of my life: one evening, walking home after a concert given by Karl Friedberg, one of the leading pianists of the period, I decided that I could never reach a standard of playing comparable to his, that it was impossible to do more than one thing perfectly (I had read something by Goethe to that effect) and that, therefore, the only sensible thing was to concentrate on law and to stop playing the piano in my inferior way. I regretted it ever since.

# University and After

On the other hand in Berlin it was in every respect less provincial. Not only life as a whole, but the standards of teaching and learning, the standards of demands and achievements were higher, critisism was sharper, praise was rarer, what was good in Munich was just average in Berlin. Some aspects of social life of the time, but only some were described by Isherwood and have created the impression in some minds that Berlin was a city of corruption and perversion. Nothing could be further from the truth than such a generalisation. My prime recollection is that we were hard working and that standards in every sphere of life were high. The standards of teaching in the [19] Faculty of law were incredibly high. The Faculty comprised not only the leading lights in German legal science, but also men who were splendid teachers. Bruns, Triepel Smend and Erich Kaufmann for public international and constitutional law, Kohlrausch for criminal law, Heymann, Theodor Kipp, Lewald, Rafel, Nussbaum, Martin Wolff, Flechtheim for civil and commercial law, Goldschmidt for civil procedure, – these are some outstanding representatives of a Faculty which in those years constituted the best Germany had to offer. I also remember with great admiration Karl F. Schumacher, the economist, Eduard Spranger, the philosopher whose lectures were specially instructive. Towards the end of my University studies I also attended the famous cramming courses of Siegbert Springer, an extraordinarily able, kind and interesting man whose memory deserves to be honoured, seeing in particular that he was shamefully driven to suicide by the Nazis during the war.

So in May 1930 I took my first examination. The Commission of five included Ernst Heymann, Ernst Rabel and Hermann Heller, the constitutional lawyer. I passed. In fact my mark was such that Martin Wolff immediately accepted me for the doctorate and I was offered by the Faculty the position of a Faculty Assistant. After my examination my father, my aunt and I made a long trip which began at Salzburg and ended in Venice, – Salzburg, because Franz Cohen, an uncle of my mother's and my aunt's had died shortly before and he was one of the founders of the Mozarteum in Salzburg, an institution which, I believe, he conceived and promoted and which to this day has honoured him with a memorial plaque in the entrance hall.

I then started my practical legal education. I was naturalised in Prussia (having been Bavarian before) and began my career as a "Referendar", i.e. as pupil passing through six-monthly stages of practical legal education at a County Court, a District Court, a Public Prosecutor's Office, an advocate's office, (I was lucky to be accepted by the partnership of Pinner, Walter Schmidt Kempner and Beutner, one of the leading German firms of corporation lawyers with whom I remained in close touch for a number of years) and the Court of Appeal in Berlin (where, in view of my qualifications, I was honoured to work like a slave in the First Senate dealing with final appeals in non-contentious matters for the whole of Prussia and where I learned with greater concentration and was subject to more severe critisism than at any other time in my life). But at the beginning of the winter term 1930/31 I also started as a Faculty Assistant which involved three principal duties, namely to correct papers handed in by students, to hold courses supplemental to the Professor's main course and designed to deal with and answer specific questions, and to assist him with incidental duties such as opinions he was asked to render, reading proofs etc; and during the vacation we were giving vacation courses to students who were willing to pay, which often meant a most welcome source of income. I worked mainly for Martin Wolff, but also for Flechtheim and, later, for Fritz Schulz after he had moved to Berlin in 1931. [20]

These were also the early years of the Institute which was then known as the Kaiser Wilhelm Institute and is now the Max Planck Institute in Hamburg, Heidelberg, Freiburg and Munich. I did not regularly work there nor did I attempt to do so, mainly in order to avoid Ernst Rabel who was one of the least pleasant men I ever met, who in my view (no doubt influenced by Martin Wolff) was very much overrated, and whose principal merit lay in his ability to promote new fields of research. But I spent much time at the Institute, not only because I had to do some comparative research for my own work, but also to write two articles I was invited to contribute to the Encyclopedia of Comparative Law and to assist Walter Hallstein in producing his work on "Die Aktienrechte der Gegenwart", – hence my friendship with the first President of the EEC, which survived many tribulations.

As I have already indicated, Berlin at the time was by no means that centre of sin, corruptions and crime which many people, impressed by isolated incidents, Nazi propaganda or fiction believe it to have been. On the contrary, it was a centre of research, art and academic and cultural activity such as the world has rarely seen, and we participated in and profited from it to the fullest extent. The theatre was unique. It was dominated by Max Reinhardt as a producer and by Alfred Kerr as a critic. The musical life created by Furtwängler, Bruno Walter, Klemperer and Kleiber, many soloists and much chamber music was incomparable in variety and richness. Much of my interest in visual art was provoked and fostered by Justin Thannhauser, the famous art dealer, and his wife Kaete, who became life-long friends, from whom my father bought some Vlamincks and an Utrillo which I continue to admire and love, and whose contribution to Berlin's interest in French impressionists and, incidentally, also to its social life I remember with gratitude; to Justin who died only in December 1976 I shall return in later pages.

The Thannhauser's certainly were among the people who became closest to me throughout my life, but I must mention others with whom I had contact and whose memory deserves to be kept, and in some minds is likely to be, alive.

One of them is Max Alsberg. He was the greatest defending counsel Germany has ever produced and one of the leading criminal lawyers of his time. My father had been friendly with him since University days and later maintained both professional and social connections. His practice extended over the whole of Germany. His successes were legendary. They were founded on a very quiet, but immensely persuasive type of oratory and most painstaking preparation of the case. I was from time to time invited to his splendid house and learned much from his enormous practical experience. One of his rules was never to appear in any strange town without the assistance of a local lawyer, – a principle which in Germany and other continental towns I would invariably observe in the course of my own professional activities on the Continent. One one occasion I found him surrounded by a group of young lawyers to whom he was relating a case he was just then engaged in. While he was doing so, his [21] son, then aged perhaps twelve, came up and in due course asked: "What did the man do, father?" Whereupon the father said in a severe voice: "Don't you know what you have to say? What is the man *alleged* to have done!" Alsberg was in many ways an artist: he was the author of some plays which were successfully shown in Berlin, he was a great collector of art and an excellent writer, not only of strict law, but also of legal philosophy, – I still possess his writing on Socrates, on the philosophy of defence in criminal cases and so forth. He fell a tragic victim to Hitler: in 1933 he committed suicide in St. Moritz.

Another great figure I must mention was Julius Flechtheim. He came from Cologne where as a young man he started to practise at the Court of Appeal, one of the most important ones in Germany at that time, and had a success widely regarded as phenomenal. In his early years he wrote the first and fundamental book on the law of Cartels, – then a new subject. Later he moved to Berlin where he became the legal adviser to one of the banks, a leading authority on company law, the author of a work on the subject, which to this day is in many respects still authoritative, and a professor at the University. It was in this capacity that I met and respected him and for some terms I worked for him as a Faculty Assistant. He inspired some of my early publications and showed much kindness to me. He was one of the clearest minds I have ever met. At the same time his practical experience in his own field was unsurpassed. It is a great pity that young German lawyers are so indifferent that they know little about their predecessors. Thus it was not long ago that a young professor asked me what I thought about his idea to write a book on the "State of German Companies". He was most astonished when I told and proved to him that in 1932 Flechtheim, together with Martin Wolff and M. Schmulewitz (now Clive Schmitthoff) had already published such a work.

I must, however, not forget the inestimable stimulation which the group of Faculty Assistants provided. We had our own room in the University where we met regularly and where the problems of the day, no less than legal problems, were analysed and discussed. It would be invidious to enumerate names, because most of them will be unknown outside Germany, though I must specifically refer to Werner Flume, who in 1931 came with Fritz Schulz from Bonn and with whom a life-long friendship developed. The remarkable thing about this group of young men is that with some very few exceptions they kept up the standards of the Faculty during the Nazi period, never joined the Nazi party and never engaged in those mean and contemptuous acts of cowardice, hate or baseness that characterised the most shamerul period in German history.[6] [22]

Among the Faculty Assistants was a girl who was primarily attached to the Institute of Criminal Law (where her immediate colleagues were, among others, Ernst Heinitz, later Professor in Berlin, Stephan Kuttner, later Professor at Yale and Berkeley, and Wilhelm Gallas, later Professor in Heidelberg, Richard Lange, now Professor in Cologne), who therefore rarely came to the Assistants' room, but whom I met from time to time at the house of her cousin and my friend Robert Seligson. This was Eleonore (Lore) Ehrlich. In the summer of 1930, after both of us had earned a lot as a result of our vacation courses, she decided to spend the money by going to New York for six months. She came to the Kaiser Wilhelm Institute to say good bye. We corresponded, while she was away. On her return in April 1931 we came to see more and more of each other – with the inevitable result. We fell in love. We became inseparable and, as subsequent pages will show, remained together to this day. The details of our personal story cannot be of any general interest. Neither of us is inclined to display intimate feelings. Many of them will, however, be mentioned incidentally in the course of what I have to relate. Such a procedure is, I believe, more in keeping with her reticence and my intention to "depersonalize" my story.

---

6 See on this phenomenon my article on Martin Wolff, Clunet 1953, II.

## Chapter 5 – Martin Wolff

I have so far only mentioned the name of Martin Wolff, but his standing in the German legal world as a whole, his personality and his immense influence on me were such that I have to devote a chapter to the attempt to revive the man in the minds of my readers to most of whom he cannot be more than a historical figure. He was a tiny man, very thin and frail, a hunchback, with beautiful hands but with features which, analysed singly, were ugly yet gave him a facial expression glowing with his extraordinary intellectual force. He was the greatest teacher I have ever come across and perhaps one of the greatest that ever lived. His lectures were invariably so crowded that people sat on window sills or on the floor, and this was so even if he lectured in the "auditorium maximum" which, I believe, had a capacity of more than 2000 seats. His students were devoted to him. They were and felt under his spell. For a life-time I have asked myself: how did he do it? I can say, negatively, not by jokes, not by cheap witticisms or asides, not by histrionics, not by false pathos, not by shouting or even by raising his voice. He did it by the authority and at the same time the simplicity of his personality, by the devotion to his educational task, by the obvious genuineness of his wish not to hear himself speak, but to force the students to follow his line of thought. He did not have a powerful voice, but he had a voice which, without being raised, carried to the farthest corner, – and in those days microphones were unknown or at least unavailable. His tempo, the clarity of his diction, the sparsity yet precision of words were such that anyone who took notes at the end had a readable and complete textbook on the basis of which he could turn to more intensive studies of details. Was it the instinct of the great teacher that caused him to force me to open my mouth? Sometimes I pride myself that perhaps if there was something in me that he felt worth while bringing forth. The fact is that when I was a young student, I was very shy and never opened my mouth in a discussion course. One day Martin Wolff discussed a test paper which we had written for him. He was walking up and down the front or the middle gangway of the lecture room. I was sitting at the corner seat of a row fairly in front. Suddenly he stopped, pointed his finger at me and said: "And what do *you* have to say about this?" So at that moment I had to speak and from that moment ste not only my ability to speak in public, but also my attachment to Martin Wolff, for at the end of term he asked me to join the seminar he was due to conduct the following term.

The decisive aspect of his personality, however, was his authority. His authority as a human being was felt by everyone listening to him. It is best described by telling about an unforgettable incident in the winter of 1932/3, when the political tension was great, when Nazis and Communists were fighting [24] each other, when violence was liable to break out at every point. He was giving a lecture on the law of bills of exchange. In view of the feeling of tension that prevailed a fellow Faculty Assistant and I decided that, unknown to him, we would follow him into the lecture hall and place ourselves to the right and left slightly behind him. He began to lecture to a hall which was overcrowded, so that many students were standing. After a few minutes he stopped and said: "In the seventh row there is a gentleman who thinks fit to read the Berlin Illustrated Weekly, while so many ladies and gentlemen have to stand. I request the gentleman to leave the hall at once." While there was complete silence, a young man in Nazi uniform rose and left the hall. When he had gone there was thunderous applause, but Martin Wolff continued as if nothing had happened. My heart had stood still during this scene which so easily could have developed into an ugly incident.

It was also the authority of his law that was responsible for the man's power. I do not mean so much the extent of his knowledge: it may well be that there were others who were more deeply steeped in history, who had a broader intellectual background or approach. But there were few (if any) who had a clearer preception of the structure of the law and the needs and simplifications of practical life and who could present the law more precisely and more concisely in formulations of a simplicity, yet perspicacity that were exemplary. He was very strict in so far as language was concerned and always taught that it is style that makes the lawyer. I have never forgotten it. I have tried to observe his teachings and pass them on to my own pupils. Few things gave me more pleasure than when a distinguished reviewer said of one of my own books ...

I have always felt that the great care I have taken in formulating my publications, in choosing my words, in avoiding the superfluous, in practising the astringent style of the lawyer had made far too little impression on my readers and reviewers and may, therefore, have failed in one of its purposes.[25]

As an academic lawyer, Martin Wolff was of a type that does not at present exist. His strength was the systematic, logical, coherent exposition of the law. Legal policy or the functional explanation, though by no means alien to his method of approach, were not allowed that supreme role which has led to so much misuse and to a distortion of the true judicial role. His two great works, if one disregards numerous shorter contributions, the Law of Property and Private International Law have in effect been allowed to die, though they continue to influence judicial practice. The latter work is unlikely to be revived. The former was last edited by Ludwig Raiser (1957), but he does not appear to intend to continue it, and this is a matter for deep regret and in fact wholly [25] unjustifiable. Raiser seems to have taken an intellectual development which is opposed to Martin Wolff's fundamental attitude and an article which he published about him in 1972[7] displays a certain lack of sympathy with his master. The result is that a work of unique quality and authority will die. It is a great shame and fails to do justice to the memory of an outstanding figure in German legal life who ought to have deserved better. He has fallen victim first to Hitler, then to modern tendencies of treating law as an instrument of policy, sometimes leftish policies, while he was a lawyer in the traditional sense. He, like all really great ones, the most modest of men, would not venture to do more than to expound and suggest, but to use law as policy, to see in law nothing [but] policy, this was not for him.

The respect, the prestige, in some way the fear he commanded was immense, and reflected on those who were allowed to work for and under him. To say that one wrote a thesis for him, that one was of his Assistants was in itself sufficient to confer a certain standing. At that time the Berlin Faculty did not admit in a year more than two or three students to the doctorate. To be one them was widely regarded as audacious, but to accept Martin Wolff's guidance was almost sensational. However this may be, I wrote a thesis on the payment of shares in kind ("Die Sachgrundung im Aktienrecht") on the strength of which in 1931 I obtained my doctorate and which subsequently appeared as a little book in a collection edited by Karl Geiler. A doctorate in Berlin was at the time a remarkable ceremony: On the 16 May 193 in public, under the chairmanship of the fully robed Dean, Eduard Kohlrausch, and in a white tie I had to defend three out of five printed theses. My three opponents Edward Wahl, later Professor in Heidelberg and member of the Federal Parliament, Edgar Bodenheim, later Professor of Law of the University of California and Rudolf Heirsheimer, later Uri Yadin, Deputy Attorney General of Israel and Professor of Law at the University of Jerusalem. The disputation was, of course, prepared and hardly more than a ceremony, but it was a pleasant one and continued a tradition which modern days prefer to disregard. One of the theses was to the effect that the infringement abroad of a foreign patent or trade mark could give rise to a cause of action in Germany, and thus related to a field which is still a matter of controversy and on which my interest was to concentrate in quite different circumstances. In the evening of the great day my father gave a dinner for my friends at the Hotel Bristol, – an extremely pleasant, even a splendid affair remambered by many.

---

7 Archiv fur die civilistische Praxis 172 (1972) 489

I have, however, again been led to talk about myself. My intention was to draw a picture of a great and lovable man who practised and taught severe intellectual integrity, who, though completely modest himself, demanded much himself as well as others, yet gave more than most, whose influence has pervaded my life and much of what is best in German law and whose memory deserves to be kept alive in a spirit of gratitude and humility. In due course we shall meet him again in wholly different surroundings. [26]

# Chapter 6 – The End of an Era: Emigration

One should not think that economic and political problems did not overshadow the early years I have been trying to describe. The ravages of a violent inflation had hardly receded into the background, leaving a multitude of discontented victims, when the world economic crises set in and developed with increasing force into a state of wide-spread misery caused by unemployment, bankruptcies and impoverishment. It was on such a foundation that the mediocrities, the gangsters, the criminals, the irresponsible and illiterate demagogues making up the Nazi party gained ground and, eventually, power. One saw it coming and was helpless for reasons which are nowhere better described than in the memoirs of Heinrich Brüning who was Chancellor during the crucial years and who quite rightly attributed a very great deal of responsibility to the representatives of the bourgeoisie. This is not intended to be a history of the period and it would, therefore, be wrong for me to cover ground which is common to all. But our personal life could not be kept in isolation and the decay of the Weimar Republic which its guardians allowed to happen was from day to day a heavy burden on our minds and an ever-growing cause of unhappiness and worry. The worst elements the world has ever seen were let loose in our midst. We saw it with open eyes and were helpless. More than that, – we were witnesses to the ignorance, the indifference and the contributory guilt of the world around us, – the judiciary, the police, the army, the civil service, even foreign observers, all those who ought to have known better, whose sense of critissism and justice, whose judgments ought to have opened their minds, to a large and ever increasing extent fell victim to the witchcraft that was about to take possession of Germany. I repeat: we saw it coming. The final debacle was not unexpected. The disaster was bound to happen, – though its ramifications or its demonic extent was beyond the bounds of human imaginations.

Let me interpose a thought at this point. The experience of those years carries a lesson with it. It accounts for the anxiety with which, I believe, every sensible person should regard and treat all signs of extremism. There is much in England's history since the mid-sixties that is in point, but take German terrorism as an example. The best, the most liberal and most progressive elements in Germany have shown reluctance to take effective steps, not so much against the terrorists themselves, as against "sympathisers" such as lawyers or others who gave them active or even only intellectual support, and many universities allowed even their professors and certainly their students to help and support the preachers of force, terror and violence. The example of the Weimar Republic which destroyed itself by inactivity, by exaggerated and misplaced liberalism towards sworn illiberals should forever be a warning, such as some well-meaning people in England tend to forget.

No-one saw things more clearly than Lore. On her return from New York in the spring of 1931 she was determined to go back there after having qualified in [27] Germany, she had an offer from the attorneys to the German Consulate in New York which she intended to accept. However, both she and I first had to complete our legal education. In the summer of 1932 Prussia fell victim to the infamous Paper "Putsch". It was at this moment that I received an offer from a well-known firm of Munich lawyers, Professor H. Rheinstrom and Dr. Alfred Werner and partners, to join them as a partner after my qualifying examination. I did not really intend to become a practising lawyer or to leave Berlin. But the political situation in Berlin was such that some people thought Bavaria might maintain a more orderly and less revolutionary regime. Moreover, Justin and Kaete Thannhauser, deluded by the local reputation of Rheinstrom and Werner, urged me to accept and described in glowing terms the attractions of a life in Munich. I was extremely sceptical, but decided to have a look at the proposition. So, on the night of the Reichstag Fire, February 28, 1933, I took the night train to Munich to spend three months there and form a view about the future. It was a step pregnant with far-reaching, yet unexpected consequences.

I started work on March 1st and after a few days felt that Munich was not for me. The legal climate was as parochial as I had remembered it. The practice was not as distinguished as I had been led to believe. Nor was the professional spirit what I had expected. I remember that after a few days I asked: "What happens here about legal aid cases?" When I was told that they were not accepted, I was deeply shocked, for I had been brought up by my father in the idea that, although at the time a lawyer did not receive payment for legal aid cases, the acceptance was *nobile officium* and their conduct required and was entitled to special care.

A few days after my arrival Rheinstrom had to leave for London on business. Almost at the same time things in Munich became increasingly difficult. (Thomas Mann's diary for the years 1933 and 1934, published in 1977 describes his own experience in vivid terms).

One illegality followed upon another, searches, blockings of assets and public attacks occurred, prominent politicians, prominent Jews were taken prisoner. It became obvious not only that Munich was as unbearable as Berlin, but also that

The End of an Era: Emigration

Jews could not continue to live in Germany with any degree of security. I met Lore for a weekend in Bamberg to discuss the situation. She was strongly in favour of immediate emigration. Her view was finally made up on the 1st April when we were dismissed from legal service (which meant that I could not take the final examination, while Lore who had already started it, was allowed to complete it), when she was physically thrown out of the court by S.A. gangsters and when the organised boycott of Jewish business, offices etc. occurred, I could not make up my mind so quickly. I travelled home to see my father. On the way I visited Karl Geiler in Heidelberg; I shall never forget his reassuring but typically ostrich-like words, uttered while he put his arm around my shoulder: "But my dear Mann, why don't you take shelter in my office [28] while this thunderstorm lasts?".

By this time, it was clear that Rheinstrom could not return to Munich. He asked me to see him in London. I went there early in April 1933. It was then and there that it was decided that he and Werner would emigrate to Paris and open an office there and that I would take charge of a similar office of German lawyers in London (for which, unbelievably, the then German Ambassador, Herr von Hoesch, a friend of Rheinstrom's, could, would and did procure the Home Secretary's permission). I was to work in close association with a firm of solicitors, Swann Hardman & Co., 10 Norfolk Street W.C.2. where Douglas Phillips, the son-in-law of Rheinstrom's friend Sir Albert Bennett, was a partner.

I returned to Germany to liquidate such affairs as I had, but was back in London early in May, staying at the Royal Hotel, Woburn Place, pursuing the pending applications, looking around and collecting information. It was unbearably hot, the Hotel was cheap and bad, I was surfering from hay-fever more than ever before, I was totally alone and more miserable than I can begin to describe. In this situation there came a telephone call from Lore. She had had a telephone call from "Justizinspektor Sauerbier", the man in charge of the formalities relating to "Referendar" within the District of the Court of Appeal in Berlin. He said to her amazement: "You are friendly with Dr. Mann". (How on earth did he know?) When she answered in the affirmative and told him that I was abroad, he said that a new regulation had come into force as a result of which people who had advanced as far as I had could take the final examination, that it would be a great pity if I did not take it and that she should urge me to return and obtain my qualification.

So I returned to Berlin, sat for my examination without any gusto or even interest and at the beginning of October 1933 I passed with reasonable marks, but without distinction, – not that I cared.

Lore sat for her examination a few days later, on October 11th. Hers was much more exciting, for the President of her Commission was the notorious Nazi Roland Freisler, later the infamous Chairman of the People's Tribunal which sent hundred of innocent people to the gallows. Freisler treated her very well, – her colleagues were five Nazi Storm Troopers who were ignorant and illiterate, but had to pass. Lore passed with distinction, – and this was the end of our carreer as Prussian civil servants.

Next day, October 12, we got married. Since our train was due to leave shortly afer 10 a.m., Lore had previously inquired at what time we could get married. The officer said 9 o'clock. Since we had to get her new passport, this was late. So she said: "Can it not be done earlier?" Whereupon he looked her up and down and said: "Is it so urgent?" Anyhow, we got married underneath the picture of Hitler and with Werner Flurne and Erika Kempf, later the wife of Preofessor Eschenburg, Tübingen and witnesses. We left as planned, [29] and arrived next morning, Friday 13th October, in Paris, where we spent our so-called honeymoon with the Thannhausers at the Hotel Regina. On Monday the 16th, we travelled with Alfred Werner to London by train.

We stayed in a boarding house in Golders Green and first tried to collect some money. We each had 10 marks with us, but we could encash our railway return ticket and had smuggled a little money out of Germany, mainly by sending to friends in England, Nazi literature, in which we had pasted some German banknotes. We looked for a cheap furnished flat (which eventually we found at Stanley Gardens, N.W.3 for £6 a month) and equipped the single room in which I opened an office on the ground floor of 10 Norfolk Street. We brought a secondhand table and carpet, went to Woolworth and bought a blotter and a plastic pen tray (which together with a Wilhelm Tell knife my father bought for me in Zurich in 1914 still adorns my desk in the office, – none of my clients who on occasions gave me lavish presents ever have ventured to replace my modest desk fittings with something more proportionate to the status of my practice as it developed over the years.) Since we had brought a typewriter from Germany and I was to type everything myself until an attack of sinovitis forced me to employ a secretary, I was ready to start, if there were any clients.

Almost 50 years later I came across the cash book which I opened at the time and continued to keep in my own handwriting for many years. It opens with entries on 20 October 1933 as follows:

Partridge & Cooper 3. 6. 6.
Carpet                     2. 2. -.
Book Case                  2. 5. -.
Cash Book                  -. 2. 3.
Tips                       -. 2. -.

The first receipt was on 6 January 1934, – £2.2.–. paid by Cripps Harris &Solicitors. The first distribution was in July 1934, – £130, the next one in November 1934, – £50. How did we manage to live?

I am occasionally asked with something approaching admiration or incredulity how we succeeded in perceiving at so early a date that emigration from our home country offered the only hope of salvation and survival. The answer is very prosaic. There was nothing heroic in our decision. It was an obvious one: those whom the Nazis considered their enemies had nothing to expect in Nazi Germany but concentration camps and death. Jews, Socialists, critics of the regime did not have any difficulty in reaching a view or a decision. The facts made it on their behalf. The point which has pursued me all my life is an entirely different one: can I (or anyone in my position) who was free from any present or prospective persecution, who had complete freedom of choice and who could move in either direction honestly say of himself that he would not have joined the new regime? He might not have participated in, but might have excused the worst excesses. He might not have been a member of the Party, but [30] preferred to be a sympathiser. Who has the right to criticise others if he has not himself positively proved that he would have behaved differently, that he would not have been a Party member or sympathiser, that he would have had the moral emurage to act independently, according to his conscience, his faith, according to the laws of morality? I find this a terrible dilemma. I am convinced that very many of those who shout loudest would have failed the test. I can only hope that I would have passed it. But I cannot be sure, and I feel this as one of the heaviest crosses to bear. It was too easy for me to vouchsafe what my conduct would have been in circumstances such as they applied to the vast majority of Germans.

There is a final point which I must make about our emigration. We left Germany, because we were Jews and as such the victims of attack by the most despicable group of men that ever obtained power in a civilised country. We were not, we are not practising Jews. But we felt as Jews by background, history, tradition, even though our noses are straight and our cultural status was wholly and firmly German. We did not emigrate on account of political persecution, because we were not politicians. It has unfortunately become fashionable for many refugees to present themselves in the guise of political opponents or victims of the regime rather than as Jews. For biographers, writers of obituaries or authors of entries in 'Who is Who' to conceal the true motives of their escape from certain death is a common but most regrettable failing. [31]

# Chapter 7 – The Beginning of a New Era

For those refugees who left Germany as early as we did the period up to the outbreak of war in September 1939 was in many ways less difficult than is frequently thought and than the new life was for the majority which came as the result of the steadily increasing pressure in later years, particularly if they were older, less adaptable and more wedded to the position, the belongings, the mode of life they had to give up. The history of the German-Jewish emigration, its tragedies, its in part extraordinary achievements has not yet been written nor has any great novel been published that is based upon the background of refugee life of some kind, for it is most important not to generalise.

Conditions differed not only from country to country, but also from the one to the other social level. Thus, speaking very generally, Britain was, at any rate in the early years, capitalist in its approach: the test of admission was whether the particular applicant could be expected to be useful to the country and, to assist in reducing unemployment; only much later the test was whether the applicant would not be a charge on public funds while in Britain. There were, however, always exceptions and, on the whole, it should be said that the Home Secretary exercised his discretion reasonably, humanely and sympathetically.

And as time went on, it became more and more obvious that the emigration was, so to speak, a kind of self-contained unit, a community within a community which to a considerable extent was based on mutual help. My clients were mainly actual or prospective refugees. Our doctor, our dentist was a refugee. There was in Hampstead a refugee butcher. The former President of the Berlin Police became a representative of a printing firm; so you ordered your stationary from him. If you needed a book-keeper you employed a refugee. Or if you wanted electric bulbs, you bought from a former Munich lawyer of considerable repute who maintained himself by selling them from home to home and whose wife worked as a baby-sitter. There were tailors, launderers, heating engineers who were refugees and who could rely on their fellow refugees. This is the principal reason why the excellent and moving books by Judith Kerr, *When Hitler Stole Pink Rabbit* and

*The Other Way Around* are so untypical; she describes a life completely divorced from the world of refugees and, therefore, almost unnecessarily hard.

When I look back over those six years, I feel again oppressed and terrified by one thing which, I am convinced, was the most awesome blight on our life, v on the one hand, the knowledge of what was happening and what would shortly be happening in Germany, and, on the other band, the unbelievably stupid and, I must say, disgusting reaction to it in the world around us, but particularly in England. Here was a people which simply closed its eyes to facts that everyone could see. The leaders of the Labour Party talked of conciliation with "Herr Hitler", while German Socialists were murdered in their thousands. The liberal leader, Viscount Samuel, talked about peace with Nazi Germany, while that country carried on a cruel war against the Jews. Most of the press, particularly *The* [32] *Times*, talked in sanctimonious terms while sacrilegious activities of unique horror occurred. It was the lack of moral fibre, the defeatist ignorance, the degenerating character and influence of appeasement which caused not only disgust, but also the most acute fear of what would happen at the crucial moment and what might have happened (as it did happen in France) had it not been for one single, unforgettable voice which for years had spoken in vain and which, if listened to, would in all probability have prevented most of the disasters. The contrast between reality and the English world of make-believe was a continuous and increasingly heavy, a sometimes almost unbearable burden that outweighed everything else and deprived the daily worries of any significance. At the same time we could not speak up: We were strangers in a foreign country, guests enjoying hospitality, and, moreover, we had to guard against reprisals against relatives and friends in Germany.

Yet our personal life, considered in isolation, was by no means unhappy. For a while both my father and Lore's mother would send a little money each month. Each of them also obtained permission to send us £1,000. My father could send some valuable pictures, objets d'art and furniture. And I began to earn a little, – I seem to remember a little more than £100 in 1934. Anyhow in the spring of 1934 we moved into a newly built flat in Charlbert Street, N.W.8, where we paid a rent of £80 p.a. A still-born daughter arrived in the summer of 1934, but David was born in September 1935. So in the spring of 1936 we rented a lovely house, 74 Clifton Hill, N.W.8., for £120 p.a., where we had plenty of room not only for Jessica who arrived in September 1936, but also for a constant stream of visitors from Germany. We had a married couple living in the basement so we had baby-sitters and could go out and see people, – a very necessary activity for someone who looked for clients. We had arrived in London with some introductions and were given more of them as time went on. So we met a considerable number of people some of whom became life-long friends. This did not apply, however, to Mr. Neville Laski Q.C. at whose home we were once for tea and who greatly

The Beginning of a New Era

encouraged me by telling me in no uncertain terms that it was hopeless to think that I would ever make a career in the law and there was nothing but chicken-farming for me.

Notwithstanding this advice I remained faithful to the law, however difficult it proved to be. I could not at first make up my mind whether I should attempt to qualify as a barrister or a solicitor. I had grave doubts about the former career: would a foreigner with an unmistakable accent and no connection with solicitors ever obtain a practice? Would the Home Secretary ever grant the naturalisation at that time necessary for the latter career? So in order to gain time and with an eye to a possible academic career I inscribed at the London School of Economics for the L.L.M. (Master of Laws) course, having been exempted from the LL.B. examination by virtue of my German doctorate. I took the course together with Otto Kahn-Freund, Wolfgang Friedmann, [33] Joseph Ungar, Joseph Gold, among others. My teachers were uninspiring, with one great exception. This was Theodore Plucknett, a great scholar, whose seminar on English Legal History was a source of constant and interesting instruction. I took the examination in the summer of 1935, – and failed. Professor Jolowicz, the brother-in-law of Martin Wolff, was dissatisfied with my answers in the oral examination. So I took the examination again in the summer of 1936 and passed. By that time I had decided to write a book on the law of money: a number of cases which were before the courts in those years appeared to make a systematic investigation and presentation of the subject necessary, particularly since no work on it in the English language was available. So I worked on the book and early in 1936, without anyone's introduction or recommendation, I sent the manuscript to the Clarendon Press. They accepted it. The first edition appeared at the end of 1938, the Preface having been dated to 12 October 1938.[8]

By 1938 it became clear that, after five years' residence, naturalisations were being or would be granted. Moreover, by that time my practice among the lay public had grown. So had my financial needs: two small children had to be provided for and the development in Germany was such that I might any day have to look after my father, my aunt, my mother-in-law and, possibly, others. In these circumstances the Bar seemed to offer such little certainty that I could not afford it. Moreover I feared my foreign accent would for ever remain and be a great handicap. I decided to become a solicitor, – and in many ways have regretted it ever since. Douglas Phillips articled me and I became an employee of Swann Hardman & Co., a small firm then consisting of old Hardman who had practi-

---

8  I then submitted the book to which I shall have to revert to the University of London as a thesis for the Doctor of Law and was gratified in the summer of 1939 to receive one of the very few such degrees that, at any rate at that time, the University of London used to grant.

**54**    The Beginning of a New Era

cally retired, Douglas and two managing clerks. But it gave me a foothold and scope and the atmosphere was the friendliest.

Fortunately, the Home Office raised no objection. The fear of a refusal to extend the permit to stay in England was a continuous worry which, looked at from today's attitude towards immigration, seems absurd. But England at that time was not an immigration country, it was a homogeneous and not a multi-racial society, – although I should be the last one to regret the relaxations which have taken place and although I do not wish to abuse these pages for the purpose of expressing political views, I cannot help adding my very great fears of the long term consequences of the immigration policy such as it developed during the postwar period; every thinking person will be bound to regret them with bewilderment [34] and anxiety. This, however, is very much by the way. Before the war things were very different, – so different that, for instance, Lore never dared even to apply for a permit to work in order not to jeopardize mine. Whether she could have done any work with two little children on her hands is another matter. The point here is that throughout her life she felt unhappy about our (probably unjustified) nervousness which for many years prevented her from having a professional career of her own.

The decision to take articles and to become a solicitor meant the abandonment of an academic career. The reason was purely financial. I had to make certain that I could provide for the expected flow of emigration from Germany. In fact during 1938 things reached a point at which our families could not continue to live there. My father and aunt had in 1934 moved from the small town of Frankenthal to the larger centre of Frankfurt where they were less conspicuous and closer to a friend who became a great force in their lives. This was Mr. Benno Ansbacher, a banker in Frankfurt, whose elder brothers had a financial business in Paris and London respectively; the London brother was the head of Henry Ansbacher & Co., then a stockbroking firm. The family owned the Bavarian Mortgage Bank and for years my father had been a non-executive director. It had to be "Aryanised", i.e., "sold", usually at a totally inadequate price, to a non-Jew. All these negotiations for the sale and the subsequent transfer of the proceeds were carried out by my father. The understanding, never put into writing, was that if and when he had to emigrate the family would pay him a reasonable annuity and that I would in some way be treated as if I were a member of it. My father left Germany in July 1938, my aunt followed in the autumn and after a short stay in London they settled in Oxford where they took a three room flat in Woodstock Court, Woodstock Road; they decided on Oxford, because they had friends there, it was cheaper than London and they could offer us shelter in the coming war. Henry Ansbacher and after his death his son, George Ansley (one of the most unpleasant men I ever met) paid my father £30 a month until his death in 1953. They never paid anything to my aunt or to me, but, the rent being £80

# The Beginning of a New Era

p.a., my father and aunt could live on so small an income which, after the war, I was fortunately able to supplement.

1938 was a year of general crisis. Austria and the Sudeten territory became German and in November there occurred the so-called "Kristallnacht", when well organised Storm Troopers attacked all Jewish houses, flats, shops and businesses and destroyed whatever there was. At the same time very many Jews were taken into custody, usually into concentration camps. They would not be released except upon production of a visa for a foreign country to which they could emigrate. So desperate efforts were made to procure, even to buy, visas not only from the English Home Office, but also from the most obscure countries such as Ceylon or Shanghai or Costa Rica. Postal communication with Jews in German became very difficult and even dangerous. In this situation we took a step which led to one of the most bizarre incidents I ever came across. Douglas [35] Phillips was kind enough to travel to Germany. He actually went to Breslau to see Lore's family and friends and to Berlin where he saw numerous friends and relatives and also intervened with the British and American Consul. He was still in Berlin, when the London office received a telephone call from the senior partner of a well-known firm of solicitors, Gregory Rowcliffe & Co. They required an urgent interview with old Hardman. The man came, and said that he had been instructed by a department of the Foreign Office concerned with political intelligence to convey the warning the Douglas was in great danger and he should be strongly advised to return immediately. No other information was vouchsafed. This created a great dilemma for us, but we could not take any risks. We telephoned to Douglas and asked him to return immediately. Next day his , Lore and I met him at Victoria Station. His safe return was an enormous relief, but the mystery of the message, its source and the manner of its transmission remained and could never be cleared up. Our own theory was that it was a dirty trick played by a man in M.I.5. against whom Douglas, acting on behalf of a client, had just then obtained a judgment for a substantial amount. Another explanation may be that the incident was no more than a concomitant of the policy of appeasement. After all this was the period, when Mr. Chamberlain's Private Secretary, Sir Alex Douglas-Hume (as he then was) said to a friend of mine who had gone to see him to tell him about the real conditions in Germany 'Thank you very much, His Majesty's Government prefers to accept the word of "Herr" Hitler'. And that creature – I refuse to speak of "Herr" Hitler – was denying loudly that anything untoward had happened in Germany and that German policy was other than civilised and peaceful.

The decision to prefer a solicitor's career to an academic life did not mean that I abandoned all academic work. On the contrary, I continued my studies in the fields in which I felt a foreign-born and originally foreigntrained lawyer could make the most valuable contribution, namely private international law and, later, public international law as well as their interrelationship. I shall have to say more about my academic work at a later point. At present I merely intend to relate that during the years I am talking about I spent every available minute studying the subjects that interested me, and also writing a little. An article which appeared in 1937 in the British Year Book of International Law gave me much pleasure, because it proved to be influential. In those years there also arose the idea of founding the Modern Law Review. I was one of the original guarantor members and became a frequent contributor until in the 1960's a new editorial board proved to be disinteresed in my continued collaboration.

I must emphasise, however, that it was and had to be my principal concern to build up a practice. In this I succeeded so that by the outbreak of war I made a modest living and could even take out a life-insurance policy for the princely sum of £2,000.–. My clients, as I have said, were mostly refugees, but [36] as a consequence of political developments they came not only from Germany, but also from Austria, Czechoslovakia, Hungary, Poland and other continental countries. They were frequently introduced by other lawyers. Their problems were very similar: obtaining Home Office permission or a Labour permit, formation of companies, agreements with partners, purchase or leasing of a house and so forth. Sometimes they were more unusual. They arose either from peculiar German situations or from the fear of the approaching war, the outbreak of which was never doubted by any knowledgeable German refugee. On the other hand there was the unfortunately not altogether rare case in which someone succeeded, in breach of Germany's tyrannic laws, in smuggling some valuables out of Germany at the request and for the benefit of another and subsequently refused to hand over the fruits of the enterprise. Would an action against him lie in an English court? The point which is a very delicate one was never decided. In more than one case I felt compelled with bitterness in my heart to advise in favour of a compromise. Another very typical and not uninstructive problem arose from the advice given by a well-known firm of London solicitors to its wealthy refugee clients of German nationality and repeated to me: in the event of war the property of such clients might become enemy property subject to control and for this reason and also for tax reasons it was recommended to form holding companies in such countries as the Channel Islands, Luxembourg or Monaco. The costs were high, but so allegedly were the advantages.

I steadfastly refused ever to have anything to do with such a scheme, – it seemed to me absurd to believe that England would treat refugees as enemies, and stupid to create a distant barrier between oneself and one's funds. In the event those who adopted the scheme paid dearly, because all the countries in question became enemy territory and the companies became enemies, while the real owners in England did not. The experience taught me a lesson which I never forgot when in later years complicated tax avoidance schemes were under discussion: Do not allow your client to engage in artificial, complicated schemes lacking a genuine justification – such schemes never work, because no court wil uphold them. They lead to expensive litigation and unwelcome publicity and enrich lawyers, but are unmeritarious and therefore everyone will try to do them down. This is particularly so in England, where, at a time much later than that now in view, a "legal philosophy of merit" came to dominate the scene (a phenomenon to which it will be necessary to revert at some length) but where at all times litigation is in the fullest sense of the term public. This is in fact a feature which struck me very much from the outset. In all other countries the hearings are public, but the reports of cases are usually anonymous. This is certainly so in Germany, though in other countries such as France, Belguim and Switzerland there exists a limited amount of publicity in the sense that names and points of legal interest are repeated, but not details of a taxpayer's financial situation the disclosure of which has in England a deterrent effect which I suggest is unfortunate, for in far too many cases it deters a taxpayer from litigation. [37] It is not too much to say that this may involve a denial of justice or, more particularly, so grave an obstacle to access to a tribunal as to amount to a denial of justice. But English law is even more peculiar in rendering it possible for everyone to know the size of a deceased's estate and the terms of his will, while details of Land Registry entries are not freely available. Is this not a remarkable oddity?

These were some of the early lessons I learned in those years. I took my solicitors' final examination in March 1941, but could not become admitted before I was naturalized after the war, early in 1946. [38]

## Chapter 8 – The War

In England one speaks of people having had a good war; this is a war in which a person fought actively and with distinction. I have had a bad war and for the rest of my life I have suffered from this knowledge. The war was our war, it was my war, fought to eliminate the evil we had recognised and hated long before the British people, with the exception of a tiny minority, became aware of what was happening. The war was fought to eradicate the devil himself, the men whom we had decried as the originators of all that was mean, contemptible, criminal, destructive, – and I did not stand in the frontline. How did it happen?

On the Sunday when war broke out, on 3 September 1939, we were at Oxford. We heard Chamberlain speaking on the wireless, – and I still remember the odd undertone in his speech, the certain lack of enthusiasm, the disbelief that his policy of appeasing Hitler and, perhaps, uniting with him against the Soviet Union, had failed, his personal ambition of conducting a successful foreign policy in shambles, his regret of having to take up a cause described by some of his friends as that of the Jews. On the Monday morning Douglas Phillips drove Lore and me back to London. It was a memorable drive for this reason: although registered at birth by the name of Friedrich Alexander, I was usually called Fritz. Douglas said that this would be impossible during the war. Lore disliked Frederich or Fred. So we hit on Francis and this is how my friends call me, although my official name, anglicised in 1946, is still Frederick. At the same time Lore reverted to Eleonore.

As the result of the outbreak of war we had become enemy aliens. We had to appear before a tribunal, were screened, but had, of course, no difficulty in establishing that we were genuine refugees whose heart and soul were wholly and unreservedly on the side of the British and totally opposed to Nazi Germany and all it stood for. It was pure chance that we were not naturalised before the outbreak of war or during the short period early in 1940 during which applications for naturalisation were again proceeded with. We had made the application in October 1938, as soon as possible after the expiration of the statutory period of five years, and a personal enquiry in 1940 succeeded in ascertaining that the papers were ready for signature at the very moment when the stop was ordered. What course would our life have taken had the stop occurred a few days later?

During the winter 1939/1940 we were living in a furnished cottage at Bookham, Surrey. The local police had interviewed us and both they and all the local people knew all about us. (Yet we had taught the children not to speak German in public, as they had done up to that time; Jessica could hardly talk and it created nothing but amusement when one day, travelling in a bus, David aged four called loudly acros the bus to her when she murmured something like "gaggle": "Don't you know that you must not talk German in public?") So when the Low Countries were overrun and almost all male enemy aliens of certain age [39] groups were interned, the Bookham police fought a battle with the authorities. They simply refused to intern me. They invented excuses. They adopted delaying tactics. They resisted. The effect was that I was still free when that insane policy of indiscriminate internment of Britain's best friends and Hitler's greatest enemies ceased in the summer of 1940.

In the meantime, events on the Continent had taken the course which everyone knows and I need not describe. England was in danger of being attacked and, possibly, overrun by the Germans. The experience of the fate which Continental countries had suffered and the possibility or perhaps even the probability of an invasion, made us decide to send David and Jessica to Calgary in Canada where a friend of the family had offered to bring them up. On 19 July 1940, in the company of a young English girl from a good family (who, one will not believe it, never wrote a single line to us) they travelled by rail to Liverpool, then by boat to Halifax and by rail to Calgary where eventually they were handed over to Mrs. Marjorie Palmer. It took about three weeks until we received her cable. Thinking back I find it difficult to understand how we survived that period of uncertainty. Many people will find it even more difficult to understand how we could voluntarily take leave from children of such tender age. But they cannot picture the situation as we saw it, when in the course of that unforgettable morning we walked away from Euston Station, – almost convinced that in the course of the following battles we would meet death or that if these battles should end in Hitler's victory we would seek death. So we were alone for almost exactly three years, – it was in May 1943 that the children returned via Portugal in the company of an English nurse who was coming back to England. The children who during the last eighteen months or so were with the widow of one of my father's brothers in New London, Conn., were almost completely Americanised. We had felt from the little we learned about them (only two of our American friends ever visited them, sent them a present or otherwise took notice of them, and from the photographs which reached us that their whole cultural foundation was in danger of being undermined and that, therefore, their return had to be arranged as soon as it was safe and the government could make shipping available. Did the three years do

# The War

them good or harm? I always feared that in David's case there may have been some permanent injury, – he must have been jealous of his little sister who was an unusually pretty child and who quite obviously was being spoiled by her hosts, while David was much less adaptable and missing the sentimental and intellectual warmth which even boys of eight need. This sounds ungrateful towards dear aunt Sadie, but I am speaking quite objectively, – our gratitude was always assured. But that my feelings were correct became apparent years later when aunt Sadie died and her will became known: it left a legacy to Jessica only, but she was an undergraduate at Cambridge and did the right thing by sharing the legacy with her brother.

I have to go back, however, to the memorable year 1940. Since I was not interned, it did not, as in so many other cases, become the obvious and, [40] frequently, the only method of release for me to join the Pioneer Corps. This was an inferior formation of the Army for the war service of many aliens and some other groups of second-class soldiers. I could have joined it, but did not do so, particularly because at that time there prevailed the impression, subsequently proved to be wrong, that a member of the Pioneer Corps would have to remain there for ever; in fact in later years it proved to be merely the first step in what in most cases became a normal army career. So my efforts were mistakenly directed towards joining a regular formation of the armed forces but on account of my German nationality these applications never succeeded, nor did they succeed in Eleonore's case who, having been rejected by the Air Force's women's service, ended up as a technical supervisor in Osram. In the result I gave up my attempts at offering my services, – a decision which to some considerable extent was influenced by Douglas Phillips. He had joined up in 1940 and pressed me to look after such practice as he had left behind and this I did. In the result I gave in to his persuasions. The armed forces (other than the Pioneer Corps) did not want me, – so I did what I could to help my dear friend and tried to keep the nest warm for him.

Nevertheless the fact remains: I did not have a good war and I have regretted it ever since.

After the children had left for Canada we moved back to London where we stayed throughout the war years except that almost every Friday evening we went to Oxford to have two nights' uninterrupted sleep. During the worst time of the blitz we had friends staying with us in the home, particularly Walter Berlin and his family, a Nurnberg lawyer who, in the tradition of his forbears, had continued to practise law in that citadel of Nazism until shortly before the outbreak of war and with astonishing courage fought for his Jewish clients and against the terrorism of Streicher.

The war in London which has so often been described by more competent writers than myself was a unique experience in that it created a spiritual community based on the will to resist and to share the sacrifices. Wherever we went, but most particularly on such occasions as firewatching at home or in the office, it was obvious that the common danger had brought about a common attitude. There were, it is true, differences. Although it is now almost forbidden to use the word, the main difference rested on class. The better their class the more indifferent to danger people were. The top class would not spend a night in the security of an underground station. On the contrary, they would not take notice of air raids at all. Our neighbour at Clifton Hill would take a bath at 2 a.m. in the middle of an air raid. If I was not on firewatching duty I sat up working on the most abstract problems of law or playing chess with Otto Kahn-Freund who at the time spent many nights in our house. One lived, in Churchill's words, under the impregnable ceiling of the law of averages. But these are small matters One of the more important elements responsible for the spiritual strength of [41] England was the remarkable rationing system which secured to everyone the same entirely sufficient and fair, yet far from excessive amount of all necessities of life, – a system that operated efficiently, however serious the degree of nightly destruction may have been. It was a real miracle. And, in addition, life continued as if nothing had happened. The underground and the buses were operated, work continued, staff turned up, however much their nights may have been disturbed, the courts functioned even if they were sitting in underground shelters while flying bombs were overhead.

A typical example is provided by the circumstances surrounding the birth of our youngest child, Nicola. She was born in a London nursing home on 20 June 1940. The first signs of her arrival occurred while we were huddling underneath an air raid "table" which we had installed in the dining room. The ambulance arrived punctually. I left Lore in the nursing home at about 1 a.m. Her gynaecologist arrived soon afterwards. I began to walk home, – all this while the V.1.'s were falling around us. I could not get a taxi. I walked until about 2 a.m. I met a taxi and stopped it. The driver was reluctant to go my way and said to me: "Have you been a bad boy?" When I told him that I was the very opposite, he drove me through the noisy night to our part of London which was far away from his own destination.

Or one came to the office in the morning and said to one of the Secretaries, "Have you had a good night?" She replied: "Not particularly, our house was destroyed".

For some reason Oxford was never attacked. So during the war we spent most weekends there. In particular David and Jessica were sent there, when Nicola's arrival was imminent. They stayed there until could take them to Manchester, where friends had put a house at our disposal and where they joined up with Lore who after Nicola's birth had had a very difficult time: after a few days in the nursing home the V-l attacks compelled her to leave London with the baby in the

# The War

fullest train I have ever seen to go to an isolated fishermen's hotel in Forest-in-Teesdale where the cot did not catch up with her, so that the baby slept in a drawer lined with old copies of The Times. (Thirty-five years later Nicola and her family visited the place again to see "where Mummy slept in a drawer"). She then spent a few days with friends in Bradford, where the child slept in a suitcase the lid of which was tied to the back of a chair, but eventually she could take possession of the Manchester house where the four of them spent a reasonably comfortable, though lonely few months, David going to local school and Jessica getting used to the little sister and overcoming her jealousy ("I knew you would be nice to the baby, but I did not think you would be so nice to her".) In about November we were re-united in London and risked V.1.and V.2. together.

Oxford remained the weekend refuge, but for me Oxford had other attractions too. On Saturday mornings I used to work in the Codrington Library. The [42] afternoon I spent with Martin Wolff. And in the evening, after dinner, I visited Fritz Schulz and his family in their house at Tackley Place. The Sunday belonged to my father and aunt. This routine continued on very many weekends after the war until 1953, when Martin Wolff died in July, when Fritz Schulz suffered a stroke and was completely paralysed in August and when my father died in September.

The relationship with Martin Wolff during those years was completely different from that which had existed in Berlin before 1933. I was no longer the pupil who sat at the feet of his teacher. An old master now conversed with a young friend. We talked about the things we were doing. Martin Wolff, to the eternal shame of Oxford University, was never allowed to teach. He was given a room in All Souls College and had an annual grant of £300 from the Clarendon Press on account of his book on Private International Law which he was writing for them and on many aspects of which I was allowed to assist by discussion, suggestion or provision of material. The first edition appeared in 1950, the second in 1953. It was an excellent and very successful book. It is a great loss that it was allowed to die. (This is another story: on two occasions the Clarendon Press wanted me to edit it. But Martin Wolff's widow had been persuaded to entrust Kurt Lipstein, a Cambridge don who never had had any connection with Martin Wolff, with the task. He accepted it, but did not carry it out. I was not surprised. Nor was I amused by this second unhappy encounter with the Jolowicz family. And the world of learning will forever remain impoverished.) But Martin Wolff also took a great interest in my own academic work and, in particular, in my growing preoccupation with public international law. The debt I owe him for his support and stimulus, for his friendly criticism, for his continuous insistence on stylistic purity and even astringency is immense. Whenever I have the opportunity I try to discharge it and to keep his memory alive.

Fritz Schulz was an entirely different personality. A Roman lawyer, a legal historian of the greatest distinction, but also a man imbued with the most broadly based general culture, a fighter by nature he had first gone to Holland, where the University of Utrecht had offered him some opportunity for research, but on 2 September 1939 he and his wife suddenly appeared at our house in London and after a few days went to Oxford where the Clarendon Press under Kenneth Sisam provided Schulz with £300 p.a. on account of books he was to write and did write. Before leaving Germany Mrs. Schulz had taken numerous foreign students as paying guests into their beautiful house in Berlin on the understanding that payment would be made to me. By this means, naturally illegal under German law, she could ensure the education of her four children in England. All of them made good. But how often did they come to us to collect a few shillings for cleaning a pair of trousers or similar purposes! It was a continuous battle and frequently I had to advance a little money to bridge a gap. The schools were aware of the situation and all too often prepared to wait for payment of the term's fees. And all these goings-on were totally unknown to Schulz, one of the [43] most unworldly of men. His last achievement in Germany had been a course of lectures on Principles of Roman Law, which in truth and substance was nothing but a veiled attack on Nazi despotism and lawlessness. In England, very fortunately, he became fascinated by Bracton, and his writings on Bracton, particularly on Bracton's famous chapter on Kingship are to my mind of quite outstanding general interest, particularly because he succeeded in tracing the sources from which Bracton drew and thus displayed a range of knowledge and sense of academic detective work which are of the rarest and never received sufficient acknowledgment. Here again much may be due to the jealousies of colleagues who lacked the generosity of paying tribute to a unique master. This applies in particular to David Daube who obtained the Oxford Chair of Roman Law and occupied it for many years, without ever calling upon a lonely scholar of the greatest eminence whom he ought to have respected but whom he presumably feared. When Schulz died on November 12, 195 nobody felt the urge to write a few words of appreciation of a man who had done so much for the elucidation of English legal history. A short Obituary which I contributed The Times of ......... was intended as an attempt to alleviate the grave sins of omission others were guilty of.

This, however, was much later than the period I really am concerned with and may give the impression that during such period life had continued quite normally and that the war, so to speak, passed us by. Nothing could be furter from the truth. We felt deeply involved and fully committed, though, as I have explained, we could not do much ourselves. In 1942 or 1943 there arose the completely new, unforeseen and unforeseeable event of the systematic extermination of Jews in gas chambers. The horrors of that crime (when, as I, learned very much later, several near relatives and innumerable distant ones, friends lost their lives in the most frightful circumstances) continue to weigh upon me more heavily and more frequently than I can say and than most of my readers will believe. But it is a fact that all too often I am obsessed by idea that Auschwitz is the place to which I belong, where I ought to have met my fate and which, to my eternal shame, I have done nothing to revenge. The spirit of Auschwitz is a great burden and a great challenge I suffer from both. There is no more terrible and at the same time more dignified expression of the feelings I am trying to describe than in Jerusalem's Yam [....?]. All that a sensitive person feels about those frightful events is expressed in that monument of incredible beauty and simplicity.

As the war progressed and the end appeared nearer, the question of the post-war status of Germany and the reform of German law aroused acute interest. The former led to endless political discussions which do not justify repetition. But the latter was studied at many levels. I was a member of a number of Committees which were concerned with it and, in particular, was throughout consulted by the relevant department of the future military government of [44] Germany, which was headed by an excellent man, Sir Alfred Brown, with whom I co-operated closely and in perfect harmony. The poison of Nazism had pervaded German law to such an extent that the task of cleansing it was immense. It was relatively easy to enumerate the legislative measures which had to be abolished, though the retrospective or prospective effect of abolition sometimes raised considerable problems of policy. But to eliminate the specific interpretation which Nazism had put on general German law and which led to its degeneration was a much more difficut matter. It could only be dealt with by means of a general formula the scope of which required much thought and discussion, particularly with the Americans. The result was Proclamation No.1 which came into force immediately upon General Eisenhower's troops occupying German territory.

And so, eventually, that unforgettable day, 8 May 1945, arrived. The war was over. The devil had been eradicated, though at immense sacrifice and costs. Again a new era was to begin. [45]

# Chapter 9 – A Last beginning: Germany 1946 and After

Shortly after the end of the hostilities in Europe there occurred one of the events which may come to be recognised as one of the turning points in the history of the world. I am not speaking about the atom bomb and its use (which I always regarded as one of the regrettable necessities of warfare), but about the election of a Labour Government in England in July 1945. Never in the history of the world has the decay of a country been so rapid and so complete as England's decline between 1945 and 1975. At the end of the war England was impoverished in material resources and to some relatively slight extent physically damaged by air raids. But England's spiritual condition was excellent the heart of its people was at the right place and beating strongly, its prest in the world was enormous, the goodwill was rich and full of promise and opportunity. Thirty years later, after a mere generation, England is at the bottom of the league, it is a poor and backward country which has lost its influence and has been far overtaken by its former enemies, Germany and Japan, in spite of the death-like condition in which the former found itself during the first two of these thirty years, 1946 to 1948. If one looks for external signs in 1945 the £ had a value of $4.20, in 1975 of $1.75., the internal purchasing power of the pound was in 1945 [......] in 1975 [....]. When there were signs of the pound rising a few cents as against the dollar, the press demanded intervention by the Bank of England to keep the rate down and thus the rate of exports up, – as if German and Japanese exports had not continuously risen in the face of a steadily rising currency. The reason, of course, is that customers do not necessarily buy what is cheapest. They pay for quality, promptness of delivery, service and maintenance after purchase. But English suppliers, like so much else in England, have become unreliable, for England has been ruined by its trade unions and their uncontrolled monopoly power resulting in continuous wage increases unrelated to productivity and by the abuse and misapplication of the welfare state. If after the war English policies had been directed to the recreation of wealth and therefore of investment, if people had been encouraged and indeed compelled to save and had not seen their savings taxed away or diluted by inflation, the result, thirty years later is likely to have been wholly different. As early as 1947 a fundamental mistake was made by the Exchange Control Act 1947 which perpetuated war-time exchange control and thus created a siege economy, while England with its enormous financial expertise as it then existed (but has since been lost) could have become what Switzerland now is. To support the needy is one thing, to promote scroungers is quite another. A state of affairs where a printer in Fleet Street earns £300 working on Friday, Saturday and Sunday and receives unemployment benefit for the rest of the week is intolerable, but typical. That the families of strikers are being paid damile benefits which the head of the family is under no duty of repaying is a peculiarity of the English system which cannot be justified by any reasonable [46] argument. But reason or reasonableness cease to operate where the carefully created and disingenuously supported lawlessness of English trade unionism prevails. This is not the place to describe its pervasive influence and its destructiveness or the responsibility of those politicians and intellectuals who have promoted it. All I must record is my conviction that the election of 1945 was the root cause of the condition which in 1978 every honest observer is bound to recognise. It is pointless to reply that the same would have happened had there been a Conservative victory. This is unproven and unprovable. We must judge what has happened, not what could, would or might have happened.

What I have said is by no means a digression, but, on the contrary, provides the key-note to much of what will have to be said in later chapters. In July 1945 those multifarious implications were, of course, not discernible. On the contrary, hopes were high and since Douglas Phillips, having at the end been a Lieutenant-Colonel in the Eighth Army, was demobilised at a very early date and since I was naturalised early in 1946, we resumed our common work, though we changed the name of the firm to Hardman Phillips and Mann.

We had hardly done so, when Sir Alfred Brown approached me with the urgent request to fill a gap that had suddenly arisen in the British Element of the Allied Control Council in Berlin and to go to Berlin on a temporary basis as the British Delegate on Inter-Allied Legal Committees. I accepted with alacrity and in about April 1946 flew, for the first time in my life, to Berlin in the uniform of a Lieutenant-Colonel of the Control Council of Germany, popularly called Charlie Chaplin's Grenadiers.

I arrived in Berlin, for the first time since 1933, on a Sunday. It was a wonderfully warm spring day. I was met by car and driven through scenes of unbelievable destruction and misery to a very comfortable flat of two rooms, kitchen and bathroom in a block near the Officers Club, the "400 Club", at Breitenbachplatz in Dahlem. I inspected my new home. I unpacked. I decided to walk through familiar grounds and look for houses and places known from former times. The house where I used to live in Hubertusallee was destroyed. The house where Lore used to live in Lynarstrasse was very largely destroyed, its owners had left. Altogether the destruction surpassed my wildest imagination. I sank into a state of stupor. Yet the sky was blue, the sun was shining on a town which seemed to be mysteriously quiet. Suddenly I noticed a piece of paper with typescript nailed to a tree. I looked and saw an "advertisement" of a concert to be given that evening by the Chamber Music Ensemble of the Berlin Philharmonic Orchestra in a house in the Podbielskiallee in Dahlem. I went there in the evening. The former library of a large villa, an enormous room without roof or windows, served as a concert hall. There were large numbers of folding stools and I was lucky to find one. Very many people were standing. They played Schubert's Octet and Beethoven's Septet. They played beautifully. But, quite apart from the excellence of the performance, it was one of the most moving [47] concerts I ever attended. The public, in spite of its obvious worries, its shabbiness and, I felt sure, its hunger was devoted to and taken up by the music to such an extent that the whole "room" had an atmosphere of uplift and dedication such as one rarely comes across. I can never forget the contrast between the beauty of the music, the grimness of the surroundings and the singlemindedness of the players and the listeners. The last of many deep impressions obtained in the course of this first day overwhelmed me completely and it was with difficulty that I found my way back to the new "home" I had acquired a few hours earlier.

Next day I reported to the office at Fehrbellinerplatz. The Chief of the Legal Department was Mr. N.L.C. MacKaskie Q.C., his Deputy one Pereira neither of whom appeared to me particularly attractive. But they left me alone and took little if any interest in the work I was doing.

This was mainly concerned with the reform, i. e. the denazification of German law through Control Council legislation which was prepared by Inter-Allied Committees. These consisted of a representative of each of the Four Powers, assisted by Secretaries and Interpreters. The American Delegate was my old friend Max Rheinstein, at that time already Professor of Comparative Law at Chicago University. I have forgotten the name of the French Delegate who was a former judge from Alsace-Lorraine and the Soviet Delegate was a Major whose background and qualifications remained mysterious. There were a number of Committees on the reform of German law in general, and on more specific subjects such as the law of German nationality, criminal procedure and so forth. We met about three times a week in the building of the former Kammergericht (Court of Appeal). On many aspects I required, of course, instructions from our Head Office, which was situate in Bad Oeynhausen and there were many occasions when Head Office sent a representative to attend particular meetings. Progress was extremely slow. This was exclusively due to Soviet intransigence, ignorance and suspicion. Although we know that the Control Council and its organisation continued to exist and to some extent to function until April 1947, when the Soviet General walked out and the Berlin blockade began, it was clear to me already in 1946 that co-operation with the Russians was impossible. Nothing that since then has happened in the world has tended to remove that impression. It was just for this reason that my time in Berlin, about ten months in all, was of the most interesting in my life. Never again have I come so near the deep cleavage between West and East, which I consider unbridgeable and which no talk about détente, human rights, Helsinki or whatever other misleading embellishments may be used will ever be able to overcome. Many incidents could be related to support what I am saying. Two stand out in my memory. Both occurred during a month of British chairmanship, when, accordingly, I acted as Chairman.

The first occurred in the Committee on the reform of German law. We were, at Soviet request, systematically scanning the statutes to ascertain whether they included any Nazi element, – a procedure which to the mind of any knowledgable [48] person was in itself senseless. We came across a proviso according to which in certain circumstances service can be effected by a "town-crier", This may have been a suitable method in certain cases in 1871, when the statute came into force, but had since then become wholly obsolete. The provision might just as well be removed. The Soviet Major regarded it as a truly democratic feature which should be retained. A discussion ensued. In the course of it Rheinstein whose strong academic leanings and attitudes always came to the fore made a little comparative survey, describing practices prevailing in ancient Rome, in France, in the American States and so forth. He then said: "And as to Soviet law I have no knowledge". At this moment I felt that the atmosphere had become icy. I noticed the Soviet Major collecting his papers. I was puzzled but almost immediately my interpreter came up to me and said: "She translated: As to Soviet law I do not care". This explained it. Where others would have laughed, a diplomatic indident had arisen. In fact it took me the rest of the morning and all my skill to straighten matters out and to pacify the Major. A sense of humour, or of proportion was entirely alien to him. We spoke different languages.

The second incident occurred during a big meeting, also under my chairmanship, of the legal division, internal security, police and foreign relations. There were perhaps eighty people in the room to discuss a new law of German nationality which was necessary in preparation of the first elections which were intended to be held. The issue was whether and to what extent people of foreign nationality who happened to be in Germany should be treated as, or should be allowed to become, German nationals. The specific points concerned the nationality of people from Danzig. The Russians wished to treat them simply as Germans. I had clear instructions from the authorities in the British zone of occupation that as matter of fundamental principle we could not agree to impose nationality upon any person against his or her will. We could agree only to an option. The discussion on this point went to and fro between the enormous, fat, red-cheeked Soviet Colonel opposite and myself. Eventually the Colonel asked me: "How many people are involved?". I replied in accordance with my instructions that we had no exact figures, but believed about 20,000 to be concerned.

[unreadable, text covered]

1. 33 (1947) Transactions of the Grotius Society 119 or Studies in International Law p.634
2. International Law Quarterly 1947, 314; Jahrbuch für internationales und ausländisches öffentliches Recht I (1948) 127.
3. Süddeutsche Juristenzeitung 1947, 463.
4. International and Comparative L.Q. (1967) or Studies in International Law p. 660; in German: Juristenzeitung 1967, 585, 617.
5. See on the history of these events Walter Schwarz, Ruckerstattung nach den Gesetzen der Allieerten Machte (Munich, 1974) pp. 23–67. lt may be that the oppodition of. the British was stronger than Schwarz believes.

[49] One question which I remember particularly vividly related to the restitution of the property of victims of Nazi prosecution.[9] Already in 1946, the American occupation authorities were preparing laws to secure restitution. They were anxious to promulgate the same legislation in the three Western zones simultaneously. They failed in their objective and their own law was introduced on 10 November 1947. The British took their time and followed suit on 12 May 1949. In the meantime furious discussions went on inside the British administration about the principle of the policy. My Chiefs, Messrs. Mackaskie and Pereira were violently opposed to any measure of restitution. I never had the feeling that their sentiments towards Jews and Jewish problems in general were friendly or even neutral. Nor did they ever display any sympathy with or understanding of the fate Continental Jews had suffered between 1933 and 1945. Nominally their opposition stemmed from the upheaval and the ill-feeling which restitution was expected to cause and which might make life uncomfortable for the occupation authorities. That there existed a strong feeling among very many Germans that elementary justice required the undoing of injustice and the return of property that in the sense of the moral law had been stolen would not occur to them. Such discussions as I was allowed to share and such papers as came to my notice conveyed the impression of opposition to American proposals or at least of passive resistance. The justification put forward was legalistic, even specious and opportunistic. The only argument which did make a certain practical sense in view of the then desperate economic situation of Germany was that in the

---

9 See on the history of these events Walter Schwarz, Rückerstattung nach den Gesetyen der Allieerten Mächte (Munich, 1974) pp. 23–67. It may be that the opposition oft he British was stronger than Schwarz believes.

foreseeable future property in Germany would be worthless. It was a reasonable, but in the light of subsequent events a staggering error. Who could foresee in 1946 that six years later Adenauer would supplement the allied policy of restitution by most generous measures of indemnification as a result of which Germany paid to victims of Nazi persecution more than 100 billion DM up to the end of 1978?

Life in the Control Commission was, on the whole, far from hectic. I had time to go to concerts and to the theatre both of which revived astonishingly quickly in often very primitive surroundings. I spent much time with Rheinstein and other friends in the American element. I saw old German friends (although, strange to say, "fraternisation" was not allowed) and managed to provide them with drink, chocolate and cigarettes which they could exchange for more necessary items. In particular I saw and tried to help Eleonore's cousin Suse Meyer (now Veith) whose husband, formerly a journalist with Ullstein Publications, had died during the war. Since he could not be transported, the Gestapo did not remove them from the room in which they lived and which they had rented from a ladies' [50] hairdresser, Arthur Veith. The moment he had died they called to take Suse away to a camp, but Veith had organised her escape. He had provided her with the papers of a deceased woman and arranged for her to be hidden by altogether ten different families in different places while the war lasted. In the end she worked in the house of a landowner not far from Berlin. When the Russians arrived, they shot her protector in front of her eyes. Having survived the war and the dangers to which her status of illegality exposed her and her courageous hosts, she returned to Berlin and eventually married Arthur Veith to whose generosity, courage and foresight she owed her life. (Her only son was brought up in Scotland, served in the British Army and in the autumn of 1945 succeeded in visiting his mother, almost unrecognisable to her eye. He is now a Professor at an English University.)

It was also possible for me to undertake several trips. I went to Marburg where I gave a few lectures to students and met some old colleagues, in particular Walter Hallstein. I went to Frankfurt where in the house of Walter Lewald I again met Hallstein and Ernst von Caemmerer. I also visited my father's old maid whom he had set up with an annuity in Frankfurt and who throughout the Nazi period (and after) had behaved with exemplary faithfulness and integrity. And I went to Nuremburg, where I was allowed to spend almost a week to attend the great trial of Goering & Co. I was present during part of Goering's crossexamination and was reluctantly impressed by the strength of his personality. The trial itself was then and has since become a topic of much discussion among lawyers. I never had any doubt that it was necessary and, indeed, inevitable to have such a trial and that, on the whole, it had to end as it did, that it vindicated the law and that it created an effective and useful precedent. To describe it as victor's law or as a miscarriage of justice seems to me comment that is completely oblivious of the uniquely horrific offences of which those men were convicted. The only doubt

A Last beginning: Germany 1946 and After

which over the years has become increasingly strong arises from the participation of Soviet judges, seeing that the Soviet Union itself has been and is guilty of no less heinous crimes against humanity than those which were ventilated at Nuremberg. Those who criticise the trial are called upon to answer the question what they would have put into its place. Kill the principal criminals without trial? Let them go scot-free? Both solutions were from every point of view impossible. Was there a fourth one?

While in Nuremberg I re-established contact with members of the Plochmann family whom I mentioned earlier. And in Berlin I had the visit of many old German friends (so that, incidentally, my unconcealed contact with Germans led to some difficulty with certain British authorities in charge of antifraternisation). Thus I saw Eduard Wahl, later Professor in Heidelberg and member of the Federal Parliament, but then in a desperate state after the death of his first wife, the murder of his brother in a concentration camp and the suffering of his children from tubercolosis caused by undernourishment. I would not mention it if there had not been a remarkable incident. We talked about the [51] world, the war, Hitlerism, general conditions. Towards the end of our conversation about the war he uttered the memorable words: "Yet, you know, great things were done". I was dumbfounded. Nothing of the kind happened with our old friend Gudrun Scherling, then a lawyer at Naumburg in the Soviet zone, later a judge at the Federal Labour Court. She came twice to see me in Berlin. Her husband had survived the war, but was then starved to death in a Soviet concentration camp, – another victim of Soviet brutality whose behaviour during the Nazi period had been exemplary and who would have amply deserved a kinder fate. I also saw a good deal of Eduard Kohlrausch and his family. Although never a Nazi, he was for some reason I have forgotten excluded from the University and felt extremely bitter about it. Yet he constituted my last and only link with the old Faculty.

Why do I recall all these personal meetings?

To explain the reasons, I must mention the trip to Germany which I undertook eighteen months later, in the spring of 1948, just before the German currency reform of June 20. I was then acting for Baron Heinrich Thyssen-Bornemisza. Since communication with Germany was still almost impossible, it was decided to send me there to ascertain the state of the Baron's German affairs. After enormous efforts the Foreign Office granted me a visa and travel facilities and I proceeded to Cologne, Berlin and Düsseldorf. In Cologne I was collected by a car, driven by a coal-burner, to see the Thyssen works at Hamborn and talk to the Managing Director, Mr. Roehlen. I was received in great style: lunch was served in the great conference room, it consisted of a sort of bean soup accompanied by the most exquisite Moselle I have ever had, the cellar having been left undamaged. In Berlin I negotiated about the release of the Thyssen interests from military control, – without success. I travelled by train through the totally destroyed Ruhr territory and along-side the wiped-out Krupp works in Düsseldorf to negotiate with the Coal and Steel Administration. I stayed very comfortably at the Park Hotel which was reserved for Allied personnel. I mention this only because during this stay I had, after fifteen years, my first and memorable meeting with Flume. He had refused to join the Nazi Party and therefore could not adopt the academic career for which he was predestined. He became a tame lawyer in an industrial concern. This brought him into contact with tax law, so that he had the unusual distinction of combining Roman and civil law with tax law. He had just been appointed to a Chair in Göttingen. Walking about Düsseldorf (for I was not allowed to take him into the Park Hotel and I had no German ration cards to go to a German restaurant) we discussed not only the past but also the future, – his, mine, Germany's. We analysed the enormous and challenging task that lay ahead. It became very clear to me that people, particularly academics in my position and with my background had a considerable responsibility towards Germany. German youth was, and was likely to continue to be, cut off from the developments in the West. Twelve years had to be made [52] good. The right direction had to be shown. Young Germans had never met a Jew. Hitler's errors and crimes had to be shown up by the living example. The ideals of the rule of law, of justice and of law had to be revived. The task was enormous, promising and multifarious. It was a duty to perform it. The many refugees who preached the theory of never setting foot on German territory again but who later on were only too happy to accept German money paid by way of indemnification avoided it and failed to discharge the specific obligation of supporting the few, far too few who had offered resistance, as well as those young people who had not participated in Germany's crimes. Collective guilt, a perfectly legitimate concept, did not mean that everyone was equally guilty. It meant that the vast, almost total majority had supported the regime, as was the fact, and was responsible for its crimes, but did not exclude support to be given to that tiny minority which was entitled to hold its head high, or to those who were too young to have been infected.

It was with considerations such as these in mind that from an early date I tried to do my bit to assist in rebuilding a sound intellectual standard in Germany. From 1946 to 1978 I lectured at German Universities. In fact there is hardly any German University where I did not give a lecture. I addressed the German branch of the International Law Association (1950), the German Lawyers Conference in Hamburg (1953), the Karlsruhe Forum in 1965, and in 1960 I was appointed Honorary Professor of Law in the University of Bonn, where every summer term I gave a course of lectures on English law, on International Commercial Law and, once or twice, on the law of Money and Credit, and where, in particular, I invariably held a seminar on International Commercial Law. This was of particular importance and satisfaction to me, for more than anything else it gave me the feeling of imbuing the young with knowledge and tradition such as I had acquired from my great masters. The seminar produced some excellent work, part of which was published, and some young men who made their way honourably and successfully in the new Republic. At the end of my days I look back with a measure of satisfaction upon the academic work which I could do in Germany and which England never gave me the opportunity of doing. Nor did I hesitate to contribute to the development of the new German law. I wrote numerous articles on a great variety of subjects. Twenty contributions to private international law were republished in a single volume in 1976. The second edition of The Legal Aspect of Money was translated into German and appeared in 1960. I wrote numerous book reviews and the occasional article for newspapers such as for the Handelsblatt on the reform of company law in England or on the extraterritorial effect of American tax legislation and for 'Die Zeit' on Kronstein's unpleasant 'Letters to a Young German', one of the most distasteful books I have ever come across about which I did not mince my words, although the review consisted almost exclusively of quotations from the author himself. And when I reached three score and ten in 1977, not only did the Federal President confer the Great Cross of the Order of Merit upon me, but German [53] scholars and publishers also took the initiative in publishing a splendid volume of essays in my honour, and the University of Kiel, with its splendid tradition in international law conferred an honorary doctorate on me. I mention all this to show that my initial decision was proved to be right by the recognition which it received.

I have, however, always refused to have anything to do with Germany east of the wall. I have never set foot on East German territory, as I have never entered any totalitarian territory anywhere. It was not the fact that the lawyers of Carl Zeiss may have been in jeopardy. Nor was it the fact that my academic contributions on Germany's legal status, just because they proved to be influential in the West, were abhorrent to the East. It was simply my hatred for fascism, whether coming from the right or the left, that kept me away physically and mentally, and my conviction that the Eastern regime was to a large extent a continuation of Hitlerian abuses. In no sense could there be any common cause with them or the spirit behind them.

It is, of course, my hope that my work in post-war Germany helped in recreating the new picture of the German Jew in Germany's mind. But I frequently ask myself whether it did. A new generation has grown up in Germany. They did not know what happened. They do not want to know. Most of them have never had any contact with Jews. The deliberate killing of six million Jews is an abstract statement to them – they had not personally known a single one among them. A single tragedy personally experienced is more telling than a figure too stupendous to be appreciated. [54]

# Chapter 10 – England 1946 and After

It was pure coincidence that I have told about my post-war activities in Germany before relating my life in England. Nothing I have said is intended to give the impression that the centre of my life after the war has not been firmiy fixed in England, – I who has succeeded so often to make people in reality domiciled in England non-domiciled to secure great tax advantages for them have to confess that, speaking technically, I am firmly and unequivocally domiciled in England, however disadvantageous this may be. I have not even re-acquired German nationality, although this again would have had advantages, but to acquire (or lose) nationality for financial reasons is a thing not to be done: one does not trade nationalities. I certainly do not wish to have any nationality other than British, however expensive it may be, for I am British and I owe my life and all I have become to Britain. To be truthful, I have to confess that the wholly monstruous rates of taxation which for some years have prevailed in England, which are wholly unique to this country and which compel me to pay up to 83 % on my earned and 98 % on my unearned income, a high capital transfer tax and capital gains tax on what is nothing but an inflationary increase of values on my savings have often caused me to contemplate emigration, but so far I have rejected the idea.

The centre of my life is in England, in the first place because my family is firmly settled in England. After leaving Stowe, David served for two years in the British Army, then went to New College, Oxford, to read history, and is now established as a banker and married to Pauline Vogelpoel, a Director of the Contemporary Art Society. Jessica after leaving St. Paul's went to Newham to read archaeology, became the wife of Professor Charles Thomas, the archaeologist and has four children and some seven detective novels, together with much other work for the B.B.C., the Times Literary Supplement and others, to her credit. Nicola also went to Newham after St. Paul's, read English and is the mother of four children, – perhaps one day she will do more than write the occasional book review for the observer. So I have four grandsons and four granddaughters and a great joy they are. But it is typical for England in the last quarter of the 20th century that a chief worry is how I can provide for the education of my grandchildren without getting involved in heavy tax liability. Should these intelligent and gifted children be compelled to be kept down to the level of the majority whose education they would have to share were they to attend comprehensive schools, as our socialist masters dictate? And the joke or rather the tragic dishonesty is that many socialists dictate it for others, but their own children are too good for comprehensive education.

So the family firmly belongs to England and I belong to the family. So does Eleonore, – even much more than I do. She is even a socialist, though she draws lines. Thus the education of her grandchildren is sacred and not even socialist doctrines are allowed to deprive her grandchildren of the best education money [55] can buy. Her outlook is, so I fear, tainted, for in 1955 she qualified as a solicitor and, after working for some years for a variety of others, in February 1966 she did something about which I cannot speak highly enough or with sufficient respect. She opened an office in Portobello Road for the specific purpose, not of making a profit, but of helping the poor (though, as a result of legal aid, she would after a time make just enough to cover her expenses). She is still carrying on the office, seeing often ten or fifteen people a day and carrying the burdens of the outcasts of humanity. At the age of seventy-one it is a heavy load, even though she now concentrates on matrimonial and rent cases. She sees a part of life that is completely unknown to me. She even sees a part of legal life about which I know nothing and which the authorities have mis in an astonishing manner. Listening to her stories in the evening I am everytime amazed at the ignorance of facts which characterises our bureaucracy, yet does not disqualify it from imposing its will. The same ignorance is responsible for the defects of our rent legislation which has become a political issue and is therefore no longer governed by considerations of merit, reasonableness or social advantage.

I belong to England also because I belong to English law. It is unfortunately true that I have never been able to achieve the recognition connected with an academic post, either full-time or part-time, though I have been greatly honoured by being elected a Fellow of the British Academy (which includes only about twenty-five lawyers) and a Member of the Institut de Droit International (which has only about ten British members). In 1945 Dr. Goodhart offered me a fellowship at University College Oxford, but the pay was wholly insufficient to maintain a family with three children or contribute towards the maintenance of my father and aunt. In 1949, supported by Dr. Cheshire, Sir Hersch Lauterpacht and Sir Valentine Holmes Q.C., I applied for the professorship in international law in the University of London. The short list of three included Mr. Mervyn Jones (who since died) and Professor (then merely Dr.) Clive Parry. The Committee included Lord McNair, Sir Eric Beckett, Sir David Hughes Parry and a few others. A few days after the interview on October 3 we received letters to the effect

# England 1946 and After

that a decision would be made in due course. In fact the chair, at that time one of five in the United Kingdom, was left vacant for ten full years until, without fresh advertisement, it was filled by the appointment of David Johnson. At the time I learned that it was felt difficult not to appoint me, that one did not, however, wish to appoint a lawyer of foreign origin and that therefore one preferred – not to make any appointment at all. So I had or have no official academic status in England. But I am glad to say my academic work has been extensive and, I believe, has contributed to the progressive development of English law.

I have frequently asked myself what my life would have been like if in 1949 the Committee had decided in favour of my appointment. One thing is [56] certain. I would not have pursued my academic work in that state of intellectual isolation from which I have suffered all my life. Apart from Sir Hersch Lauterpacht to whom I shall presently refer there was only (Sir) Otto Kahn-Freund with whom in earlier years I regularly corresponded. We frequently met and talked. We read each other's manuscripts. We argued. We criticised. We made suggestions. As time went on, this very pleasing and valuable exchange of views ceased almost completely. We remained good friends. I have the greatest admiration for his intellectual stature, his great knowledge, his wonderful ability to formulate and present his thoughts. Our deep-seated divergence on politics, our differences in the approach to law such as his contempt for "mere" law and my comtempt for "socio-legal" thoughts and practices have not at any time interfered with our intimate personal relationship, – a miracle and, perhaps, a monument to civilised behaviour, which I gratefully acknowledge. But my law is not Otto's law, and so I have in every respect remained a loner. I did not find it a happy state, for by nature I am strongly inclined towars the Socratic method, the human and intellectual contact, the give and take of discussion in the Senior Common Room.

My principal academic effort has been to keep *The Legal Aspect of Money* up to date. A second edition appeared in 1953, a third one in 1971. As I write these lines, I am beginning to think about a fourth edition which the Clarendon Press would like to publish in 1981. Habent sua fata libelli, – the fourth edition will be very different from the earlier ones, mainly because in a vital respect English law has undergone a radical change. The old English practice was that you could not recover foreign currency in an English court, but only sterling and that the foreign currency had to be converted into sterling at the rate of exchange of the day when the money fell due. This worked reasonably well while sterling was strong, although even in such circumstances some of the results were very odd. I attacked the whole doctrine and its foundation in all editions of the book. After the war I caused the Monetary Law Committee of the International Law Association (of which for twenty-one years I was *rapporteur*) to consider the subject on an international level and on a comparative basis. The outcome were the so-called Dubrovnik rules of 1956 which established a set of principles in line with

**80**                                                            England 1946 and After

Continental practice and the submissions in my book. By that time I was a member of the Lord Chancellor's Private International Law Committee under the chairmanship of Mr. Justice Wynn-Parry. I succeeded in having the Lord Chancellor refer the subject to the Committee. It reported in 1961 (Cmnd.1648). The majority, including Richard Wilberforce and Geoffrey Cross, very much under the influence of Lord Justice Megaw, came out in favour of the old English rule. I wrote a long minority report in part of which Colin McFadyan joined. The report was much influenced by the fact that in 1961 the House of Lords[10] had strongly upheld the old English practice and rejected the argument [57] of Richard Wilberforce (who was instructed by me) to limit its scope. It was a case which I have always regarded as most remarkable, because on a point of great importance to modern commercial life Viscount Simonds had regarded it as "decisive" that many centuries ago in claims for foreign currency a certain form of action used to be employed. However this may be, in 1961 the reform of English law looked hopeless. So I tackled the problem from another angle. I induced the Council of Europe in Strasbourg to set up a Committee for the purpose of considering and possibly drafting a Convention to give effect to the Dubrovnik rules. The British government was so peeved at this fresh attempt to overturn a report of its Committee and a decision of its House of Lords that it refused to participate in the work of the Committee. But this appointed me as its Consultant So for some two or three years I participated in its deliberations. They ended in 1967 with a draft Convention on Foreign Monetary Obligations[11] which in effect adopted the Dubrovnik rules. Yet once again the English did nothing. It was only the dramatic fall of sterling and the effect of inflation which compelled a Court of Appeal under the presidency and leadership of Lord Denning in 1974 deliberately and perhaps impermissibly to depart from the law laid down by the House of Lords, to disown what Lord Denning had said himself in giving his opinion in 1961 and to accept the submissions in the third edition of my book. Provoked by this unprecedented initiative the House of Lords two years later, this time under the presidency of Lord Wilberforce, at last followed suit[12] although with some reservations. But then years later[13] even these were thrown overboard. A battle for common sense justice begun forty years earlier had come to an end.

There were two other fundamental changes after 1971 which will make the fourth edition of the book a very different work. In the first-place inflation, hardly recognised in 1971 and certainly not explored by other scholars in their academic work, had assumed proportions by 1978 which created a grave social

---

10  *Re United Railways of Havana and Regla Warehouses*, [1961] A.C. 1007
11  Reports of the International Law Association (47th Conference, 1956) p. 29[?]
12  *Miliangus v. George Frank (Textiles) Ltd.*, [1975] A.C. 443
13  *The Despina R.*, [1979] A.C. 685

problem. The word "inflation" had been ignored for so long that English law appeared to lack any equipment for dealing with it. Whether it can be devised remains to be seen and depends to some extent on the question whether it will prove possible to contain the problem. Unfortunately, this seems highly unlikely, since the trade unions which have caused it and which have aggravated it by extracting by force of monopoly wage increases unrelated to the extent of productivity will not change their policy. Hence the law will have to afford relief in a certain type of case. Its definition will lead to much debate and I can only hope that the fourth edition will make a useful contribution. [58]

The third change in the breakdown of the international monetary system and, indeed, of almost all standards of value since 1971. The gravity of this wholly unsolved problem is not generally appreciated, nor has anyone been able to suggest an effective remedy, least of all the International Monetary Fund which, I fear, has completely failed as an international monetary institution. It is heretical, yet by no means unlikely that in the end a return to gold as a standard of value will appear as the only solution.

The book thus refutes the old English rule that no living author can be cited to or by a judge. It was frequently cited both by the Court of Appeal and the House of Lords, though judges of first instance have been more conservative and refrained, sometimes in remarkable circumstances, from referring to material which, though it had been drawn to their attention, was unworthy of judicial notice.[14] Incidentally, although my German students used to laugh when I told them about the old English rule, it is a matter for consideration whether to some extent and in certain cases there is not a lot of wisdom in it. When you remember that German lawyers, often for substantial payment, publish articles to influence the result in pending cases, you will at least concede this much: recent law review articles, if used at all may, depending on the identity of the author have to be treated with a measure of circumspection.

The book, however, has not been by any means the only outlet for my research. The conflict of laws has remained my special field and over the years a large number of articles appeared. They have not been collected in a single volume such as many of the German ones have. On the other hand, those on public international [law], or the majority of them, did appear in 1973 in a splendid volume published by the Clarendon Press under the title *Studies in International Law*. In this context I must say a few words about the great debt which I owe to the unforgettable Hersch Lauterpacht. It was in 1943, after a lecture I had given to the

---

14 See, e.g., Browne Wilkinson in Multiservice Bookbinding, (1978) LW.L.R. 535, whose judgment reflects Counsel's ample references to my book, but who does not mention it. Or see Lord Wilerberforce in [...] who approved Dicey – Morris – Kahn-Freund who in turn had acknowledged to do no more than to formulate what is said in my book

Grotius Society and he had attended, that I suddenly received a letter from him suggesting a meeting. From that first approach there stemmed a friendship which lasted, developed and grew until his premature death in 1962. No week passed when we did not exchange one or two letters or met for lunch at the Athenaeum. He was the kindest of men, the warmest of friends, the greatest of idealists and at the same time the sharpest of lawyers. And he had an uncanny ability to stimulate, suggest and provoke. In so far as I am concerned it is due to him alone that I have become interested in public international law and can now with some humility, describe myself as a student of and perhaps, as an expert in public international law, – I speak with hesitation, because the subject is now [59] so vast that none can claim to have a command of the whole of it. What is even more important is that Hersch Lauterpacht has determined my attitude towards international law, its character and limits. No wonder that he can be said to have founded a school, – his disciples (the most prominent being Richard Baxter, now Judge at the International Court of Justice) are all over the world and always ready in gratitude to acknowledge his pervading influence. The pity is the greater that the school has to a large extent failed the master. In England in particular, the study of international law has declined. The apparatus which in the modern world is enormous and which Lauterpacht created or kept in being has almost disappeared. The splendid textbook founded by L. Oppenheim and last edited by Lauterpacht in 1955 is probably incapable of being revived. If I look at what I have done I cannot help feeling with some satisfaction that within my limits I have not failed him.

It so happened that many years after his death I felt with much regret and reluctance unable to follow him on a point of law upon which I feared he had allowed his feelings to have precedence over strictly legal reasoning. In 1973 the Court of Appeal (Lord Denning M.R., Buckley and Orr L.JJ.) decided in the case of *Oppenheimer v. Cattermole*[15] that the notorious Nazi Decree of 23 November 1941 depriving German Jews outside Germany of their German nationality and confiscating their property was effective in England. In particular, public international law or public policy was not considered sufficient to disregard law recognised to be obnoxious, – a most extraordinary result. The problem was a famous one. It had arisen in numerous other countries. Lauterpacht had at an early stage written an article advocating a result which involved the recognition of the expatriation so as not to force upon the victim a distasteful nationality.[16] In all the earlier cases the recognition of statelessness was to the victim's advantage. In Oppenheimer's case the rejection of expatriation, i. e. the continued recognition of German nationality was to his advantage. When I saw a report of the decision it

---

15  [1973] Ch. 264
16  Jewish Year Book of International Law (1949) p. 164

# England 1946 and After

was mainly the jurisprudential aspect which caused me to write an article which appeared in April 1973 in the Law Quarterly Review.[17] I did then know that an appeal to the House of Lords had been prosecuted and that in fact by the time of the publication of my article the argument had been closed, some of the opinions had already been written and that the result, expected to be in favour of the appellant was likely to be announced any day. What happened was that some of the law lords had read my article. As a result, but without express reference to it, the unusual step of re-opening the hearing was taken. At the fresh hearing the case was sent back to the Special Commissioners for a new investigation of the German law. Eventually the case came back to the House of Lords, was re-argued and ended in the appeal being dismissed.[18] The essential [60] reason was that by Article 116 of its Basic Law the Federal Republic itself had recognised the expatriation of those non-resident Jews who were still living – an extremely doubtful line of reasoning, for it meant that, contrary to all its fundamental teachings, the Federal Republic had re-imposed its nationality upon non-residents over whom it had no jurisdiction. However, the majority of the House of Lords, making some very restrained acknowledgment to my article, in clear terms rejected the idea that an English court could ever recognise a decree such as that of 23 November 1941 which constituted a violation of human rights and international law. So on the jurisprudential aspect I had been successful. Yet it must not be overlooked that Lord Pearson, like before him Buckley and Orr L.JJ., adopted the typically positivistic attitude of the English lawyer: for him, a German law duly enacted by the German lawgiver was law which no English court could disregard. It is an attitude which in due course I shall have to note more than once and which is expressive of the traditional English legal mind or, more specifically, of the English approach towards statute law. It is probably due to the deep-seated, though wholly mistaken, belief in the inexorable omnipotence of Parliament or, indeed, of any lawgiver, which prevents any kind of judicial review.

It is rare in England that academic work has such rapid and unexpected an effect upon the decision of a case and the evolution of legal thought, but it is plain that during my lifetime the influence of academic work in general has become much more penetrating. Acadamic law is no longer treated with that contempt or at least indifference which used to characterize the English legal scene. In 1961 I had a case in the House of Lords in the course of which Counsel for my opponent cited the decision in *Kahler v. Midland*,[19] one of the most unfortunate and most unjust decisions ever rendered by the House of Lords. I had sharply criticized it

---

17 89 (1973) L.Q.R. 194
18 [1976] A.C. 249
19 (1950) A.C. 24

whenever the occasion arose, particularly in my book. (I must add for the sake of frankness, but with great shame that Herbert Smith & Co., long before I joined them, acted for the unsuccessful appellant and cannot be acquitted of their share of responsibility in the outcome which a different, more learned and more sustained argument might well have prevented.) When that case was mentioned, Viscount Simonds interrupted Counsel (Mr. T.G. Roche Q.C.) and said: "You know that this case has come in for a great deal of academic criticism and may have to be reconsidered". Whereupon Counsel replied: "Fortunately, my Lord, I never look at the stuff". This was a typical reaction, but I doubt whether today it would be allowed to pass without some judicial rebuke.

Although my work has concentrated on public and private international law and the relationship between both, I have on occasions ventured outside these fields. I mention such excursions here, because I have to leave that part of my work in a more unfinished state than any academic work is necessarily in, and it may be that someone who reads these lines will feel stimulated into taking it up. In 1959 the Law Quarterly Review published a contribution of mine entitled [61] 'Outline of a history of expropriation'.[20] I think (and my dear friend Arthur Goodhart, the then editor, thought so) that this is one of the best and most interesting things I wrote. It led to little reaction, but was intended as the first chapter of a great book on expropriation. Such a book, on a broad comparative basis, still deserves to be written. Its absence accounts in my view for the obscurity and uncertainty which surrounds very many parts of the international law of expropriation. If, for instance, people ask what basis there could be in international law for a rule prohibiting confiscation without just compensation, the answer is likely to be that the municipal practice of most states yields a compelling analogy upon which the international rule rests. Or if it is asked what "just" compensation means, a very detailed and comprehensive review of municipal legal systems would probably establish that there exists a wide measure of agreement about the extent of compensation and its calculation. Indeed, the very term "taking" is in great need of investigation: there exists in many countries a rich municipal practice on the question what constitutes a "taking" of property, and that practice would provide much guidance to the international lawyer. A book of that kind is an enormous task. It is unlikely that in present circumstances a single scholar can undertake it. I can only hope that in due course someone will pick up the threads which I could not combine into a complete work.

Very similar remarks apply to another hobby-horse I took up at a late stage of my life. The occasion was the Blackstone Lecture which Pembroke College, Oxford, invited me to give in 1977. I decided to speak about Britain's Bill of Rights.

---

20 75 (1959) L.Q.R. 188

The lecture was published by the Law Quarterly Review in October 1977.[21] Its main point, to put it with exaggerated shortness, was to draw attention to the paradox which precluded English judges from the judicial review of legislation, but entrusted it to a body of frequently second-rate foreigners from Cyprus or Portugal, Turkey or Iceland, Greece or Luxembourg, Malta or Finland. At the root of the trouble is the fact that in truth England has no constitutional law and, indeed, prides itsef in the so-called sovereignty of Parliament which is omnipotent and can, for instance, abolish everything, including itself. After the lecture had been given, there appeared the Report of the Select Committee on a Bill of Rights (House of Lords) and the volume of evidence given to the Committee. Neither affected the argument of my lecture, but the extraordinary mental gymnastics which English lawyers have to undergo when they discuss such problems as entrenchment or judicial review impressed me deeply and since they are so wholly inappropriate to the 20th century I decided to do some more work on a Bill of Rights, and its constitutional implications. But it will require an even greater abuse of parliamentary sovereignty and bureaucratic stranglehood before the British people will be prepared to trust its own judiciary rather than the Strasbourg authorities.

It cannot be of any general interest to explain why and how everyone of [62] my articles – well in excess of a hundred – was written. But it is important to say that, although there have been periods, usually short periods when I felt at a loose end and did not know what to do next, on the whole I have always had more ideas, plans and commitments than I could cope with. When I exclude the commitments – such as contributions to Festschriften, lectures at Universities here or abroad, courses of lectures at the Academy of International in the Hague (1959, 1964, 1971) or the Institut des Hautes Etudes Internationales in Geneva (1977) –, I owe it to my practical experience that I knew what to do. This is a lesson for many academics. Purely academic law is liable to become sterile. The demands of an extensive practice are such that they always lead to some fruitful starting point for research. It is rare that practice directly brings up the wish to explore a particular problem. What arises in practice is usually on the fringe of some central topic. Or when reading something up for the purpose of solving a specific, probably very narrow problem, one suddenly comes across or sees a much wider subject worthy of exploration. But it is life in practice that provides the fertile ground for work which, the author feels and some believe serves a useful purpose.

While speaking about the origin of my academic work, there is one further message which I am anxious to pass on. As a firm general rule, lawyers should never publish anything, unless they have something new to say. Mere repetition or the mere compilation of known material merits publication only in the most

---

21 (1978) L.Q.R. 512

exceptional case. The observation of the rule presupposes that before publication every conceivable effort has been to ensure that everything published on the subject has been read and that every relevant contribution has been cited. For the public and private international lawyer this means that he must be able to read (and to have access to) at least French, but preferably also German and Italian literature. He is most particularly exposed to the risk that what he believes is an original thought in England has occurred to others abroad. If this happens it may, in special cases, still be possible to publish in English, but the manner of presentation must be different. There is in any case nothing more humiliating than to find after publication that something important has been overlooked or even that somebody else has said the same thing before. In such an event an early opportunity must be taken to disclose and rectify the error. The true scholar will not hesitate to confess his errors. But he will also remember that the printed word is permanent and that few things justify permanence.

I have frequently been asked how I managed to combine my academic work with an extensive practice. I find it difficult to answer the question. In my case no less than in that of the rest of mankind the day does not have more than twenty-four hours. I must somehow have fitted it in. We would see friends, but we would not lead what one would call a social life. I would go to a theatre or a concert, many concerts, though I would select the best only. For the second-best my large collection of records was an adequate substitute. In the early [62] years I would spend even many an evening working on papers for the office, though in more recent times I have not done so. Nor did I go to bed much later than 10 p.m. Nonetheless, on principle I worked for myself in the evenings and during the greater part of the weekend, though Saturday mornings were invariably spent at the library of the London School of Economics or, more recently, the Instite of Advanced Legal Studies. The result seems to prove that, oddly enough, within the limits of the time thus found, I had enough leisure to do what I did. And there were always long holidays during which I did not do any work.

There is another activity which I must mention and which stands midway between academic life and practice of the law. Since 1952 a very great deal of my time has been spent on membership of national and international Committees and working parties. From 1952 to 1964 I belonged to the Lord Chancellor's Committee for the Reform of Private International Law. When coming to power in 1964 the Labour Government allowed it to become defunct without a single word about its existence or its disappearance being mentioned by anyone. Subsequently I was a member of numerous working parties usually set up by the Law Commission, such as the working party on the codification of contract law, on jurisdiction in divorce and nullity and the recognition of foreign divorce and nullity dec on the private international law relating to obligations, on the country's accession to the European Judgments Convention of 1968, on a Convention with the United States of America about the recognition and enforcement of judgments and so forth. At the same time I was the British member of a Council of Europe Committee on the unification of the law relating to the place of payment. I mention this work, because most people are unaware of the enormous amount of preparation and consultation which usually precedes legislation in the legal field. It is time-consuming work, because the amount of paper that has to be read before each meeting is heavy and the meetings themselves often occupy a whole day. It is a type of work which I find congenial, because it involves putting to use not only legal knowledge, but also legal imagination. But it is a remarkable feature of English life that one is expected to do such extensive and time-consuming work in the midst of an active professional life. That it is unpaid and unrecognised does not matter in a period of confiscatory taxation.

This is perhaps the place to mention one of the many other side-lines which brought variety and intellectual entertainment to my life. I happened to be in New York when the Alger Hiss trial took place. I was deeply shocked not only by the kind of publicity and press comment the case attracted, but also by the manner in which it seemed to have been conducted, which I believe to was typical of American procedure and so strange to the English lawyer's sense of justice, decorum and strictness. I felt grave doubts about the case and these were much increased when perhaps a year later I happened to meet at the house of the Thannhauser's Robert Benjamin, the lawyer who argued the appeal. In the result I received not only large parts of the record, but also came into touch with Chester Lane, the devoted lawyer who fought until his early death for a reopening [64] of the case and for whom I could do a little work of investigation in England. Later the press reported that Earl Jowitt was writing a book about the case. I wrote to him offering my help. This is how I came into close contact with Earl Jowitt and although he did not allow me to help him in any way in writing the book which in 1953 he published under the title of *The Strange Case of Alger Hiss*,[22] he asked me to read and criticise the manuscript and to check certain points for him.

It was a great pleasure to work with Jowitt in this way. He had a very sharp legal mind, but in particular he had an outstanding forensic experience and to discuss the frightful aberrations of American procedure with him was for me an illuminating experience. I cannot say it often enough: critics of the English system of judicial admonistration should keep their mouths shut so long as they have not made a prolonged and detailed practical study of foreign procedures. It was only years later that I personally met Hiss. That he was wrongly convicted has been my firm view for more than thirty years. Nothing would give me greater satisfaction than to live to see it proved right.

---

22 E. Jowitt, *The Strange Case of Alger Hiss* (1953), Doubleday & Company, New York.

Nothing I have been saying must give the impression that my academic work, that is to say, my research, my writing, my lecturing, was other than purely incidental to my practice. It was my practice which I was determined to build up. It was my practice which required my full attention. It was my clientele which was my primary concern and which had to be looked after and which was very perhaps unusually, demanding. The extent to which I succeeded will appear from the second part of these memoirs. By 1955 a solid basis had been created. At that moment a great misfortune occurred. On 20 May 1955, by the absurdest of motor car accidents, my dear friend Douglas Phillips was killed. I lost a faithful and warm-hearted friend, an intelligent colleague imbued with commonsense, but also with enthusiasm and energy. He was only fifty-five years old. For a time I felt almost paralysed with grief and also with worry, because from then onwards the practice and, in particular, the acquisition of a good clientele rested almost entirely on my shoulders. The rescue came when in the summer of 1957 Herbert Smith & Co., then a relatively small firm with nine partners and a staff of about sixty, approached me with a view to amalgamation. We quickly came to an agreement and as from 1 January 1958 the amalgamation took effect. It proved a happy marriage, free from any tension or difficulty, and it was a very successful one, for at the moment of writing Herbert Smith & Co. has more than forty partners and a staff of almost four hundred and is certainly one of the largest and most highly reputed firms of solicitors in the country.

In the new surroundings the type and rhythm of my work changed very quickly. It became the exception that I dealt with a matter alone and at all its stages. I had assistance from some ten or twelve younger lawyers who formed part of the various departments into which the firm is divided and who, under my continuous supervision, attended to the detailed work. I hardly ever saw clients alone. The younger partner or assistant was present throughout. While the mail came in [65] the first instance to me (so that I was informed about the progress of every matter), I passed it on. We met to discuss policy or, on occasion, details. In the result I did much more than before, but I did it differently and, I believe, more efficiently. As time goes on the role of an older partner changes. His personal practice is liable to become very specialised, but also within the firm his status becomes more and more that of a consultant in that younger men come to discuss their problems with him. In my experience this is one of the great advantages of a large firm. People talk things over, – they have the opportunity of doing so and, moreover, in so far as I personally am concerned I have always encouraged a continuous exchange of views, for it is this method which more than any other enables an older man to pass on his experience, the know-how which cannot be read up in books and, most particularly, his standard of professional work and attitudes. By this I do not only mean matters of etiquette, though they are not to be underrated. I also mean the approach to a case, the

# England 1946 and After

method of investigating and handling it, the formation of conclusions. Lawyers in a large firm are far too readily inclined to regard it as an institution which is bound to exist for ever, while in truth it may go downhil more speedily than it could ever be built upon. It is important to hammer it into their heads that even a large firm is a professional one, that it is conditioned by the quality of its partners and that the outlook of a professional man is fundamentally different from that of either a businessman or a civil servant. The lawyer must not have any interest other than that of his client at heart, subject only to the demands of propriety. And he must have them completely and unreservedly at heart, – the responsibility is his, not, for instance, Counsel's. It is one of the disadvantages of the English legal system that solicitors are far too ready to believe in the wisdom and knowledge of Counsel rather than to think for themselves. I shall never forget the case of the large Italian firm which consulted one of the leading London firms and, through it, the most fashionable commercial silk of the day in a case involving thirteen million dollars. He advised in two written opinions that there was a case. Thereupon the Italians came to me. I looked at the case independently, with my own eyes, uninfluenced by anything that happened before. I found that the earlier approach had been wrong in that the wrong question had been asked, namely what F.P. Neill Q.C. subsequently instructed by me called a "bizarre" question which had nothing to do with the issue. We started proceedings. The point anticipated by the great man was not even taken against us. After fifteen days we recovered judgment in full. Why? Simply because I had used my own brain and refused to be led or misled by anyone else. This is what a large firm has or should have, to offer. The specialised knowledge and experience, the independence of judgment, the critical attitude towards what counts as authority. Try again! Never give up!

In recent years it has unfortunately become fashionable to consult merchant [66] banks not merely on matters of pure finance, but much more generally on policy, on legal possibilities and methods, on commercial matters and their legal implications. Merchant banks exist to make money. They are not professional men whose primary duty is a fiduciary one. This is what distinguishes them from lawyers. This is what one day will cause them grave difficulties, the conflict between their own interest and the interest of the client. The lawyer has no interest of his own. Yet merchant banks charge scandalously high fees. They are usually unaware of their correspondingly high responsibility.

While it is my sincere hope that Herbert Smith & Co. will maintain the standards of efficiency and integrity which it has reached in my time, and while I am sure that many of the large firms in the City of London will follow successfully a similar course, I am, on the whole, very pessimistic about the future of solicitors in England. In my time I have witnessed a considerable lowering of professional attitudes. Excessive levels of taxation, inflation and continuously rising over-

**90**  England 1946 and After

heads will lead to the erosion of professional probity such as it used to exist. There exists a strong political element which is determined to undermine the Bar which, on the whole, has been a safeguard against abuse. The same elements are opposed to "the establishment", to authority, to tradition. Thus there are many solicitors who believe that they ought to be allowed to do the barrister's job, but they never ask themselves whether the average solicitor has the knowledge and ability to argue a case of any importance or what the consequences of the abolition of the present system would be. In 1977 I tried to describe them in an article which appeared in the Law Quarterly Review.[23] But none of those who shout the loudest has vouchsafed a reply or otherwise tried to meet the challenge. In my time I have seen a good bit of litigation and legal practice in the United States, Germany, Switzerland, France, Austria. I have no hesitation in saying that, as regards quality of the decision and the decision-making process, speed of decision and efficiency of procedure, the English legal system is far superior, – but this point among many others derived from almost fifty years of practical experience had better be left to the second part.

Before I turn to it there is one fact which I must record. In course of time my work brought me into contact with a great many lawyers, mainly members of the Bar, who became firm friends and who remained friends, when they went to the Bench. In fact most of those who are now on the Bench are at least well nown to me. It would be tedious and tactless to enumerate all the names, or to speak of acts of kindness or recognition which so many of them have shown me. In many cases, such as those of Mark Littman Q.C. and Sir Michael Kerr, future chapters will provide me with an opportunity of talking about my relationship with them, – a relationship which continues on the most intimate terms and is a source of great satisfaction to me. But there are three people who I feel have deserve being specially mentioned. [67]

In the first place I must mention Lord Denning. I met him in the early years of the war, when I consulted him on behalf of a client of Douglas Phillips. An English woman, while in France shortly before the outbreak of war, became insane and was held in an institution in France. Her English property was being administered by a Receiver appointed by the Court of Protection. Was she resident in France, so that the Trading with the Enemy Act applied? Since then I have met Lord Denning on innumerable occasions and in many different surroundings. I have the most charming letters from him, – all written by hand. To give a single example, when I spoke highly[24] of his partly dissenting opinion in *Rahimtoola v. Westminster Bank*[25] (of which he later said[26] that he had never taken so much

---

23  Law Quarterly Review 1977, 367
24  21 (1958) Mod. L.R. 165
25  *Rahimtoola v. The Nizam of Hyderabad* [1958] A.C.

England 1946 and After

trouble over an opinion as in that case) he wrote me a latter saying that my remarks were an encouragement for him. In short, I owe him innumerable acts of personal kindness. In particular he readily accepted the suggestion (not made by me or with my knowledge) that the annual F.A.Mann lecture which on the occasion of my 70th birthday a number of friends initiated and the first of which was given by Lord Diplock in October 1977 and the second by President Benda of the Federal Constitutional Court of Germany, should be held under the auspices of the British Institute of International and Comparative Law. But the reason why I am specifically referring to Lord Denning in the present context is the enormous debt of gratitude which all English, indeed all British lawyers of my generation and of many future generations owe him as a unique stimulator: he the law moving, he made innumerable suggestions for changes and improvements, his sense of justice frequently ran away and overcame legal restraints but his his reasoning, his intellectual and moral process always is fascinating and challenging and his English style invariably superb. It does not matter whether his decisions, always expressed in the most beautiful English, were "right" or "wrong", – they frequently were "wrong". The point is that they were always interesting, usually progressive and possibly anticipating what may become the law in future years. Lord Denning's achievement which I cannot adequately define is immense and I am sure that a large part of it will in due course meet with universal acknowledgment, even though in our time it is open to criticism. To that achievement I would like to pay tribute.

The second name I would like to mention is that of Sir John Foster Q.C. Lord Radcliffe one day said to me that John had never received that public recognition which was his due. I agree and would like to make amends to the limited extent that is within my power. I first met John before the war through Douglas Phillips who was a friend of his. In due course he became my regular Counsel, but he also became much more than that. He became a great friend and, somewhat unusually, one of my chief sources of interesting work. He is a man [68] who knows everybody in the world who is of any consequence. In particular he knows foreign countries and most of the important people in each one of them. Thus it came about that foreigners frequently wished to consult him, but in those days not even foreigners could have direct access to members of the Bar, so he sent a good many clients to me. In fact some of my most valuable clients were directly or indirectly introduced to me through John. Working with him was always a great pleasure for me. His mind is one of the quickest I have known. He is a man of ideas. His intellectual powers are outstanding. The trouble is that he cannot make his abilities apparent. He is a poor speaker. His advocacy is not impressive. But what he says in his sloppy, inarticulate way persuades by the force of his argument, the

26

simplicity of his reasoning and his concentration upon the essentials of a case or a point. But he also has many interests outside the law. He has done a lot for refugees. He has supported many good causes in his life. He has a wholly independent mind and he speaks it. No wonder the establishment never allowed him to get as far as his intellect and the integrity of his character required. Just before the Conservatives came back in October 1951, I had a case in which Sir Walter Monckton K.C. was leading John, then a young silk, and Mark Littman. It was confidently expected by all three and, indeed, by all who believed to be in the know that Monckton would become Attorney-General and John Solicitor-General. We know that Monckton became Minister of Labour and John Under-Secretary of State in the Commonwealth Office. The latter was a most regrettable appointment. Two years later John abandoned the idea of a political career and returned to the Bar. It was the country's loss and my gain.

Lastly, I have to refer to a great friend who I am sorry to say is no longer alive, J.G. (Tom) Strangman Q.C. He retired early from the Bar, never having reached the heights which were his due. He was one of the best advocates I ever met and a splendid cross-examiner, but somehow did not gain general recognition. I owe him a great deal, not only because he achieved the almost unbelievable feat of winning for me no less than seventeen cases consecutively, but also and mainly because I learned so much from him. He was a great tactician. He knew (and taught me) all the tricks of litigation. He proved that in England a lawyer engaged in litigation must devote himself to the case in hand wholeheartedly, give it exclusive attention and know it so completely and intimately that at any given moment he can appreciate, find and exploit the required point. This is the traditional approach which has become all too rare. Far too many members of the Bar (and solicitors) believe that they can simultaneously have their fingers in several pies. The truth is that nobody can and that the hybris of many a fashionable silk has cost their client dearly. Tom retired at a relatively early age and lived in the country growing orchids and forgetting the law. I have not forgotten a great master of the law in practice. [68a]

# Eleonore

She was called Lore Ehrlich. Her real name was Eleonore. Her mother chose it on account of an almost childish admiration for Eleonora Duse, the actress.

She must have been a precocious child. William Stern in his work on the Psychology of Children records the "little Lore E." as the child with the earliest memory. She was an outstanding pupil, primarily interested in and gifted for mathematics. Her love for her father who died in 1926 was deep and lasting. Her feelings towards her mother who died in Israel aged ninety-three were ambivalent and at times approached hate and hostility. As a child she suffered from her mother's oddities, her narrow-mindedness, her prejudices, her intense dependence upon the very bourgeois milieu of her family, of Jewish society in Breslau, her unusual capacity of turning small matters into big issues, to fuss and worry and make mountains out of molehills. Getting away from this setting became almost an obsession. The right to have short hair, what at the time was called an "Eton crop", was the anxiously awaited sign of emancipation and came only when she was about sixteen, in 1923.

I met her, I think, in 1929. As I have already mentioned, we were both Assistants at the Faculty of Law in Berlin, though at first this did not mean much because she was attached to the Institute of Criminal Law which to a considerable extent led a life of its own. But she also had a cousin, Robert Seligson, whom I had met in Geneva and who was one of my best friends, and we met frequently in the house of his parents. She was a very attractive girl, good-looking but not "pretty", very vivacious, dashing, full of zest, curiosity, vivacity, *joie de vivre*, ready to laugh, at the same time highly intelligent, critical, willing to argue and to challenge, sometimes merely to provoke, amusing but not superficial, clever but not showing-off. As time went on she changed, but I am now speaking of our early days.

There was nothing special that brought us together. We accepted and respected each other, perhaps we even enjoyed our meetings, but there was nothing in the nature of a "special relationship". In the summer of 1930, as was usual at the time, we both held vacation courses for law students, for which we were paid by the faculty. She was a particularly popular lecturer and teacher, attracted large classes and therefore made a good bit of money. In September 1930 she unexpectedly came to see me in what was then called the Kaiser Wilhelm Institute housed in the former Imperial Palace and is now the Max Planck Institute in Hamburg. I was working there on my thesis for the doctorate. Why she decided to look me up remained a mystery. Ostensibly she came to tell me that she had decided to spend the money earned by vacation courses on a trip to New York, where she proposed to stay for six months working for an American lawyer. She had called to say good-bye. The result was that I collected my papers and left with her. We talked. We had dinner together. We spent a pleasant evening. We parted and she was due to take the train for Hamburg the next day. [68b]

And then, some weeks later, out of the blue I received a letter from her in New York. It led to regular correspondence. More than that: I can say we fell in love by correspondence. She returned in April 1931. We were firm friends and soon we became lovers. We remained lovers and, as I have already recounted, got married at 9 a.m. on 12 October 1933 underneath a photograph of Hitler and emigrated an hour later. She never returned to Berlin or to Breslau.

We stayed together for a little more than 47 years, until her death on 20 November 1980. For months it had been obvious that her health was failing. But she steadfastly refused to see a doctor, – apart from gynocologists on the occasions of her pregnancies she had last seen a doctor in 1934, nor had she ever been ill. At long last, on 14 November 1980, she went to see Dr. Peter Meyer, one of our closest friends. He found that she had lost almost two thirds of her blood. Next day I took her to the London Clinic, where she was given blood transfusions. Then tests were made. She was told that there was a growth in her bowels. I was, but she was not, told that it was cancer. An operation was necessary. The surgeon was to see her on the 19th. Having talked to Jessica rationally and affectionately for about an hour, she left the Clinic in her own car at 11 a.m. She went home. She tidied up her affairs. She collected some money. Under a false name (Mrs. Addison) she went to a hotel. She took an overdose and, reading a detective novel, went to sleep, never to wake up again. She was found next day. There was a note giving her real name with detailed instructions. There was the following letter addressed to me, – a letter which deserves to be quoted in full: –

19.11.1980

Dear Francis,

I wish I could spare you this but it is really quite impossible for me to go through with this operation. You know how I hate having medical attention of any kind. It is not the actual pain involved so much as the indignity of becoming a mere object. I simply cannot face up to it. This may be a cowardly way out but I had decided long ago that in case like this I would choose death rather than the alternative. In any case, even if the operation were a success one would then spend the rest of one's life having check-ups for secondary cancer, and if you remember the letters from the Auburns between Walter's operation and his death you must agree that it is better to die quickly. You know my views on Euthanasia and my dread of becoming old and helpless.

I am more sorry than I can say that I cannot postpone it till Jessica has left but she certainly will understand my motives. I want people to remenber me as I am, and believe me, once you have got over the first shock you will realize that in spite of Peter's firm words and reassurances this is the better way. I am completely unsuited to being an invalid.

What more can I say? I cannot write a letter full of noble sentiments as Virginia Woolf left for her husband before she killed herself.

I am deeply unhappy to have to hurt you like this. Forgive me for doing things my way and being true to my principles. Please try to understand me. I have had a long and full life and I do not regret leaving it while I am still the same person I was.

I hope the children will understand and the grandchildren can be told that I died of a serious illness which is of course true.

I need not tell you that I don't want any fuss about cremation which would [68c] probably cause you less trouble than arrangements for my body to be used for research.

Leave all the arrangements to the children. When I had begun to feel ill and exhausted I hoped I would die quickly of a heart attack which is why I let things slide.

With love to you, the children and the grandchildren

> Yours L.

And to our friend and medical advisor, Dr. Peter Meyer, she wrote as follows: –

Dear Peter,

I am more sorry than I can say to cause you all this trouble. You know my views on Euthanasia and my dread of being old and an invalid and although you disagree with me you can probably understand my motives. Look after Francis, I wish I could have spared him this.

Thank you for all your great kindness to me during all these years.

With all my love to you and Eva

> Yours Lora.

As throughout her life, she spoke the truth. Her integrity as well as the strength of her character and convictions were complete. She had often said that she was not prepared to become a burden to anyone and would prefer to die rather than lead the life of an invalid. We did not take it altogether seriously. But she was serious. I recall the almost whimsical expression in her face when we urged her to see a doctor. She could not face illness, invalidity, helplessness, dependence. She was determined to be the master of her own life. She preferred to take it while she could do so rather than to prolong it in circumstances which might render her incapable and a useless burden. This was her philosophy. She lived and she died according to its rules. She did not give medicine a chance, because medicine might not give her a chance. In fact she had no chance. A post mortem examination the results of which came to light during the Inquest established that she was riddled with secondaries and had nothing to expect but a painful death within a few weeks. It was a devastating shock to all of us. But we must respect her for principles, for the nobility of her character, the obstinacy of her resolution, for the moving feelings expressed with classical stoicism and dignity. There was an element of selfishness in her decision. In truth she was the most unselfish of persons, full of love and concern for her children and grandchildren, for the poo for mankind. And she was of extraordinary shyness, and so modest that she was almost obsessed by her anxiety not to inconvenience anyone; hence her written instructions: "No mourning, no letters, no flowers."

I hope I will be forgiven for having said, even at the risk of some repetition, a few words of a very personal character about the woman who for almost 50 years was my wife. My purpose was to introduce the person who also led a double life, – a second life which had not received the recognition it deserves and which the public, in particular the legal public ought to appreciate. [68d]

At heart she was a professional woman and, while in the old days she was greatly interested in law as such, in the theory, the logical games which reminded her of her original interest in mathematics. She qualified as a solicitor in 1953, when the youngest child was nine years old and over the worst. She then took odd jobs, helping here and there in the West London area, near our home in Addison Aveaue, as a sort of *locum tenens.* In February 1964 she opened her office in Portobello Road, one of the poorest districts of London with a population consisting of many different nationalities. She did so, not for the purpose of making a profit, but simply to help. At the time there was no Neighbourhood Law Centre in the district, there were only one or two other solicitors in the area, who, naturally, had to work for a living, while, as she frequently said, she could work for altruistic purposes because she had a husband who was earning. She devoted herself to helping the poor. She never accepted a case other than a legally aided one. She soon became a focal point in North Kensington, generally recognised for her unfailing willingness to help, her generosity, her interest in humanity, her absolute professional integrity, her generosity. What she saw and heard influenced her deeply. She became a left-wing socialist. She lost interest in the type of work I was doing. She could not see that there was a different world outside the confines of North Kensington, which had an equal right to be served. She became an almost fanatical believer in simplicity, in the sordidness of privileges, in the inadequacy of our social services, yet she did not fail to recognise and condemn abuses of the system, of which she saw more than most. For about seventeen years, when she came home in the evening, she would entertain me with the iniquities and scandals which during the day she had come across. Often her stories were such as to require and deserve publication, but she never published a single line, – she would not believe that her voice carried any weight. Her modesty, her humility developed into the suppression of her individuality. She became overwhelmed by her daily experience which filled her mind and heart and reduced her interest in everything outside her world. Such energy as she had was primarily devoted to fighting poverty and injustice from the little world of two small rooms at 204 Portobello Road. Let these few pages be a monument, the only monument to a devoted friend of the under-dog. If ever an individual served the public and deserved, but never received recognition of these services, it was Eleonore. While she would fight for others, she became the most self-effacing person one can imagine, and also so selfless as to deny herself what others could not have. In the last years of her life she would not travel with me, for she disliked the sort of hotel I would frequent. She would not buy clothes except to the necessary extent. She would dislike restaurants except the simple ones.

Nevertheless, as I have said, she led a double life, because she also had a private life, namely her life as a housewife, mother, grandmother, friend, – a [68e] life which most would regard as a full-time task, but which she managed on the side. More than that, – there were the papers she read and there was about a book a day that she succeeded in reading. I have never been able to understand how she did it. She was most reliable, fullyinformed source of knowledge about new books, new plays or films, about new scientific developments, about every cultural activity other than music or the visual arts. This all-embracing knowledge had a serious effect on me. I came to appreciate it to the full extent only after her death. I saved a great deal of time in that I could merely glance at newpapers and magazines, relying on her to tell me about books, theatres and other pieces of news that she thought I should know about or I would be interested in. Her private life, therefore, was equally full, – indeed she was the beloved centre of her family, the provider, for her household always displayed the highest standards, there was always good, but not extravagant food, there was always something special for the grandchildren, she would never visit a child without bringing a suitable present, she would never run out of any of the necessities of life. What for others would have been a life of its own, and a full one at that, was for her only a second life, yet a complete one. She proved that by intelligent organisation you can make the apparently impossible possible. She was a considerable personality. Her family will forever miss her.

What I owe to her is a thing about which even now, long after her death, I cannot talk publicly. But it is only fair to record the fact that without her I would not have been able to lead the successful double life I am describing in these pages. That life was only possible, because she relieved me of all work in or about the house. Moreover, she made no demands on my time. It was only on rare occasions that we went out to see friends or to go to the theatre, to concerts or films. Usually she allowed me to work. Immediately after dinner and on weekends. She was full of understanding that I had to read papers for the office or was doing some research with a view to preparing an article or a lecture. Or I had to read proofs. Or I had to review a book. And so on. She respected, promoted and supported the curious life I had to lead to give it the quality it had. Few wives would have put up with what appeared to be neglect, but in truth was a common attitude of responsibility for progress and improvement. I recognise and pay tribute to the enormous contribution she made to everything I did and, perhaps, achieved.

She will forever live in our memories and fill our minds and hearts. [69]

**Part II: Cases**

# Chapter 11 – Expert

It was only natural that it was in my capacity as a German lawyer that I had my first contacts with litigation in England. The very first case I ever had brought many lessons. In particular it taught me how to lose a case within the first few minutes.

At some time early in 1934 there was a knock at the door of my ground floor room in Hastings House, 10 Norfolk Street, W.C.2. The visitor was Mr. Frederick Graham Maw, the senior partner of Rowe & Maw, who had seen the words "German lawyers" written on the door. He came to consult me in the case of *Sommer v. Mathews.*[27] Dr. Albert Sommer, a Jewish industrialist in Dresden, had in 1932 insured his property with Lloyds against "loss of and/or damage to the property, directly caused by requisition and/or confiscation or wilful destruction by the Government". After Hitler had come to power on 30 January 1933 and while Dr. Sommer was on a business trip to the United States of America Storm troopers possession of the property and turned it into a so-called "Corruption Bureau". At the same time "not a little of the plaintiff's wine was drunk, ... quite illegitimately, ... and that was really pilfering". This state of affairs continued until 1 June 1933, the criticial date under the policy, and probably longer. Mr Justice Roche held that, while there had been requisition (as opposed to confiscation), there had been no "loss", but only damage caused thereby. It was the plaintiff's leading Counsel, Mr Stuart Bevan K.C., lead Mr D. N. Pritt K.C. and Mr H. L. Parker, the later Lord Chief Justice, who failed to do justice to his case. He opened it by speaking about some people called Storm Troopers who occupied the plaintiff's house, drank his wine, used his ch, slept in his bed, so that after a few minutes the Judge asked: "This is trespass and no doubt damage, but where is the loss"? That any Jewish property the Nazi Storm Troopers took was lost to the Jewish owner was an idea which the Judge could not grasp. Had the case been fought a few years later the outcome would probably have been different. The report is incomplete in one very important respect. The essential point which we

---

27  49 (1934) Ll.L.R. 154

**102**                                                                                              Expert

tried to prove and which is inherent in the finding of requisition was that occupation by Storm Troopers was occupation by a State authority. As the report
indicates, Rheinstrom and Wer were called as experts, but there was also the
expert evidence of no less a lawyer than the eminent Hans Kelsen whose services I
had procured. Even he, however, did not succeed in conveying to the Judge a
picture of the reality of conditions in Germany, – the Judge thought of Germany
as a civilised country, could not really appreciate that if a group of people called
Storm Troopers occupied a house and turned it into a Corruption Bureau this
was more than trespass or that drinking the plaintiff's wine was anything other
than "pilfering". Although the outcome of the case was unsatisfactory to the
plaintiff, [70] I benefited from it, for it was the first time that I could observe
expert witnesses giving evidence and being cross-examined by no less an advocate than Sir William Jowitt K.C. whose conduct of the case was extremely skilful
in that it made you think of Germany as a country where the rule of law was
supreme.

In the following years there were many occasions when I had to give expert
evidence by affidavit, the most celebrated case being the decision of Mr Justice
Morton (as he then was) in *Ellinger v. Guiness Mahon & Co.*[28], my first encounter
with the intricacies of 0.11, where the Judge held, inter alia, that, notwithstanding
a contractual clause conferring jurisdiction on a German court, the Jewish
plaintiff could not in the then-existing circumstances be expected to find justice
in Germany. But my first and very important test of oral expert evidence occurred
in February and March 1940 in the case of *Ginsberg v. Canadian Pacific
Steamships Ltd.*[29] To put it very shortly, my client Mr Herbert Ginsberg formerly a
banker in Berlin and a well-known collector of Chinese art had paid in Reichs-
mark some £2,500 to Canadian Pacific Steamships Ltd. under a contract governed
by English law to pay for a world cruise which was due to begin in January 1939,
but was eventually cancelled. Having emigrated from Germany he claimed repayment of the fare paid by him. Numerous defences were raised. From a general
point of view the most important point, probably, was one which is not always
remembered. Some of the essential documents were overstamped: "No refund of
value whatsoever may be made outside Germany", – a clause which, so the Judge
very significantly held, had no contractual character, but merely gave notice of
some of the effects of some German exchange control restrictions. Their implication was in fact the main issue in the case. I was called as expert behalf of the
plaintiff and my friend, Dr Alfred Kauffmann, formerly a very distinguished
lawyer in Hamburg, was the defendants' expert. The Judge, Mr Justice Atkinson,
accepted my evidence. He decided in favour of the plaintiff who was living as a

---

28  (1939) 4 All E.R. 16
29  66 (1940) Ll.L.R. 206

Expert 103

refugee in Holland and, with the most enormous difficulties, had been given a permit by the Home Office to come to London to attend the hearing and give evidence. (After the low Countries had been overrun he managed escape to the United States and after the war he once came to visit me.) The case was in many respects fascinating. The Judge was known to be a plaintiff's judge and he certainly was in this case in which he made no secret of his sympathies. The defendants were represented by Mr Gilbert Paull K.C. (who many years later became Mr Justice Paull). I was to come across him on many occasions. He was a good lawyer and a great fighter, but I always felt that he was lacking in judgment and fighting too hard, with far too much insistence and little elegance. The plaintiff's Counsel, on the other hand, was the unforgettable Valentine Holmes. It was my first encounter with a man for whom I was to acquire the greatest respect and, indeed, love and admiration and who was not only one of the best lawyers I ever met, but also the most persuasive [71] advocate, though he never employed persuasiveness as a weapon. He was in 1940 and remained until well after the war Junior Counsel to the Treasury, but with his tremendous capacity for work he continued to carry on a private practice so for many years I had the good fortune to work closely with a man who represented the best the English Bar can offer, – as a man, a character, an intellect, as a gifted lawyer, as a mind of complete independence and integrity. Lastly, I had my first experience of the witness box. It became clear to me that in order to be believed, a witness should be given the opportuniy of giving an answer which is unfavourable to him or his case, – in fact skilful Counsel invariably try this trick. In this case it was the Judge who gave me the opportunity which, quite unwittingly, I used: I gave a truthful answer, but did not then realise that it would greatly impress the judge. The report is muddy on the point, but the sequence was as follows. There was a question whether the German Exchange Control authorities had in law the power to revoke a permission orally. The question was first put to Dr Kauffmann. He answered that writing was necessary. The answer was very, in fact far too favourable to the plaintiff. So a day or so later the Judge turned to me and asked: "I expect you agree that writing is necessary". I said that Dr Kauffmann was in error and that a permission could be orally revoked. The Judge was visibly astonished and asked me whether I was sure. I answered in the affirmative. Later Dr Kauffmann was recalled and agreed with me. There is nothing to be proud of: a witness, whether expert or not, has to tell the truth. The point is that it is an advantage to have the opportunity of doing so demonstrably. It is normally part of the art of advocacy to bring it about, prererably in connection with a point which is not decisive, yet not entirely incidental.

German Exchange Control problems arose in a number of other cases which were not reported and the details of which I cannot remember. Some of them involved important points, but during the war paper was scarce and reporting

**104**
Expert

facilities were much reduced. I have, however, some recollection of a case which in June 1941 came before Mr Justice Tucker (as he then was). In *Amalgamated Dental Ltd.v. Schindler*[30] Dr Schindler, a Jewish dentist who then practised in Munich had purchased goods from the English company, payment to be made to its German agent, such payment was contrary to German exchange control regulations and the money was confiscated. The payment was also invalid under German law. When sued after his emigration in England, the defendant pleaded the payment – a defence on the ground that by English law it was effective. As the contract was subject to English law, the Judge rejected the defence.

All these were relatively small cases, though their educational value was considerable. A much more important and exciting case, a case which in some is of great interest arose only in October 1950 when, on the instructions of Messrs. Kaufmann & Seigal, I was their expert witness in an action by Mr. Max [72] Hinrichsen against Novello Ltd. For more than six days I was being examined by Mr. Pascoe Hayward K.C. and cross-examined by Mr. Shelley K.C. before Mr. Justice Wynn-Parry whose judicial knowledge of me was to prove pregnant with consequence since two years later he was to be appointed Chairman of the Lord Chancellor's Standing Committee for the Reform of Private International Law, of which, as I have explained earlier, I became a member, – I always fancied this to be due to my having been an expert witness in that unforgettable case. Unfortunately, it is again not fully reported and the dramatic facts must therefore be stated in a little detail. The highly respected Hinrichsen family were the owners of the famous music publishers C.F. Peters in Leipzig. The Hinrichsen's were Jews and in November 1938 the father and one son were held in the Buchenwald concentration camp. It was made clear to them that they would be released and allowed to leave Germany if they "sold" their business to a nominee of Goering, a Dr Hermann. They had an "Aryan" manager, Mr. Petschull, who acted as a go-between and gave evidence in the course of the London trial, – evidence which made a deep impression upon everyone and would be worthy of the pen of a more skilful narrator than I am. He described how the Hinrichsen's brought directly from the concentration camp appeared before a notary in Berlin, Dr. Phillip Mähring who in post-war Germany became a prominent lawyer at the Federal Supreme Court, a professor at more than one University, the recipient of Festschrift and altogether a highly respected personality. They signed a contract by which they sold the business to the purchaser for a trifling sum. They were then released and went to live in Holland where in 1940 they were caught by the Germans, taken to Auschwitz and killed. Max Hinrichsen who had previously come to England was appointed as administrator of the estates of his parents and

---

30 I shortly referred to the case in *Studies in International Law*, p. 441 note or 1943 L.Q.R. 16 N. 73

Expert **105**

his brother. He brought an action for the return of the non-German copyright in the C.F. Peters edition, which just before the war the defendants Novello & Co ltd., had bought from Dr Hermann. Numerous questions of German law arose, apart from questions of English law on which the judgments of both Mr. Justice Wynn-Parry[31] and the Court of Appeal[32] are reported. The matter was complicated by the fact that, while Leipzig was under American occupation, Max Hinrichsen who had served in the British Army succeeded in getting there and obtained from the Military Governor certain confirmations which were said to have the effect of re-vesting the business of C.F. Peters in him. But the principal point was whether under German law the contract made before the Berlin notary was valid. It was made at a time when according to the views of those in power and the large majority of the population it was in the highest degree meritorious in the interest of the community. How could it twelve years later be said to have been invalid ab initio so as to be incapable to transfer title to the purchaser and through him [73] to the defendants? At the time of the hearing German restitution legislation was not yet in force. There was a decision of the Berlin Court of Appeal to the effect that according to the true, undistorted conceptions of German law such contracts were at all times contra bonos mores and invalid, and there was at least one decision of a District Court to the same effect. Another District Court decision expressed the opposite view. My opponent, E.J. Cohn, relied heavily on the latter and dismissed the ample academic material which supported me as unrepresentative of German legal practice. In the result the Judge could not be persuaded to adopt a view which was so inconsistent with the positivist approach and literalism characteristic of and traditional for an English lawyer, – there are no more positivistic lawyers anywhere than in England. He felt that logic required him to hold the contract valid. Nevertheless, it was, of course, clear that he would not decide in favour of a defendant who presented so undeserving a case. He held that the contract was in substance confiscatory, and could not therefore have extra-territorial effect so as to dispose of non-German copyright.

From a jurisprudential point of view the decision – if only it had been reported! – is fascinating. Subsequent events confirmed the evidence I had given the Federal Supreme Court developed its famous theory of the absolute injustice, the "non-law", and of the continued and permanent existence of the fundamental conceptions of the true, "purified" German law which no legislator, no dictator, no "lawgiver" could displace, – a theory which has met with far too little attention from legal philosophers outside Germany and which is one of the great achievements of the Federal Supreme Court, for it was the basis which enabled

---

31  68 [1951] R.P.C. 243
32  [1951] 1 Ch. 515

**106**  Expert

both in civil and criminal matters to treat as wrongful acts which according to Nazi heresies were lawful. Some ten years later, supported by the wealth of material which had accumulated in Germany, I was called upon to give evidence, again before the Foreign Compensation Commission on behalf of Baron Rothschild. The Commission had no difficulty in accepting my evidence that notwithstanding a "sale" in 1938 he had remained the owner of a large estate and was entitled to compensation for its taking by Czechoslovakia. But in 1950 Mr. Justice Wynn-Parry felt safer within the shell of traditional positivism. The second comm which that great case provokes is that, as I always felt, E.J. Cohn acted improperly in giving evidence in favour of the Nazi view. At the time all of ... greeted the Berlin decision and the discussions it provoked as an act of intellectual liberation. All of us were arguing that it was impossible for the law of the Federal Republic to uphold the validity of Nazi legislation and Nazi ideas of law. It was a great crusade in which all homines bonae voluntatis participated and I am convinced that in his heart Cohn himself belonged to the school which in Germany was represented by Gustav Radbruch and which one may describe as anti-positivistic. At any rate a Jew could not possibly adopt a different attitude and defend the continued validity of conceptions which had caused untold miseries to the Jewish people. No ethics of the profession compelled [74] him to take such a stand. Even if he had been Counsel rather than an expert witness he could not accept, for instance, the defence of Goering. Similarly he ought not to have accepted the defence of legal views which Goering propagated. Perhaps I am wrong in my criticism, but the point is of some general interest, and it is for this reason that I felt it right to make my opinion on it clear.

A case which in one important respect had a certain similarity with Hinrichsen's case and also lacks a full report was *In re Wippermann v. Boch*[33] which in the course of the year 1953 came before Mr. Justice Holroyd Pearce (as he then vas). The late Mr Wippermann, a manufacturer at Hagen, was a German "Aryan" who had nothing to do with politics. He seems to have had one passion in his life, namely to smuggle as much money as possible out of Germany and put it into a safe in one of the Zürich banks. In course of time the Exchange Control authorities became suspicious and started an investigation. He denied everything. In particular he denied having a safe in Zürich. He offered to travel with the officials to Zürich, so that they could satisfy themselves. Accordingly, three men travelled with him in his car to Switzerland. When they had reached the Swiss part of Bâle, he requested them to leave his car and offered them the alternative of driving them to a Swiss Police station. They left. He proceeded to Zürich, collected his money and eventually settled in Holland, where he started a new business near the German frontier. When Holland was overrun in 1940, he was

---

33 Incompletely reported at [1953] 1 Dec. E.R. 764

caught, sent to prison in Frankfurt and eventually put before a People's Court. The penalty from which there seemed to be no escape was death. His lawyer was a friend of his, a non-Nazi. He pleaded insanity. The court in fact did the unbelievable: it found him insane. He was sent to the notorious asylum at Eichberg and together with all the inmates killed in accordance with Hitler's decree about the extermination of lives unworthy of preservation. While he was awaiting trial, he wrote a letter to his lawyer saying approximately the following: "In the event of my death all my possessions shall belong to my sister X". The sister thus named was living in Switzerland married to a Swiss and therefore of Swiss nationallty. He had left property of considerable value in England. The Custodian of Enemy Property had taken possession of it, but in pursuance of his policy about ex gratis release was prepared to treat Wippermann as a victim of Nazi oppression and release the propery to the Swiss sister if she could establish title. This meant proving *inter alia* the existence of the letter the original of which, together with all the lawyer's documents was destroyed in an air-raid, the effectiveness of the German form (which, under English law as it then stood, depended on his domicil), the testamentary character of the letter, the testamentary capacity of a man who had been held to be insane and the law by which such capacity had to be tested.

In the course of the hearing in which the sister was represented by Mr. Jocelyn Simon K.C. (the later Lord Simon of Glaisdale) and the Custodian by [75] Mr. Walter Raeburn K.C., a sensational event occurred. The plaintiff called as a witness the judge who had presided at Wippermann's trial in Frankfurt. His evidence was simple, but most impressive. He stated in plain terms that it would have been the Court's duty to sentence Wippermann to death and that in order to avoid this he was held to be insane, although there was no acceptable evidence in support of such a finding before it. The judge admitted to a deliberate breach of the law, a deliberate "miscarriage of justice" for the sake of justice. It was an admission which left everyone deeply moved. In the result the English Judge held that the existence of the lost letter had not been established to his satisfaction. He also decided all the other questions and I seem to remember that on these his decision was in favour of the plaintiff.

I was called as expert on German law for the plaintiff and a former Frankfurt lawyer, a great friend of my father's, Dr. Rosenmeyer, was the Custodian's expert. The principal question on which differences of opinion arose was in what circumstances words used in a letter could in German law be treated as a testamentary disposition. There exists a lot of German learning on this point, which cannot arise in a country such as England which does not admit holograph wills. I have always been opposed to the principle of holograph wills (except in cases of emergency), – indeed I have been and still am strongly opposed to any form of will other than the notarial one, but would also admit a will made and witnessed by a solicitor, provided it is entered in a central register such a exists in Holland. The reason is that only such a procedure guarantees that on the death of a person it can be ascertained whether he left a will or not. Under the English or German system it happens continuously that a will is kept in some unknown place about which the testator leaves no word, so that his estate is wound up without any knowledge of his true intentions. Moreover, under the English or German system it is the easiest thing in the world for an unscrupulous person to suppress a known will, – a criminal offence which I am sure is frequently being committed and rarely discovered. Liberalism in these matters is misplaced. It is certainly less justifiable than an intestacy, provided the statutory scheme of distribution is well thought out and reasonable.

Another significant group of cases was inaugurated in 1957 by the decision of Vaisey J. in Loew's Incorporated v. Littler which was reversed by the Court of Appeal.[34] It concerned the copyright in the "Merry Widow". To put it very shortly, the authors had in 1905 made an agreement with a Berlin firm of music and dramatic agents, whereby against payment of a commission, the latter under "the sole and exclusive distribution of the opera" and obtained the exclusive right of public performance so as to be "solely and exclusively entitled during the period of this agreement to exercise the said rights either by itself or its agents abroad without any restriction". In 1906 the agents granted the English rights to George Edwardes from whom they eventually passed to the plaintiffs. Did the Berlin agents have power to assign the rights to Edwardes, [76] so that they survived him for the benefit of his estate and could be transmitted by him? English law, clinging, as it invariably does, to the literal meaning of words, had clearly given an affirmative answer in another case concerning George Edwardes.[35] E.J. Cohn who was the plaintiff's expert said German law was to the same effect. I relied on what I thought was firmly established German doctrine that agreements about the exploitation of copyright had to be construed in the light of their purpose and that an agreement with a commission agent did not transfer to him a greater slice of copyright than was necessary to enable him to perform his duty of exploitation. Vaisey J. accepted my evidence. The Court of Appeal felt that they "could find no sufficient authority or unanimity of view amongst these writers which would justify a construction which appears on the fact of it to be contrary to the plain meaning of the words of the document".[36] I never had any doubt that the Court of Appeal was plainly wrong and the victim of the superb advocacy of Mr. Charles Russell Q.C. (as he then was). It overrode not only German writers, but also

---

34 [1958] 2 All E.R. 200

35 *Messager v British Broadcasting Co. [1929] A.C. 151*

36 *P. 205*

German decisions which have since been given a statutory basis.[37] The reason no doubt was that the liberal construction with its pronounced preference for the author's interests was alien to the English legal mind which could not imagine that any sensible lawyer anywhere could hold a view different from that laid down by the House of Lords in a similar situation governed by English law. In other words the case proves the extreme difficulty in persuading an English court to accept a view of foreign law which is different from that reached by English law. It proves that an English court will endeavour so to apply foreign law as to render it conformable to English law.

I made the same experience in two subsequent cases the results of which were so wilful that they cannot be explained otherwise than by the prevalence of English conceptions. The first of them was *Berliner Industriebank v. Jost.*[38] The very complicated facts can be summarised shortly. The defendant, a German then resident in Germany, had obtained an overdraft from the plaintiff bank. He was made bankrupt in Berlin. The bank proved in the bankruptcy. The trustee in bankruptcy admitted the debt and in November 1958 had it entered in a register. In Germany this had the force of a judgment. In July 1964 the bankruptcy proceedings were terminated. The debtor was then found in England. The bank sued on the "judgment". The defendant denied that there was a "judgment" in the English sense and pleaded the English statute of limitation on the ground that more than six years had expired since the date, when the loan fell due. The bank replied that under German law (under which, contrary to English law, the debtor is not discharged by the termination of the bankruptcy proceedings) the due date was postponed until the lifting of the bankruptcy. German law was too different [77] from English law to appeal to Brandon J. who never appreciated the real point of the case. It is true that, in accordance with my evidence and contrary to that of the defendant's expert, Dr. Jaques, he held the German entry in the list to be a "judgment". But he thought that the judgment dated from entry. He failed to understand that under German law the debtor is not a party to bankruptcy proceedings, that he has no control over the admission, the rejection or the entry of debts and that vis à vis him according to the express provisions of sections 144–146 of the Bankruptcy Act the judgment does not exist or has no effect before the termination of the bankruptcy proceedings. This point, pressed again and again in my evidence, is not reflected in the judgment of Brandon J. or in that of the Court of Appeal. To me it remains a complete mystery to this day how both courts succeeded in ignoring so clear a provision of German law. I venture to think that

---

37 Section 31 Subsection 5 of the German Copyright Act 1965 and see the usual German commentaries with reference to the wealth of material rejected by the Court of Appeal.

38 [1971] L.Q.B. 463, affirming Brandon J., [1971] 2 All E.R. 117 (Salmon and Phillimore L.J.J., Lyell J. dissenting)

**110**                                                                                           Expert

once again they could not visualise a situation, or were anxious to avoid a result, wholly opposed to that demanded by English law. This tendency is still clearer in the most remarkable decision of the majority of the House of Lords in *Black Clawson International Ltd. v. Papierwerke Waldhof-Aschaffenburg,*[39] one of the many cases in a series of litigation to which I shall have to revert in another connection.[40] Black Clawson had brought an action against P.W.A. on bills of exchange in the courts of Munich. The defendants pleaded that the claim was statute-barred. The Munich District Court so decided and dismissed the action with costs. The plaintiff started a similar action in England. The defendants asked for service out of the jurisdiction in accordance with 0.11 to be set aside on the ground that the plaintiffs having had their claim dismissed in Germany could not show a good arguable case in England. The Court of Appeal recognised the German judgment on the basis of s.8 of the Foreign Judgments Reciprocal Enforcement Act 1933, and set the writ aside. The House of Lords reversed. Lord Reid's opinion which I believe was the last he ever delivered is so odd that it can be disregarded. The majority, very surprisingly led by Lord Wilberforce whom everyone would have been prepared to describe as a progressive internationalist, not only gave the narrowest possible construction to s.8, but also entirely ignored the AngloGerman Convention as a guide to construction. Lord Wilberforce quoted in some detail my evidence on the German law of limitation and held that, notwithstanding differences in classification, the plea of limitation in German law did not destroy the right, – he thus completely pushed aside that part of my evidence in which I had explained that once limitation had been pleaded and the defence had succeeded so as to lead to the dismissal of the action the right was gone: the plaintiff cannot any longer recover. Only Lord Diplock in his dissenting judgment saw the point clearly and expressed it with his usual persuasiveness. The majority was in the last resort enthralled by the English idea about the nature of a plea of limitation even after it has led to a judgment denying the [78] claim, as had been decided more than a hundred years earlier in a decision of questionable strength.[41] Long before the House of Lords rendered a decision which I fear constituted a breach of international law[42] and which, as I happen to know, was so regarded in Germany, I had submitted a memorandum on the point to the Law Reform Committee and when in September 1977 its twenty-first report[43] on limitation of actions appeared I had the satisfaction of reading in paragraphs 2.92 to 2.96 that, while the Committee felt unable to make recommendations on a subject which related to the conflict of laws rather than limitation they were

---

39 [1975] A.C. 591.
40 Below p.
41 *Harris v. Quine* [1869] L.R. 4 Q.B. 653
42 See my article in the British Year Book of International Law 1975–1976, 21
43 Cmnd. 6923

Expert 111

impressed by the fundamental argument I had presented. Since then nothing has happened in a field with which I had so unfortunate a connection, so one can only hope that in years to come something will be done to put English law back on a course of greater logic and justice.

The PWA case was also one of the many which led to my acting as an expert on English law in German courts[44]. In the course of the years this happened quite frequently, but the unique event of this part of my life occurred in 1961, when I appeared before the Federal Constitutional Court in a case involving the merge of Feldmühle A.G. with another German company the shareholders of which launched an attack on the law regulating the conditions to be offered to the merged company. Feldmühle was and probably still is controlled by Friedrich Flick and his group who had engaged a whole batallion of prominent German lawyers. I was asked to assist by explaining to the Court that the relevant German law did not substantially differ from English legislation and English practice. I participated in many pre-trial conferences and eventually addressed the Constitutional Court at some length. About a year later the attack against the constitutional validity of the German law failed.[45] The experience was an interesting one, particularly because the hearing before the Constitutional Court in Karlsruhe once again made it very clear to me how inferior in quality and effect oral hearings are in the German legal system. The Court proved to be an entirely silent tribunal which did not ask a single question or enter into any discussion or argument at all. Moreover, with one single exception the speeches of the German lawyers were pathetically poor, – they were verbose, almost invariably beside the point, lacking in precision and formulated in unpolished terms which failed to be in any way persuasive or impressive. The single exception was the speech made by Dr. Hans Hengeler, a leading German company lawyer from Dusseldorf who alone among the whole group was worth listening to, because he had something to say. My impression that even in the highest tribunal of Germany oral hearings are little more than farcial was greatly strengthened. [79] It is a most regrettable decline, even decay which cannot be without farreaching influence upon German law and the administration of justice in Germany.

---

44 See below p.
45 BVerfG 14, 263 (decision of 7 November 1962)

# Chapter 12 – Divorce

Douglas Phillips' practice before the war was almost exclusively a family practice including a good deal of divorce when he was called up, I carried it on and so it happened that for a number of years I used to do a good deal of divorce work. In those days such work was quite different from what it is at present. Defended cases were more frequent. Arrangements about property were easier, because the court's discretion was not as unlimited as at present, the rules of practice or, perhaps, of thumb were firmly settled and the wife's claims upon the husband's savings and earnings were more limited. In almost all cases an element of human interest attracted the lawyer's attention. I do not regret an experience of a professional activity which in later years became wholly remote from my work.

Cases of real legal interest were rare and I can remember only one. I am not thinking of a petition in which John Foster, instigated by me, tried to revive the old remedy of jactitation, but obtained the more modern relief of a declaration and thus caused this to become a very usual method of procedure in a certain type of case. Rather I am thinking of the great case of *Apt v. Apt*[46] which established the important point that English law recognises the validity of proxy marriages celebrated abroad. Curiously enough the King's Proctor, through Colin Duncan as his Counsel, strongly argued in favour of validity, although the consequence of such a rule in certain circumstances may be far from desirable; in the 1960's and 1970's they could have produced a flood of immigrants had not the legislation of 1971 introduced the conception of "patrial" and thus eliminated the foreign spouse's automatic right to join the spouse resident in England. The result of the decision was not surprising, seeing that many civilised countries recognise marriages by proxy and that therefore it would have been difficult to hold them contrary to English public policy. What was disturbing, however, was the fact that in the Court of Appeal approval was given to Scrutton L.J.'s unacceptable statement twenty years earlier that to hold foreign law to be contrary to public policy might be a "casus belli". It is difficult to believe that so eminent a judge

---

46  [1948] P. 83

**114** Divorce

could ever talk such nonsense and that in 1948 it could be repeated by three no less eminent members of the Court of Appeal.

A third case which on the wholly incidental point of the husband's liability to provide security for an appeal found its way into the law reports[47] is a more interesting example of human behaviour. Mrs. Roman for whom I acted was the respondent in a petition for divorce on the ground of cruelty. It appeared from the petition that the husband was asking for the Court's discretion, i.e. that he had committed adultery. In accordance with then prevailing practice the contents of the "discretion statement" were not made available to us before the hearing. [81] When we saw the statement Mrs. Roman's Counsel, Mr. Barry Q.C. (later Mr. Justice Barry) asked for and obtained leave to amend by cross-petitioning on the ground of the husband's adultery. The Judge, Mr. Justice Barnard, however, granted the husband a decree on grounds which I thought wholly untenable and almost absurd and which were so bad as to determine me to get an appeal on its feet. Although we lost the application for security the wife somehow found the money to enable me to brief at a very moderate fee the redoubtable Mr. Gilbert Beyfus Q.C. He agreed with my view of the Judge's findings, fought a great battle in the Court of Appeal and won. Mr. Roman's petition was dismissed, Mrs. Roman obtained a decree on the ground of her husband's adultery. The consequence in those days was that he was liable to maintain her. The husband petitioned the House of Lords for leave to appeal. The petition was dismissed. I returned from the House of Lords to the office where Mrs. Roman was waiting. She was overjoyed. I discussed the next steps with her to secure the largest possible amount of maintenance. She left me with many expressions of eternal gratitude, a very happy and satisfied woman. Two days later I received a letter from other solicitors informing me that for unexplained reasons they had been instructed by her and asking me to hand over the papers. It was unfortunately not the only time that clients for whom every possible effort had been made with great success showed themselves so ungrateful as to leave a memory of bitter disappointment. Professional success does not always imply human satisfaction.

I have just mentioned discretion statements. They are now a matter of the past, but in my time they were a very important feature of a divorce lawyer's life, for it was the duty of the solicitor to ensure that the client was frank with the court. Odd though the institution was, it did not lack an element of fairness: why should a guilty party be allowed to succeed against a party who was possibly much less guilty? In fact, however, clients did not usually disclose their own adultery if it was unknown to the other side and could not be found out. Even in undefended cases a discretion statement properly made could cause great difficulties with certain judges and on occasions much skilful persuasion was necessary (but not always

---

47 [1947] 1 All E.R. 434

Divorce                                                                                    **115**

sufficient) to obtain a decree. I remember one particularly difficult case of the wife of a very prominent City personality, for whom I was acting. With the knowledge of her husband she had had an affair for many years with another equally prominent man. The problem was solved not only by a cleverly drafted discretion statement, but also by instructing Mr. Seymour Karminski Q.C. (later Lord Justice Karminski) to appear in this undefended case and to have it fixed for 3.45 p.m. on the last day of term before Christmas before a Commissioner rather than a regular judge, – the sort of arrangement which under the curious English system the efficient clerk of a prominent leader can achieve. Need I add that a decree of divorce was duly granted and that there was no publicity?

The case I have spoken about might have had the same outcome had the parties [82] been so poor as to be legally aided. But no person of moderate means could have afforded the money required to prepare it and see it through to a successful end. Another memorable case where money produced victory was the case of *De Stempel*. Mr. De Stempel was, I seem to remember, a Russian emigré who married the daughter of a very wealthy Englishman. The marriage bacame unhappy and the wife suspected that her husband was committing adultery with a member of one of the great English noble families. Detectives were instructed. They had an extremely difficult task. Nothing definite, apart from a close association, could be proven. The detectives at one time rented a flat above that of the husband's and installed a microphone. They followed him on his journeys all over Europe. There were several volumes of reports. Yes, a close, a very close association existed. But always separate bedrooms, no hard evidence of adultery. Three extremely prominent firms of solicitors specialising in divorce were consulted. Each of them consulted different Counsel of eminence. The advice invariably given to the wife was that there was insufficient evidence of adultery. In this situation she came to me. I formed the view that there was enough in these interminable reports to put forward a case which had to be answered, so that the husband and the lady in question would have to go into the witness box and submit themselves to cross-examination, and that this risk might deter them from fighting. I instructed Mr. Holroyd Pearce, then a junior, later Lord Pearce. He agreed with me. He settled a petition which he used to call his "novel", – it was almost a book with innumerable particulars from which adultery could perhaps be inferred. The case became defended. It dragged on and eventually the hearing was fixed for the beginning of January. Dozens of dectectives and enquiry agents from all over Europe were to be called. The case was expected to take some weeks. And what happened? A few days before the great day we were told that there would be no defence. So we obtained a decree in an undefended case. It was the easiest thing in the world. Whether there was in fact adultery the gods only know. It may well be that as a result of the great financial power of the wife's father an injustice was done. But it did not both me greatly, because the wife had the grace not to ask for maintenance.

One of the cases which was really fought to the bitter end is memorable not only for the superb cross-examination of the respondent's wife by my client's Leading Counsel, Mr. R.F. Levy Q.C., but also for the fact that the hearing took place in the summer of 1944 in the cellar of the Royal Courts of Justice while the flying bombs were falling around us. My client, the petitioner, was one of the star pilots of the Battle of Britain. The wife was a woman whom he had married somewhere in the East and who was, as our investigations proved, an adventuress. One of the relatively minor pieces of material which we had against her was that we had procured her birth certificate and could establish that in the marriage certificate she was said to be twenty-nine years old, while her true age was thirty-nine. When she was in the box to be cross-examined Mr. Levy [83] started by asking her: "When were you born?" She immediately became flustered by this unexpected question and after a second's hesitation answered: "I am thirty-seven". In the quietest of voice Mr. Levy said: "I did not ask how old you were. I asked: when were you born?" She hesitated for quite some time and eventually repeated: "I am thirty-seven". Mr. Levy again pressed her very quietly. Eventually she said: "I was born on 15 January 1907". He then put the birth certificate to her. She accepted that it related to herself and that her real birthday was 15 January 1897 and that in the course of the marriage ceremony she had given a false date. With pain in his quiet voice Mr. Levy said: "Why?" By the end she had to admit the real and obvious reason. She never recovered her poise and Mr. Justice Bucknell granted my client a decree. There is another reason why I have never forgotten this case. After judgment had been given and everybody was on the point of dispersing Mr. G.O. Slade K.C. (the later Mr. Justice Slade) who had appeared for the wife came up to me, congratulated me, asked me to give his good wishes to my client and said that he had never had any confidence in his own client's case. I always considered this a fine tribute to the tradition of the profession.

Another case with a much less happy ending also belonged to a class that could not now occur. The petitioner was a serving soldier. In his absence his extremely pretty wife fell in love with a much older man, an art historian of repute, and began to live with him. The husband removed from her their infant son and sent him to his parents in the United States, – whether the wife ever saw him again I know not. The husband started proceedings for divorce which were, of course, undefended. But he also asked for damages against the co-respondent, as was possible under the law as it then stood. This claim was defended by us, at any rate as to quantum. The husband asked for £2000, – then an enormous sum which my client was quite unable to pay. All efforts to settle at less than this figure failed. So with a heavy heart we came before Mr. Justice Barnard. We argued that in the circumstances the award of damages was in the nature of a penalty rather than

Divorce **117**

compensation for loss of a wife. These were always very difficult and delicate cases. Our argument failed, as we had expected, but the unexpected happened in that the Judge did award exactly £2000. I had every sympathy with my poor client, but he had none with me and blamed for ever after. Yet I also had the opposite case in which, in very similar circumstances, but in the manner typical for lawyers my sympathies were entirely with my client, the innocent husband. He also was a serving soidier, a refugee in the Pioneer Corps, who had married before the war an English woman of substantial means, with whom he had three children of tender age. The wife had bought a large farm in the West country where they lived together until the husband joined the army. The wife fell in love with a farm labourer employed by her, a very common, uneducated and vulgar man. After every effort to get this Lady Chatterley away from her man had failed the husband started divorce proceedings and also asked for an order that the wife should settle a [84] substantial part of her property on the children, – an order which even in those days one could obtain in somewhat exceptional circumstances. The wife instructed Mr. Gerald Russell, the senior partner of Charles Russell & Co. with whom I had one of the most unpleasant interviews I have ever had with a colleague, – or rather with a solicitor, for at the time he was a solicitor of great standing, while I was an unadmitted clerk. He tried to tell me that the order for which we were asking was something so monstruous that no respectable person would ever ask for it or allow a client to ask for it. When I drew his attention to the authorities according to which the order was meant to cover the very type of case with which we were concerned he became quite abusive and more or less demanded a withdrawal of the application for the sake of the husband and his relations with the children. I have forgotten the outcome, but I believe we did withdraw the application, because the husband feared that an order would in the end so antagonise his wife against both himself and even the children that it was wiser to forego it.

Divorce necessarily entailed a certain amount of practice in making infant children wards of court, a procedure which was then brought in the Chancery Division and was quite distinct from the Divorce Division. Such cases were usually very uninteresting, but time-consuming and disproportionately expensive. The most prominent one I ever had was that of Deborah Kerr, the actress, who had left her husband. Although the matrimonial home was in California, she became the respondent in very unpleasant ward-of-court proceedings in England. The only redeeming feature was that I saw a lot of this charming woman and the man with whom she then lived and whom she married after her Californian divorce had come through, the writer Peter Viertel. We have remained friendly ever since that time. Another of these cases could safely be left where it is were it not for an incident which is instructive. I was acting for the wife who had left her husband for another man and who was allowed to have access to the only child of the marriage during specified periods. On one occasion she kept the child longer than she was entitled to. She had told me on the telephone about it and I had advised her in the strongest possible terms against the course she proposed to take. When the case eventually came before Mr. Justice Wynn-Parry the husband's Counsel made the most of this unfortunate incident. The Judge pressed the wife's Counsel about it. He was Mr. Gerald Upjohn K.C., later Lord Upjohn. The poor man could only offer apologies, but this was not enough for the Judge who became very angry about the incident. Eventually Mr. Upjohn adopted the position that the wife had been badly advised and that this should not be held against her, – a defence which was totally unfounded and which he had not been instructed to fall back upon. The Judge then criticised the solicitors, i.e. me in strong terms. The lessons from this incident are twofold. In the first place, Upjohn acted wrongly in that, albeit in defence of his client's interests he said something which he had no instructions to say. Secondly, he acted in violation of his duty towards the court in that he said something that he knew to be untrue. He was an eminent Counsel and became a splendid judge. But this was an occasion, when Homer nodded, and did so very markedly. [86]

# Chapter 13 – Advice and Negotiation

What I have said so far and what will follow is liable to give the impression that the only or at least the main part of my work was of a litigious character. This would probably not be entirely incorrect. Yet it might be somewhat misleading, for so much of every lawyer's work is advisory and my experience was not different. The trouble is, however, that advisory work is almost invariably unsuited for publication. It is necessarily secret and very often it cannot be recalled even anonymously, for the persons concerned could perhaps be identified by some processes of clever combination of elimination. Such a risk, however remote, must be sufficient to impose restraint. A professional man is bound to observe the strictest reticence and to allow this part of his work to remain covered by the seal of secrecy, so much so that he cannot even disclose the identity of the persons who came to ask for his advice. It is, incidentally, the same with arbitration in which I was in recent years very closely engaged both as advocate and as arbitrator. It is one of the main functions of arbitration to keep a dispute from the eyes of the public and it would therefore be quite wrong for anyone connected with it to disclose facts or events which relate to arbitration proceeaings, however interesting or instructive they may be. (I have therefore always had grave doubts about the propriety of reporting in such publications as the International Law Reports awards rendered in arbitration between a Stae and a private person in the absence of the consent of all concerned.) In the case of both advice and arbitration it is different only where litigation follows and where the publicity of proceeding removes the lid of secrecy. We shall in due course come across some such example.

The restraint by which I feel bound is in many ways regrettable, for some of the events which I could relate if I were free to do so are of great human interest, quite apart from the fascinating legal problems or techniques they frequently involved. Just consider a case such as the following: a surgeon operates upon a woman patient. After the operation she is seriously ill. The surgeon opens her up again and finds swabs which in the course of the first operation had inadvertently been left in her abdomen. He comes to you in a state of great anxiety and excitement and asks whether the neglect comes within his or the nurse's and therefore the hospital's responsibility and whether <u>he</u> can make the hospital liable for any damage to his reputation. In the course of the conversation with him he states that he has left the patient in the dark, does not propose to enlighten her and is even thinking of charging her a fee for the second operation to complete the cover-up. You tell him that it is his plain legal duty (quite apart from the morality of the matter) to tell the patient the truth and that if he charges for the second operation without telling her and if she subsequently learns the true facts she can recover the fee, possibly on the basis of fraudulent misrepresentation. Whereupon he leaves you in a state of indignation, because, so he says, he came to obtain advice on his [87] rights rather than on his duties. He does not pay your modest bill and talks about you to all and sundry in the most derogatory terms.

Negotiations about contracts, the terms of bond issues, the reason why wills were made or not made or made in this sense and no other, tax schemes, the structure of companies, – these are just a few of the matters which on occasion gave rise to memorable incidents, but I cannot think of one which I could tell about. On the other hand there is the case of the Rosenfelder family which can now be told, which occupied a great part of my time during many years and in which for reasons that will become apparent my role was very largely an advisory one. Emil and Oscar Rosenfelder were brothers who had founded the Vereinigte Papierwerke A.G., a highly successful paper manufacturing company near Nuremberg, its principal products being Tempo paper handkerchiefs and Camelia sanitary towels. They owned the large majority, but by no means all the shares. When Hitler came to power, they very quickly saw the necessity for securing their future outside Germany. So they went to London and consulted Mr. Herbert Oppenheimer whose firm had a very large German-Jewish clientele. He devised a scheme the details of which I cannot remember exactly but which was approximately as follows: Oscar's son Hans came to London and managed a newly formed company, Chiswell Paper Co. Ltd., which, with the help of finance provided by English business friends, took up manufacture in England. At the same time the brothers entered into contracts with their German company as a result of which they became entitled to very large sums by way of salary and pension. Furthermore the German Company granted a Power of Attorney to Hans enabling him to dispose of and deal with the whole of the German company's non-German assets, particularly patents and trademarks. When the danger became acute, Emil and Oscar and their respective families escaped from Germany, while Hans, acting under his Power of Attorney, transferred to the English company the whole of the German company's foreign assets and started proceedings in Holland, Switzerland and other countries to stop the German company's exports which infringed the patent and trade mark rights now vested in the English company. It was an ingenious, politically appropriate, but in law

Advice and Negotiation

indefensible, though at first fairly successful scheme, particularly because the Nazis failed to pay the money allegedly due to the Rosenfelders, appointed a curator to administer their property and confiscated whatever they could lay their hands on. In short, in principle they took action such as was typical in thousands of cases, except that in this particular case there existed an element of provocation in the Rosenfelder's defensive measures. In due course proceedings against them were started in England. I cannot remember their precise nature or the identity of the plaintiff, – was it the English group which had financed the English company or was it the German company which in the meantime had been bought from the curator by the Schickedanz Group which after the war was to become one of the most powerful enterprises in the Federal Republic? In either case the principal [88] issue was the validity of Mr. Oppenheimer's scheme and in particular the validity of the Power of Attorney under German law. Mr. Oppenheimer and his firm refused to act, but sent the clients to a firm specialising in criminal law, Myers & Co., who instructed Mr. Owen Stable K.C. (the later Mr. Justice Stable) and Sir Geoffrey Jones. I was throughout employed in an advisory capacity and as one of the first steps had John Foster added to the team. Mr. Oppenheimer not only refused to act (an attitude which one can perhaps understand and justify, although in all he did he was supported by opinions rendered by the Marquis of Reading K.C.) but he also refused to appear as a witness, did not accept service of a subpoena and went to Egypt, when shortly before the trial an agent attempted to serve it personally. The case seemed hopeless and at the door of the court Sir Walter Monckton K.C. leading for the plaintiff agreed to a compromise the short effect of which was that the Rosenfelders lost almost everything Oppenheimer's scheme was to achieve for them. Let me add at once that it was only long after the war, in about 1955 that the German restitution proceedings got under way as a result of which Mr. Schickedantz paid a substantial, though in my view wholly insufficient sum which had to be accepted, as one member of the family insisted on an immediate settlement in preference to what he believed would be long-drawn out proceedings against a powerful and influential opponent. But this was almost twenty years after the events in connection with which I acted as a continuous advisor on litigation which, nominally, was conducted by other solicitors. At that time there existed also the very acute danger that the Germans would institute extradition proceedings or would obtain judgments in Germany which might be enforceable in England. The whole complex of the Hosenfelder case and its implications was a textbook case: few branches of the law and of professional etiquete remained outside its scope.

There were many other instances which proved that escape from Germany did not by any means always allow the refugee to enjoy complete freedom. The Nazis had a habit of sending officials to England to inspect the books and records of refugees who had started a new business here. This led to many and serious difficulties and on one occasion I knew no solution other than to let the client pretend an illness. My activities in these and other connections must have become known to the Nazis. Fortunately, I never returned to Germany before 1946. And after the war I learned that the authorities had issued an arrest warrant against me.

It is for very unfortunate reasons that it is possible to tell about one of the most fascinating successes that I ever achieved by way of friendly negotiations. The story is in many respects so instructive that it is justified telling it in some detail. In the early part of 1956 I was consulted by a group of five of the most important German banks comprising the Deutsche Bank, Commerz & Privatbank, Frankfurter Bank, Burkhardt & Co. and Getreidehandelsbank, later known as Invetstitions – und Handelsbank. They had financed a Frankfurt company [89] known as Internationale Tabak Gesellschaft in regard to the importation from Turkey of tobacco worth altogether about DM 18 million. The principal security obtained by the banks was a Lloyds policy of insurance issued to the importer and assigned to the banks. The policy covered loss or damage caused, inter alia by detainment and/or revocation of export permit (although I cannot remember precise terms of the policy). The German buyers wanted to pay for the tobacco by the price which they had paid into the German-Turkish Clearing for goods they had purchased in Turkey. The Turks, on the other hand, insisted on the price for the tobacco being paid cash against documents and pending acceptance of this withheld an export permit for the tobacco. In this situation the German bank alleged that the policy monies had become payable. Lloyds denied liability. Two of the banks' tame lawyers came to consult me and were shocked and amazed when I told them that in my view they seemed unlikely to have a case. The issue, if I remember correctly, turned on the single word "revocation". Refusal of or failure to grant an export permit was not the same thing as the revocation of a permit. The Germans argued with me: what about the "equity"?, "Treu und Glauben"?, The intention of the parties? I had to tell them that unambiguous words could not be explained away. I developed a plan of action for them which they accepted. Accordingly, I went to see Sir William Charles Crocker who acted for Lloyds. I told him that my clients were probably the most important German banks, that they had taken an assignment of the policy under a misapprehension as to the legal position, that it was in the interest of an institution such as Lloyds at an early stage of the rapidly developing international trade of Germany not to be too technical and narrow and that it would pay them in the end to settle on a generous basis without litigation. A week or so later Sir William, having obtained instructions at the highest level, informed me that Lloyds accepted my approach and were prepared to pay the DM 18 million in full on the basis of principles which were outlined to and discussed with me and which I explained to all my clients in the course of a large meeting in Germany. They accepted with alacrity. A

Advice and Negotiation

completion meeting took place in Hamburg. Two of the banks' lawyers collected me at the airport. Their first question was whether I had the cheques. I told them that the Lloyds' lawyer would have them. Everything was done as arranged. The Germans received DM 18 million to cash. I returned to London and felt that I had had a great success. So did my clients who thanked me in the most generous terms and paid my bill. A month or so later Sir William telephoned me. He said that he had to discuss a matter of importance with me and asked for lunch at the R.A.C. Club. When I came, he told me that some of the German banks had failed to carry out the agreement and refused to do so, inter alia, on the ground that in agreeing to some of the terms I had acted without their authority. I was greatly shocked, particularly because my clients had of course copies of all relevant documents. My enquiries led to some unpleasant and disappointing correspondence. My consolation was that, although Sir William suspected something in the nature of a conspiracy on the part of the Germans, [90] he never questioned my good faith. Eventually Lloyds brought proceedings for breach of contract against three of the German banks in England. Their representatives came to see me, – not to instruct me, but to ask me to support their case by evidence. I refused. They attacked the jurisdiction of the English Court, but the Master, the Judge and the Court of Appeal rejected their application. The judgment of the Court of Appeal is reported.[48] Hence I could tell many, though not all aspects of the story upon which I cannot even at the present stage offer any comment, but which constitutes one of the most striking experiences of my professional life.

If my negotiations on behalf of the five German banks were at the same time most gratifying and most disappointing, another negotiation on behalf of Weidenfeld and Nicolson Ltd. was the most amusing, and since George, now Lord Weidenfeld, is in the habit of telling the story to all and sundry, there is no reason why I should not tell it here. Weidenfeld and Nicolson had published a book by a former high Nazi official who then lived near Salzburg and who had dealt with espionage during the war in Hungary. (I have forgotten both the author's name and the title of the book.) In the book there was a chapter on a named woman whom he described as a "high-class" prostitute and a double agent and whose activities were related in great detail. A year or so after publication of the book a firm of London solicitors made a claim for damages for libel for an enormous sum of money (I seem to remember that more than £100,000 was mentioned) on behalf of the woman who was then living somewhere in South America. Fear of a defence of justification seemed to offer the only hope of achieving a reasonable settlement. So the author was instructed to collect all the former German officers and officials who knew about the woman and to bring them to Salzburg, so that I could take statements of their evidence. George and I travelled several times to

---

48 *Gibson v. Commerz und Creditbank,* [1958] 2 Ll.L.B. 113

Salzburg to interview these men who used to hold the highest ranks in the Nazi hierarchy and most of them, oddly enough, lived in the surroundings of Salzburg. We even found one man who was prepared to confirm that he had made use of the sexual services offered by the woman and paid her a handsome sum for them. And then we found some witnesses in Munich who spoke about the woman's activities in the interest of the Soviet army. In the end I had twelve or fifteen signed statements which made out a respectable case of justification. I went to see the solicitors and allowed them to see all these statements. The case was very quickly settled, I believe by the payment of £1,000. But the amusing and probably unique part of the case was the contact with all those Nazis. I had never met or still less dined with high S.S. officers whom, on the one hand, George and I had to humour to obtain their evidence, and who, on the other hand, were so very anxious to assure us of their ignorance and innocence of all the atrocities in which they had no doubt participated to the fullest extent. It was rather a para-doxical situation. [91]

It is fitting to conclude this chapter with the one fairy tale that occurred in, and has for many years given much pleasure to, my professional life. In the early 1950's a partner in a small firm of City solicitors came to see me. He had been consulted by the typist employed at £9 per week by surveyors. She was a war widow with one little daughter then about seven years old and lived in very restricted circumstances. The daughter, so he told me, had inherited some money in Germany. Neither he nor his client could read German nor was there money to have the German letters translated. I looked at them and ascertained that the little girl had inherited a third of the estate of one of the great German industrialists who had died intestate and whose deceased sister was the paternal grandmother of the child. It was obviously an enormous fortune which, in particular, included a third of the shares in a well-known German industrial undertaking. Would I take the matter over? I said that I would be delighted to assist or act as his agent. This suggestion he rejected indignantly: he knew nothing about such matters and it would be unfair for him to remain in any way connected with the case. He wanted me to take it over as a whole. I asked whether he realised what he was giving up. He assured me that he knew what he was doing. So I accepted, but may add at once that when I received my first [...] in the matter I sent him a large case of fine wines. In any event I did take over. We were faced with the fact (so incomprehensible to a Continental lawyer) that in England a parent has no power to act on behalf of an infant child in administering her property. So we had to apply to the Court under the Guardianship of Infants Act for appointment of guardians who acted under the supervision of the Court. I repeatedly went to Germany and had a lawyer appointed a non-executive director of the company's Board to look after the child's interests (which led to other friendly discussions about English notion on conflict of interests, since the lawyer soon began to act on behalf of the company whose interests were not necessarily identical with those of the infant. But it was a very pleasant and satisfactory matter which lasted until the girl reached the age of twenty-one. The interesting part is that here is an extremely rich young woman about whose existence and wealth no newspaper ever discovered anything. Let me conclude by recalling a not untypical conversation with the German company's tame lawyer whom I met in the course of my first visit. He asked me about my background and history and I told him about my family, my father, and those who perished during the Hitler régime. Whereupon he said: "Yes, during the last days of the war I also had a terrible experience. A bomb fell into my garden and shattered many of my windows." [92]

# Chapter 14 – War and Litigation

It is in the nature of things and of the· human character that war inevitable leads to litigation of a type which, had there been no war, would not have occurred. On the one hand there are specific legal problems to which war gives rise. What is much more frequent, on the other hand, is human frailty, meanness and dishonesty which in wartime find opportunities that in less unusual circumstances do not present themselves. From the early days of the war I saw innumerable examples of this type. Some of them, not necessarily the most telling ones, may be retold.

Already in 1942 it was decided[49] that if a German refugee, as a result of the outbreak of war, is interned, his employer may summarily dismiss him. But the case of Mr. Hugo Heidecker was different. He had been the owner of a substantial manufacturing business in Nuremberg, managed to come to England and by a contract made after the outbreak of war was employed by a company in Wales as the manager of their local factory. In 1940 he was interned for a few months, but the employers alleged that the mere fact of his internment justified them in terminating his services. So we brought an action for wrongful dismissal, alleging that at the time of the conclusion of the conract temporary internment had been within the contemplation of the parties. Mr. Valentine Holmes who appeared for the plaintiff thought we had an unanswerable case. I remember well that when a few days before the trial we had a conference with him he said that there was absolutely nothing that he had to say or to ask, – it was all in the brief and the case was clear. It was in 1941 or 1942 that we came before Mr. Justice Lewis. Mr. F.A. Sellers K.C. appeared for the defendants. The case went very well, the cross-examination of my client was feeble and failed to shake his case. But the Judge was decidedly hostile and I was very puzzled by his attitude when I left the Court at the adjournment in the afternoon. On leaving the Court Valentine Holmes asked me to meet him at his Chambers. I went there straight from court and asked my client to meet me at my office. When I saw Holmes, he said to me that the Judge was a

---

49 *Unger v Preston Corporation* [1942] 1 All E.R. 200

rabid antisemite, that he was very sorry to have to say to me frankly that it was impossible for a Jew to win before this Judge, that objectively the day had gone very well and that therefore he might be able to settle the case on some terms, however unsatisfactory they might be. He added that he felt so ashamed by what he had to tell me that if necessary he would renounce his fees. He also explained that there had been no point in telling me earlier about this Judge, because we did not know before the afternoon of the preceding day that we would come before him, that by that time all the costs had been incurred and that he had decided to see how the Judge would behave before disclosing facts to me which embarrassed him greatly. The upshot was that, with the full knowledge and consent of my client, we withdrew the action, the defendant paying its own costs. For both Mr. Heidecker who remained a faithful client throughout his life and who, fortunately, after the war recovered his very [93] substantial property in Germany, and for me and no doubt for the incomparable Valentine Holmes this experience was one of the bitterest of our lives. Are there Judges with the same or similar prejudices on the Bench today?

Early in 1943 Mr. Otto Boll was very much luckier. He had been the owner of a printing works in Berlin and escaped to this country a few days before the outbreak of war. He possessed nothing except a secret process for producing plastic printing plates. Late in 1939 he succeeded in interesting C. & E La., a large printing firm which no longer exists. He entered into a home-made agreement with them, consisting of a few words only. He was to instruct them in the process which they were not allowed to use without his consent. They would pay him 5 % of the sales prices of all plates made by them and incorporating his process. In the summer of 1940, after having worked with Layton for about six months, Boll joined the Pioneer Corps. In the course of the following winter he came to London on leave and went to see Layton to ask about his account. They were so short of staff that they had no time to look into the matter. In the summer of 1941, he again came on leave and saw a Mr. Coterell. He took him to a pub at the corner, explained that they had no time to prepare accounts, but gave him a drink and and a £1 note "on account". Boll then began to write, but always received evasive answers. Eventually he went to see a solicitor. He asked for a payment of £30 on account. Boll did not own more than about £3 in the whole world. Someone then sent him to me. I wrote to Layton demanding an account. I received a reply from old Mr. White, the very nice senior partner of Smiles & Co. He denied any liability, but on the basis of paying for nuisance value offered me £25 in full settlement. I refused and, although Boll could not make any payment, instructed Mr. Valentine Holmes to settle a writ and statement claim. This alleged, inter alia, the failure to render an account or to payment other than £1. After I had served the writ Mr. White telephoned me, pointed out that this was no time for litigation (which was, indeed true) and offered me £50. I refused. The defence admitted the manufacture of plastic printing plates, but denied use of the process, and admitted the payment of £1, allegedly as a gift. We came to discovery. Mr. White offered me £250. This was more serious. Although he did not have a bean and I had nothing on account, he refused and I was willing to go along, because by then I smelt a matter of some gravity. We came to fix the date for trial. Mr. White invited me to the National Liberal Club for lunch and offered me £500. I refused. The day of trial arrived. Under the door of the court, Mr. White offered me £2,500, and all the costs. After consultation with Holmes I refused. We came before Mr. Justice Cassels. The defendants were represented by Mr. Blanco White K.C. and Mr. E. Holroyd Pearce (later Lord Pearce). The trial took three weeks. Much turned on the expert evidence. Our principal expert was Mr. Alexander Gill, senior partner of Gill Jennings and Every, patent agents. In February 1943 the Judge awarded Boll a declaration that he was entitled to 5 % on all plastic plates made by Layton. I remember one unforgettable phrase in the judgment: "Never in the history of [94] litigation has so much been said about so small a sum as £1". And Mr. Holroyd Pearce said to me that never had he seen Mr. Holmes so angry as in this case. Next day I received a cheque for almost £9,000. For many years, until he agreed to accept a capital sum in full settlement, Soll received substantial quarterly payments. Early in 1945 he was discharged from active service for reasons of health. He formed Plastetype Ltd. and with some financial support from Douglas Phillips and myself began the production of plastic plates. In the course of years, the business grew. Boll became the recognised expert in the field, was made an O.B.E., but shortly after retiring from the firm died in the 1960's. Plastetype is going from strength to strength. The shareholders have no reason to complain.

The period of this worrying, but in the end very pleasing fight saw another great case in which Mr. Holmes was instructed by me and Mr. Holroyd Pearce appeared for the defendants and which I must mention for a specific legal reason I acted for Messrs. Bamberger and Stapenhorst who had financed Mr. Sommerfeld, the inventor of the famous wire-netting used for temporary airfields. We claimed an account of profits on the basis of a partnership. The remarkable feature of the case which was in the end settled arose during discovery. I received the defendant's affidavit of documents from which it appeared that he had no documents whatever, all of them having been transferred to a company formed immediately before the institution of proceedings for the purpose of acquiring the defendant's business, the directors and shareholders being the defendant and his wife. Fraud could not be proved, because there was evidence that the defendant acted under legal advice and for tax reasons not connected with the pending proceedings. We alleged that nonetheless the defendant was "in control" of the documents. We won before the Master and Mr. Justice Stable. (On leaving his court Mr. Holroyd Pearce wittily exclaimed: "How can anyone win against

Man and Superman?") The Appeal came before Sir Wilfred Greene M.R., Luxmoore L.J. and Mackinnon L.J. They made very short shrift of it: the company was a separate legal entity which was in sole control of its own property, so that no director or shareholder, acting singly or as a body, would be said to have control. Unfortunately, this remarkable judgment was not reported. Even today the point has not been finally settled.[50] Yet in Sommerfeld's case the defendant's victory was a pyrrhic one. For Valentine Holmes advised me to serve a subpoena on the company and to tell them at the same time that if they produced the documents only during the trial so as to render an adjournment necessary we would apply for an order for costs against it. I seem to remember that it was this ploy which led to a settlement. But in the meantime, we had consulted Mr. Wilfred Hunt on some questions of partnership law. This established a relationship which lasted until that great man's retirement from practice at a time when he was well in his eighties. I saw a lot of him, because we used to meet on our way to or from Holland Park Station. He had a very unusual routine: he came home at [95] seven, had dinner and then slept until 9 p.m. He was woken with a cup of tea, worked until midnight and then went to bed. He woke at 5.30 a.m., worked until 8.30, was in Chambers at 9.30 and in court at 10.30. His standing at the Bar was unique. At the same time he was the kindest of men. Early in 1945 David was seriously ill with pneumonia. This was before the time of penicillin. I told Mr Hunt about my worries when coming home in the evening. Next morning Mrs.Hunt appeared at the door, – she was a complete stranger to us. But she brought some eggs which they had, because they kept chickens in their garden and which she shared with strangers whose child was ill. Such acts of kindness should be recorded so as to serve as a shining example to future generations.

The end of the war brought with it a completely new field of activity, namely a flood of foreign clients whose property was in the hands of the Custody of Enemy Property and who, relying on the Custodian's generous policy of release were trying to obtain the return of their property or its proceeds. The Custodian did not normally retain the property of an enemy national who at all times during the war was resident outside enemy territory. Nor did he retain property of enemies who were the victims of Nazi persecution, provided the original owners or their successors-in-title had left enemy territory. In effect such a policy which was subject to less broadly stated additional conditions meant the release of all the property of Jewish owners, and, although in some cases the policy did not apply and was therefore occasionally exposed to criticism, it was executed with great fairness and sympathy. I had probably hundreds of such cases. They were usually introduced by foreign lawyers. Most of them, unfortunately, involved a prior Grant of Representation, since the original owner had been killed during the war

---

50 See *B. v. B.* [1978] 3 W.L.R. 624.

# War and Litigation

in a concentration camp. Some problems of identification arose, as in the case in which a Pole had taken a safe at Selfridge's under the pseudonym Armel Futter (meaning sleeve lining in German). Sometimes there was the question of the order in point of time of death within a family. Sometimes it was necessary to trace the property, as in the case of the Romanian Kormos family: a New York lawyer instructed me that relatives had always indicated that there was a property in England. Could I find it? I asked myself with which bank a Romanian Jew was likely to have banked and wrote to some of them, including the Swiss Bank Corparation which in fact turned out to have had a large sum paid over to the Custodian. Sometimes one came across a grave fraud as in the unforgettable case of Mr. Michael Burg: he had had an account with Barclays Bank and a safe with the London Safe Deposit Company. A nephew in England knew of the existence of both, but did not possess any other particulars. He swore to the death of Michael (for which little more was necessary than evidence that the de cujus had been in a certain concentration camp and had not been heard of for some time) and obtained Letters of Administration on the footing of an affidavit that he was the only relative surviving. Equipped with the Grant he obtained the substantial assets and used [96] them up very fast, no doubt after having paid a share to the solicitor who had assisted him and who subsequently emigrated to Israel years later Mr. Michael Burg who had survived in Hungary came to London and ascertained that his assets had disappeared. He came to me for advice. We started proceedings against the bank and the Safe Deposit Company who in defence relied on the protection afford by the grant of Letters of Administration. But we thought that the law was clearly to the effect that the statutory protection did not operate where there had been no death of the owner at all. The point was, however, never decided, because the defendants paid up in full after the case had reached the Court of Appeal on some legal point relating to discovery and in response to the argument of Mr. Glyn-Jones K.C. (later Mr. Justice Glyn-Jones) the Court had intimated views very favourable to our case.

Fraud or something akin to it was rampant during the war and it is a sad comment on human nature that there were many who felt entitled to exploit the misfortune of others for their own advantage. Some of the most striking cases of this kind merit the attention of my readers.

There is the case of Mr. Gompertz which should be told under the motto: advocacy by silence. Mr. Gompertz and his cousin Mr. Meinrath were the owners of a button factory in Hanover. Meinrath came to ßngland and formed Gompertz and Meinrath Ltd. in which Gompertz had a share of, I believe, fifty per cent. Gompertz went to Brussels where he survived the war and occupation in dreadful circumstances. For more than two years he and his family lived in a small cellar in the house of Belgian friends who shared their rations with them. When Brussels was liberated, Gompertz wrote to his cousin Meinrath one of the most pathetic letters I have ever read. He said that he had absolutely nothing apart from the few clothes he was wearing, that he had no money, no home, no food or means of subsistence. He assumed that during the war dividends on his shares had been paid, and asked to use that money to send him parcels and if possible, cash. In reply Gompertz received a letter from a firm of solicitors. It read approximately as follows: "Mr. Meinrath has instructed us to reply to your letter. Your reference to shares is not understood, since you do not own any shares in Gompertz and Meinrath Ltd. Nor are any dividends held for your account. Yours faithfully, XYZ." After some further, wholly desultory correspondence Mr. I Gompertz instructed me. My investigations proved that during the war the shares of Mr. Gompertz had been transferred into the name of Mr. Meinrath and his associates, – I cannot remember precisely how it was done, but I believe that the Custodian of Enemy Property agreed to a transfer for a certain price paid to him. In due course we started proceedings. In about 1949 the case came before Justice Wynn-Parry. Mr. Valentine Holmes K.C. (by then he had taken silk) and Mr. J.G. Strangman appeared for the plaintiff, Sir Andrew Clark K.C. was for the defendants. Holmes opened the case on a Monday morning. At about 12.45 he reached Mr. Gompertz's letter which I summarised above. He read it extremely slowly, but without any emphasis or pathos. Nor did he comment on it. He merely [97] said with the utmost quietness: "The reply is on the next page". He then read the solicitors' letter, again in a deadpan manner. He did not comment on it. He simply fell silent. Nothing was said for perhaps three, four or five minutes. Nothing in the court moved. Nor did the Judge say anything. The longer Holmes was silent the redder the Judge's face became. The extraordinary tension was relieved when the Judge said: "I adjourn now to two o'clock". We left the court. At 2 o'clock Sir Andrew Clark said to Holmes that he wanted to come to terms. In fact the case, one of the most memorable in my experience, was settled on terms which gave us all we wanted.

The Koreska case which soon afterwards came before Mr. Justice Lloyd Jacobs was not entirely dissimilar in character. The Koreska brothers, no Jews, had a factory in Vienna for carbon paper, typewriter ribbons and similar goods. Well before the Anschluss they formed Kores Ltd. in England and started manufacture here. Shortly after the Anschluss in March 1938 one of the brothers came to London and consulted the company's solicitors to discuss protective measures in the event of war which they thought was imminent. The solicitor devised a scheme which was adopted and which up to a point was successful. The solicitor bought the shares at par. The German exchange control authorities were pleased to receive a small sum of sterling and gave their consent. At the same time the solicitor handed to Mr. Koreska a secret document whereby he undertook at any time upon request by Koreska personally to resell the shares to him at the same price as that paid plus stamp duty. When after the war Koreska came and asked

# War and Litigation

for the return of his shares, he was met by the answer that he had no rights at all, because the war had abrogated all contractual ties between the parties who had become enemies; the existence of such a rule was undeniable. Deeply shocked and, indeed, horrified Mr. Koreska consulted a firm of solicitors who took the opinion of a Mr Frederick Hallis. He confirmed the solicitor's view and advised that there was no remedy. A puzzled Mr. Koreska could not believe that this was English law and went to another firm of solicitors. They obtained the opinion of Mr. Gerald Gardiner K.C. (later Lord Gardiner). But he gave the same advice and ended his opinion with the memorable words: "A letter might be written to demand the return of the shares". Mr. Koreska then came to me. I was convinced that was right, that the fiduciary relationship with the solicitor created a trust and that the purely contractual rules about abrogation of contracts did not apply to property, including equitable rights. Tom Strangman (J.G. Strangman K.C.) so advised, so we started proceedings with Mr. R.O. Wilberforce (later Lord Wilberforce) and Mark Littman as juniors. The preparation of the case took considerable time. I was frequently in Vienna and elsewhere to search for documents and to obtain the statements of witnesses to prove the equitable relationship. Eventually the trial started on a Monday morning. There was a formidable team against us. Sir E. Milner Holland K.C., Mr. Gilbert Paull K.C. (later Mr. Justice Paull) and Mr. Charles Russell K.C. (later Lord Russell of Killowen) appeared for the defendants who were not only the solicitor, but also [98] some of the company's directors who had obtained some of the shares from him. Tom Strangman's opening speech took the first week, because the documentation had become very comprehensive. On Friday, shortly after two o'clock, Mr. Paull handed Tom a slip of paper saying: "String it out until four. We are giving in and can agree details during the weekend". This is precisely what happened. By Monday the Koreska's had their shares back, the solicitor and his firm were thrown out of the company, the Board of Directors was reconstituted. The company was to pay our costs. And partly to protect the Koreska's, partly to reward me I was made Chairman at an acceptable fee and was appointed solicitor to the company. The success was complete and the beginning of a very pleasant relationship with Kores Ltd. It lasted until the late 1960's, when apparently some sort of reconstruction of the Koreska group took place. At any rate out of the blue I received a curt letter from another firm of solicitors demanding my resignation as a director. I complied. No golden handshake for me!

A third case of this type was *Gordon v. Gonda* which reached the Court of Appeal. The parties had in Hungary entered into a partnership for the exploitation of the defendant's patents. The latter came to England and succeeded in selling his invention. The plaintiff stayed behind, went through several concentration camps and eventually, long after the war, came to the Argentine. When Hungary became enemy territory, the partnership became dissolved and the

**134**                                                                    War and Litigation

question arose whether a specific patent sold by the defendant was partnership property. After a trial of eight days Danckwerts J. in January 1954 decided in the plaintiff's favour and directed an enquiry as to damages.[51] The case which was won by Strangman Q.C. entirely turned on the facts which are not of general interest. But on taling accounts the further question arose whether certain shares which the defendant had received for the patent were upon the dissolution of the partnership held in trust by him, so that he became liable to pay interest on the proceeds of sale. The Court of Appeal (Sir Raymond Evershed M.R., Hodson and Romer L.JJ.), affirming the Judge, answered in the affirmative,[52] though in doing so they departed slightly from what is usual in a partnership action. The point relating to the interest was, of course, a minor one. The plaintiff's success in the main action was an eminently satisfactory vindication of justice and a great relief to all who had heard the plaintiff's dreadful story. [99]

It is almost with relief that, finally. I can come to the litigation with the Custodian of Enemy Property or rather the Administrator of national enemy property which during those years was a prominent feature and is of the highest legal, though free from any human, interest.

The last case of the kind which it is convenient to mention first was *Fischler v. Adminstrator of Roumanian Property.*[53] The essential facts were extremely simple. Fischler was a merchant in Bukarest who had suffered terribly in Nazi and Communist concentration camps, but eventually made his way to Israel. The Anglo-Roumanian Clearing Office had had a credit of the princely sum of £2193 which stood in the name of the Commercial Bank of Roumania, which was paid to the defendant and of which the plaintiff claimed to be the owner. The defendant was quite prepared to let poor Mr. Fischler have the money, for he was indeed a victim of Nazi persecution. But could he prove that it was he rather than the Commeicial Bank who was "the owner"? Mr. Justice Glyn-Jones answered in the affirmative, but the Court of Appeal reversed him. Fortunately, we obtained leave to appeal. Mr. Fischler obtained help to finance the appeal. John Foster opened the appeal, but when Eustace Roskill K.C. (later Lord Justice Roskill) had concluded his argument for the respondent on a Thursday afternoon, it seemed most likely that we had lost. John asked for permission that his junior, Mark Littman, might reply on Monday morning, since he was sitting as a Recorder at Oxford. Mark's reply was the only reply I have ever heard which swung the court completely. It did not take more than forty-five minutes. But it was a masterpiece of precision and conciseness (and incidentally directly led to Mark applying for an obtaining silk). We won. Since the case is little known, it is worth pointing out

---

51  Reports of the Patent Cases 71 (1954) 121
52  [1955] 2 All E.R. 762.
53  [1960] 1 W.L.R. 117

War and Litigation

that it contains not only a masterly analysis of the payment clearing system, but also is an authority on the status of banks in regard to assets which, under a system of exchange control, they hold as "beneficiaries". Moreover, Lord Denning had some interesting things to say about the remedy of restitution (which more recently seem to have been rejected) and about *Rahimtoola's* case which, as he rightly discerned, came back with a vengeance. Finally, the case is the most vivid illustration of the enormous intellectual gulf which separated the much overrated Lord Reid from Lord Radcliffe. The opinion of the former is as diff s as most of his opinions are, while Lord Radcliffe's is crystal clear, cogent and compelling.

The greatest case in the field and, indeed, one of the greatest cases in English law is *Bank voor Handel en Scheepvaart v Slatford*.[54] It came to me in 1947 through Henry Hyde, a New York lawyer who had been recommended to me by John Foster and with whom I was to co-operate on may occasions in subsequent years. The Bank in Rotterdam was owned, through many holding companies, trusts etc., Baron Thyssen-Bornemisza, a brother of the German industrialist Fritz Thyssen. He was a Hungarian national who for many years had lived in Villa Favorita in [100] Lugano which also housed his world-famous collection of paintings. The Bank had in 1940 gold and bank accounts with London banks. As soon as Holland became enemy territory the Custodian got hold of these assets and sold them for a total of £1,984,120, which he invested from time to time in the purchase at a discount of Treasury Bills, producing between 1940 and 1950 £151,454. The case had from the start a very odd feature. If the Dutch Bank was the owner of the assets then, of course, at the end of enemy occupation of the Netherlands the assets were to be returned to it. If the Baron was the owner then it would normally have been Government policy to release the assets to him, because he was at all material times resident outside enemy territory, namely in Switzerland and in such circumstances the British Government did not usually enforce its charge upon assets which in strict law belonged to an enemy national. But the authorities were very suspicious of the name Thyssen. They suspected activities during the war for the benefit of Germany, co-operation with the vast Thyssen industries in the Ruhr basin and a close connection with the enemy's war effort. Also, no doubt Britain would have preferred to retain so large a sum as more than £2 million. Hence the case was fought. On the Dutch side, on the other hand, the Government took from the beginning the keenest interest in the case, because Holland was short of foreign exchange and badly wanted the £2 million. The Dutch Government not only appointed an English solicitor as a sort of watch-dog to check all our activities and I had to keep him informed about all major developments, but they also called us for conferences in The Hague in the

---

54 [1953] 1 Q.B. 248

**136**                                                                                           War and Litigation

course of which it was made clear to us that they were very skeptical about the outcome of the case which they would have liked to settle. My clients, however, were optimistic and did not want to settle. In these circumstances there was, behind the scenes, a continuous tug-of-war about a sum which at the time seemed enormous but which at the moment of writing has almost become a common occurrence. If one disregards a somewhat esoteric point which is not reported, which related to the Baron's personal status and on which expert evidence from Dutch, Swiss and Hungarian lawyers was called, the issues in the case were twofold. In the first place we claimed that before the assets were sold in July 1940 they had become vested in the Dutch Government, that there was therefore a conversion which entitled us to damages calculated according to the value of the gold at the time of judgment rather than sale, and that the plaintiffs were the assignees of the Dutch Government entitled to pursue their rights under an Anglo-Dutch Treaty. Secondly, the Bank claimed to be the owner of the assets and entitled to their return, since it was always a Dutch national unaffected by the terms of the Anglo-Roumanian Peace Treaty.

On the first point we failed altogether. Devlin J. did not decide whether the assignment of treaty rights to a private individual was possible in law.[55] He refused to hold that the assets ever became vested in the Dutch Government. On [101] this point his judgment is of fundamental importance, for he held that English property was subject only to English law and could not be transferred by virtue of a foreign decree, even the decree of an allied government acting in wartime, for the protection of its national; public policy could not be used for such a purpose. These were pronouncements which, perhaps, were more novel and therefore more important than those dealing with the second point which was wholly traditional in character. It is the corporation rather than its sole shareholders that is the owner of the corporation's assets. It is in fact difficult to understand how so eminent a team as the then Solicitor-General (Sir Lynn Un-goed-Thomas, later Mr. Justice Ungoed-Thomas), Mr. Gerald Upjohn K.C. (later Lord Upjohn), Mr. J.P. Ashworth (later Mr. Justice Ashworth) and Mr. R.J. Parker (later Mr. Justice Parker) could present a sustained argument in support of the contrary proposition which, many years later, I was to meet again in the case of *Barcelona Traction.*[56]

Our success in this most important case was the result of years of intensive preparation which involved almost monthly trips to Rotterdam and The Hague as well as other places. But it also involved about three months of the most intensive and detailed cramming with Sir Walter Monckton K.C. who, on our side, led John

---

55  I later wrote on this point in British Yearbook of International Law 1954, 475, also Studies in International Law p. 360.

56  See below p.

Foster, then a young silk, and Mark Littman. Every week we met three or four times to discuss every conceivable point, to write Monckton's speeches, to analyse every authority, every refinement to him. He was not a great lawyer, – however great his reputation may have been. He did not have an original mind or a fine legal brain. He was an elegant speaker who had acquited a considerable reputation, but who, left to himself, was not of the same intellectual rank to carry on a persuasive argument with Mr. Justice Devlin, one of the finest brains that ever adorned the English Bench. So it [was] necessary to provide Monckton with notes dealing with every conceivable contingency, and this we did and he managed to see the case through. I had had my doubts about him, but it was difficult at the time to find a "super-leader". I remember that at one time I was thinking of D.N. Pritt, but when I mentioned his name to my clients, they were horrified on account of his Communist leanings. Incidentally, the choice of Devlin J. is a story that I have often told, particularly to my German students who were invariably horrified by it. For in Germany the principle that everyone has what is called his "statutory judge", i. e. a predetermined judge to whom at the beginning of the year all cases of plaintiffs are assigned whose names begin with say, the letter B, is one of the basic principles of the Constitution, a guarantee of the independence and impartiality of justice, a method of eliminating any possibility of manipulation. But in England there exists a fair measure of "arrangement". There is nothing underhand about it. There is no bribery. It is simply the empiric rule at work according to which there are horses for courses. In the Bank's case Monckton, in my presence, telephoned the Attorney-General. It was Shawcross at the time. He asked whom they should entrust with this important case. Shawcross must have asked for suggestions, for Monckton replied that there [102] were three runners, Devlin among them. Shawcross must then have asked for Monckton's choice. When he mentioned Devlin, Shawcross agreed, and Devlin it was. I am quite certain that on both sides quality was the only test.

The Crown did not appeal against Devlin J.'s judgment which was rendered in July 1951. Yet there was an important epilogue to the case. Devlin J. had held that we were not only entitled to interest from the date of the beginning of the proceedings (his remarks on this aspect should be made known to every civil servant), but also the so called fruits of the proceeds of sale, i. e. the sum of £151.454 mentioned above which, perhaps unnecessarily and, I believe, without express instructions, the Solicitor-General had conceded to be due to the Bank in the event of the principal being due. (In 1953 the Government procured an express provision, called by the Board of Trade the "lex Mann", namely s. 4 of the Enemy Property Act 1953, whereby the point was put on a statutory basis.) From this sum the Crown wished to deduct interest. We said that the Custodian being part of "the Crown" was not subject to tax. So a secend case developed which Mark Littman won before Devlin J., since both Monckton and John Foster had by

October 1951 joined the recently formed Conservative government. In the Court of Appeal (Lord Evershed M.R., Denning and Romer L.JJ.) we lost. I had great difficulty in persuading my clients to go to the Lords. Charles Russell K.C. and Mark Littman presented a broadly based, learned and most persuasive argument. The respondent's team was led by the Attorney-General, Sir Lionel Heald K.C. who felt completely at sea, Mr. J.H. Stamp, J.A. Ashworh and R.J. Parker. The memorable part of the argument was· Mr. Stamp's speech, – it did not last longer than about thirty minutes, but it was singularly impressive as a most cogent piece of legal reasoning, one of the greatest speeches I have ever heard. In the end we won three against two. Two Scotsmen, Lord Morton of Henryton and Lord Keith of Avonholme were against us while the third Scotsman, Lord Reid, and Lords Tucker and Asquith of Bishopstone were in our favour.[57] So we won with the narrowest possible margin. But the decision is a milestone in the development of the law relating to the immunity of Crown servants as well as the law relating to the interpretation and effect of the trading with the enemy legislation, – a very special field which during and after the war became one of my special interests,[58] but which, one most sincerely hopes, will never again acquire practical importance.

The only reason why, perhaps, one day I shall revert to it is that the German courts created a fascinating jurisprudential problem by a series of decisions which, I am convinced, constitute a complete distortion of Allied legislation dealing with German property. I became concerned with it in 1962 when I gave an opinion to the Dutch company AKU (now AKZO) on the subject. It was subsequently published as a little book,[59] and although it caused the German [103] Federal Supreme Tribunal in one vital respect to change its practice, it did influence the general trend of the decisions, and while the travaux préparatoires which I was able to publish had their effect upon the German Federal Constitutional Court, a decision of the German Federal Tribunal considered them irrelevant, since they had not been generally available. It is a long and sad story of chauvinistic aberrations by the judiciary.

During the period of the Slatford case the Thyssen-Bornemisza group was faced with many other problems, in particular the "decartelisation policy" which the Allies were attempting to impose upon Germany. It was my task, together with the Rotterdam officials of the Bank, to present the reasons why the concern should not be split. An interesting, but inconclusive meeting with the Allied High Commissioners took place in the Petersberg Hotel opposite Bad Godesberg. It was preceded by detailed preparation about the concern's status, finances, eco-

---

57 *Bank voor Handel en Scheepvaart v. Administrator of Hungarian Property* [1954] A.C. 584
58 See, e.g., "Enemy Property and the Paris Peace Treaties", Law Quarterly Review 64 (1948) 492
59 Zum Privatrecht der deutschen Reparationsleistung (Tübingen, 1962)

nomic coherence etc. I remember, in particular, a long session in Hamborn with Dr. Roehlen and his staff whom I have mentioned before, which lasted until about midnight. The memorable part of it is that, when I came out of the conference room there was Dr. Roehlen's secretary sitting in the ante-room. I went up to her, apologized for the late hour and thanked her for staying so late. Roehlen took me down the staircase to the car, gripped my arm and said to me: "How dare you spoil my staff like this! If I ask her to stay, she has to stay and there is nothing to thank for". Times have changed, – even in Germany, as in later years, I have had many occasions to observe.

In the course of the twenty-five years following upon the decision of the House of Lords I heard little if anything from the Thyssen-Bornemisza concern. In England they went to other lawyers and their German affairs were in the hands of a friend of mine in Dusseldorf to whom I had introduced them and who thus acquired the most important client one lawyer has ever introduced to another. It was only in 1979 that Baron Heini came to consult me in certain personal matters. I cannot help saying that after so successful an effort a closer professional contact would have been pleasing. [104]

## Chapter 15 – Families

Looking back over the years I find it quite extraordinary how large a part of interesting litigation which I conducted arose from disputes within families. Such cases are usually being fought with a bitterness and tenacity which is wholly alien to commercial litigation. Readiness to compromise is almost always missing, – compromises stem from necessity. At the same time the families involved in litigation frequently are the best known and the observer of human reactions finds much interesting material in the behaviour of the famous which is usually quite different from the popular expectation.

From 1958 until his death in 1973 I acted for Nubar Gulbenkian (and I still act for his widow). Although Nubar had other problems on which I continuously advised him, his primary preoccupation during the time I knew him was to get his own back on his father who had died in 1956 and with whom he apparently had enjoyed a most extraordinary love-hate relationship which involved much litigation and equally much reconciliation. The father, the famous "Mr. 5 %", had just before the war given up his home in Paris and emigrated to Lisbon, where he employed a lawyer, Dr. Perdigao, who became the son's arch-enemy. Perdigao made a will for the old man, which very much reduced Nubar's share in the estate but also maue Perdigao the master of the Portugese foundation to which Calouste Gulbenkian bequeathed his splendid collection of works of art. The will ignored Nubar's right to a statutory portion under the law of Portugal where Calouste was domiciled. Litigation ensued, but it had been settled by a complicated Deed of Family Arrangement before I came on the scene, – it was settled, because Nuba did not have the resources to see very complicated litigation through all the obstacles and delays which Portuguese justice created. In broad terms Nubar was left with two objects in life. In the first place he tried by all possible methods of interpretation so to read the Deed of Family Arrangement as to obtain some additional benefit. Secondly, he fought the trustee of the foundation on every possible front, and in this he was much helped by the fact that Lord Radcliffe who for many years had been a friend of Calouste's and had been appointed one of the original trustees fell out with Perdigao and resigned. Nuba did not save time or money to see whether he could not find somewhere along the line an opening for attack and innumerable conferences took place in my office or more frequently, in his flat in Arlington House, to discuss not only his personal problems (which usually involved tax and were based upon Mr. Justice Langton's decision in 1937[60] who had held Nubar to be domiciled in England). Eventually an opportunity appeared. The BBC wished to show a televised interview with Nubar. He agreed, but waived his fee and instead arranged orally with a representative of the BBC that he would receive free of charge a tele-recording. The interview took place. The trustees protested (but to Nubar's eternal regret did not bring a libel action to defend themselves against the charge of disregarding his father's wishes and mismanaging the foundation's affairs). [105] Thereupon the BBC refused to hand over the film. We started proceedings for specific performance of the oral contract. The BBC denied its existence and argued that in its discretion the Court should refuse specific performance, because the showing of the film might expose them to a libel action by the trustees. The case which is described in detail in Nubar's autobiography came before Mr. Justice Glyn Jones in July 1962. Nubar was represented by Sir Lionel Heald Q.C. - a most unfortunate choice made by Nubar personally, - his snobbishness misled him into insisting upon a titled Leading Counsel - and Mark Littman. The Judge accepted Nubar's evidence on the existence of the contract, but awarded £2 by way of damages and refused specific performance. The latter ruling was surely wrong (and the Judge later admitted as much in private conversation with me), but unfortunately Nubar lost courage and did not appeal. He never collected the cheque for £2, but framed it and put it up on the wall in his study. During the case Nubar's favourite caterers offered fabulous cold luncheons in one of the consultation rooms in court to our side, and the newspapers made the most of such unusual an event. So Nubar attracted a great deal of publicity which was much enhanced by the fact that Lord Radcliffe appeared as a witness in support of Nubar's reply to the defence that the trustees could not reasonably be expected to expose themselves to the risks of a libel action in an English court. In short, Nubar had a libel action in reverse and enjoyed himself greatly, - he [did] not mind paying the costs of the action, which he thought were worth the satisfaction he obtained.

During the period in question a second set of proceedings was pending which gave Nubar no end of pleasure. Before the war Calouste had made a settlement which directed the trustees during the life of Nubar to pay the income for the benefit of Nubar and "any person or persons in whose house or apartments or in whose company or under whose care or control or by or with whom the said Nubar may from time to time be employed or residing". By the 1958 compromise Nubar gave up all his rights under the settlement. But did he, could he forego the

---

60  [1937] 4 All E.R. 618

# Families

right of the trustees to benefit him or the rights of the person coming within the quoted words? Such as his butler or the matron of a nursing home where he might find himself? The trustee's first line of defence was that the clause and with it the settlement as a whole were void for uncertainty. This case went through all the courts. We won everywhere and in the House of Lords[61] Lord Reid made the statement which English lawyers should always have in the forefront of their mind: "But the client must not be penalised for his lawyer's slovenly drafting". (Perhaps the citizen should not be penalised for parliamentary draftsmen's well-known slovenliness.) There then followed the next stage of proceedings: had Nubar's renunciation of his own interest deprived the trust of the power to benefit him or the other persons mentioned in the clause? Mr. Justice Plowman answered in the affirmative.[62] We appealed. The Court of Appeal was quite clear that the Judge's reasoning was untenable. Yet the Court was about to dismiss the appeal for different reasons. At this point Mr. Brian Dillen [106] (who had replaced Mr. Peter Foster Q.C., later Foster J.) and Mr. Sydney Templeman Q.C. (as both then were) succeeded in settling the case on terms which were very favourable to Nubar. When the settlement was announced to the court it expressed great regret that it had no opportunity of disapproving the grounds of a decision which was clearly wrong. But when the papers were returned to us by the court, they included a draft judgment by Winn L.J. dismissing the appeal on other grounds, – I used a circuitous route to have it tactfully returned to the Lord Justice's clerk. The case is an excellent example of a thesis I am emphasising again and again: in law Nubar ought to have won, but he had no merits and every court would find means of making him lose.

Nubar was a man of some quality, albeit without depth. He was amusing, not without kindess or intelligence, but completely disinterested in the higher spheres of life. I doubt whether he ever read a book. Art did not interest him. But horses, high living, society, – these were the things he loved and pursued with wit and a measure of charm. In his will he left me £10,000, – a most generous gesture at the time when the money was much more valuable than now. Incidentally t h e m a k i n g of his will was one of the most macabre affairs I ever had to witness. It was a most carefully considered document of, rather, there were two documents, a foreign and English will and a detailed letter of instructions and advice to his wife, the principal beneficiary. Before the will was signed, he insisted upon a rehearsal in the presence of his wife: he was assumed to be dead and in his presence his wife was being instructed in regard to the various options open to her, what she should do etc. He enjoyed himself hugely, but for the others it was, to say the least, embarrassing. One of his endearing features was that he used to

---

61  [1970] A.C. 508, at p. 517
62  [1970] Ch. 408

**144** Families

argue long and hard with me, but he was amenable to reasoned advice and I had no difficulty in keeping him on a straight line except once, – and his widow had to pay for it. He devised a scheme which I considered fraudulent and refused to carry out. He consulted S.G. Warburg & Co. who, without reference to me, sent him to other lawyers who, again, without reference to me, did what he wanted them to do. Years later it had to be undone. By the time of his death Nubar was domiciled in France and his estate was wound up under French law, but since English settlements were involved there were considerable difficulties and I had to spend much time in Paris to confer with the French lawyers, but eventually everything was straightened out in a manner which would have given him much pleasure. Though he was a snob if ever there was one, he was a personality and I cannot help saying that I enjoyed acting for him. My work for him brought me on many occasions into contact with Lord Radcliffe who by that time, had retired from the Bench. He was a man of unusual intelligence and perspicacity, but at the same time one of the coldest and most remote men I ever met. But for Nubar he had a certain benevolence which was totally unexpected. In fact, there could not be two more different people than these two. Did Cyril Radcliffe feel an urge to protect his friend Calouste's son? [107]

Family troubles likewise lay at the root of S o m e r s e t  M a u g h a m's legal problems. I began to act for him in about 1961 and continued to do so until his death (and later for his executors). He came to me at the time when he decided to sell his collection of impressionists at Sotheby's. He deeply felt the responsibility for the great works of art he possessed. He did not think they were safe in his house, the villa Mauresque at Cap Ferrat, so he sold them at Sotheby's for what appeared to be an enormous sum, namely about £500,000, when Lady John Hope intervened and claimed about half the proceeds on the ground that the pictures which had produced these moneys had been given to her by her father. The money was paid into court, but was eventually paid into a joint account of Herbert Smith & Co. and the solicitors of Lady John Hope's trustees. Mr. Maugham had no faith in sterling. Moreover, he was approaching the age of ninety and did not wish to run the risk of British estate duty. He therefore wished to place the money in a joint account in dollars in New York, – a very sensible suggestion, but in order, probably, to bring pressure to bear upon Mr. Maugham, the trustees refused to agree. The Court of Appeal (Sellers, Willmer and HarL.JJ.),[63] rejecting John Foster's strong argument, agreed with them, because both the action and the money was in England and "there was nothing to choose between the interests of the two parties". The result was that Mr. Maugham settled the case. And he also gave in, when he lost a much more unusual case in France on which I had been working for many months. The decision which is

---

63 The Times, 28 July 1962 p. 4 Decision of 3 July 1963

Families **145**

reported in almost all French law reports and has provoked a great deal of learned discussion was to the effect that Lady John Hope was Mr. Maugham's legitimated daughter and was therefore entitled to object to Mr. Maugham's adoption of his close friend Alan Searle.[64] Just before I came on the scene Mr. Maugham had adopted Alan Searle before a notary in Nice. Under the law of France where both parties were domiciled the adoption was valid only in the absence of legitimate children. Lady John Hope intervened on the ground of her alleged status of Mr. Laugham's legitimate daughter. In the quaint language of the court Mr. Maugham "recon[aît] sans ambages que Lady Hope est bien née de ses oeuvres" in May 1915. But her mother, Syrie Barnardo, was at the time the wife of Henry Welcome who obtained a divorce from her only in August 1916, and was married to Somerset Maugham only in May 1917. He was then domiclled in England where at the time legitimation by subsequent marriage was unknown. This was, for the purposes of the present case introduced only in 1959 with retrospective effect to the date of marriage, but by 1959 Maugham had long been domiciled in France where Syrie had divorced him in 1929. In these circumstances the question was whether the English Act of 1959 could retrospectively affect the status of a man domiciled in France. The Tribunal de grande instance in Nice hardly touched upon the great legal problems which the unusual facts created. An appeal was lodged and I prepared an even more elaborate documentation than for the first hearing, but Somerset Maugham in January 1964 reached the age of ninety was loath to fight and withdrew the [108] appeal with the result that the world of private international lawyers was deprived of a judgment by a higher court on a fascinating point of law. On the terrace of the Hotel Negresco in Nice I negotiated an overall settlement with Lady Hope's London solicitors which worked out to everybody's satisfaction.

The family troubles of H e l e n e  R e i n h a r d t - T h i m i g were of a different kind. Germany's most famous theatrical producer of the pre-Hitler era was Max Reinhard who was unhappily married to Else Heims. He purported to obtain a divorce from her by taking up a fictitious residence in Riga, – but the divorce was invalid in German eyes.[65] Helene Thimig, the actress, had been his friend for many years when Hitler came to power and they fled to Austria and in 1938 to the United States, where Reinhardt obtained an unquestionably valid divorce, married Helene Thimig and made a will in her favour. After his death the sons of his first marriage attacked the will by proceedings in California which were eventually settled by an elaborate document. Its effect was that, with certain exceptions, the estate was recognised to belong to Helene Thimig. Early in the

---

64 Journal de Droit International 196, 562; for further reference see Batifflol Lagarde, Traité de Droit International Prové (6th ed. 196), No.

65 See JW 1932, 3844 and the German literature on the case.

1960's her brother, Hermann Thimig, the well-known actor, when clearing up the attic in his house, came across an enormous suitcase. He opened it and having removed a quantity of 1933 newspapers found it to be filled with valuable theatrical sketches and drawings. Their history came back to Helene's and Hermann's mind: in 1933 Reinhardt's secretary in Berlin had succeeded in having these drawings sent to Austria and in 1938 they were removed from Reinhardt's house and stored with Hermann who in the course of the war, the bombing, the Russian occupation completely forgot their existence. Helene who had returned to Vienna shortly after the war had been unaware of the facts. So she had the contents of the suitcase sold at Sotheby's and realised about £25,000. At this moment one of the Reinhardt sons by the first marriage intervened and claimed the money or a share in it. On behalf of Helene I started proceedings against him. He denied the jurisdiction of the English court. The Judge, unfortunately, decided in his favour. There was hardly any doubt that the decision was wrong and Michael Kerr Q.C. (as he then was) was about to argue the appeal, when Helene's Austrian advisers, much to my regret and quite unnecessarily, settled a case which in my view could not be lost. However, in connection with its preparation I had to go twice to Vienna to confer with Helene and interview such witnesses as Hermann Thimig and others. She was a great lady then in her seventies and I enjoyed listening to her talking about the old days with Reinhard, the Salzburg Festival and her time on the stage.

I cannot clearly remember what the family troubles were in the case of the M i e s e g a e s family, I only know that it was on account of some claims made by a former wife that I became involved. Mr. Miesegaes was a Dutch refugee in England during the war, but left for Klosters in 1946, since he was suffering from [109] tuberculosis and at that time the mountain climate of Switzerland was believed to be the cure. He had been divorced from his Dutch wife in Holland before the war, but the only son of the marriage was with him in England. When the father died in Switzerland in 1948, it became necessary to prove his will in solemn f and it all turned on his domicile. I had many meetings in Holland and Switzerland but what it was all about I cannot now say. A little later, however, the son was the victim of a tax case which deserves to be better known. He was a pupil at Harrow from 1947 to 1951, but spent all the holidays with his father and later with a family friend in Switzerland. Yet the Special Commissioners held that during this period he was ordinarily resident at Harrow and that therefore certain income which accrued to him was subject to United Kingdom tax. That a foreign boy who is a pupil at an English school and is present there during term time is ordinarily resident in England seemed an extraordinary and serious proposition with far-reaching consequences, yet both Wynn-Parry J. and the Court of Appeal (Lord

Evershed M.R., Pearce and Morris L.JJ.) upheld it.[66] Since then I have always felt that English schools and Universities accepting pupils who are domiciled abroad and have foreign nationality should expressly warn them that their income arising in to England may be subject to tax. In most cases, of course, the point will not arise merely because the authorities will not become aware of the income, but this does not affect the legal position which may have unfortunate consequences years after the event.

The almost insane possessiveness of a mother over her only son was at the bottom of the great case *in re Peter Fuld deceased*[67] which occupied me during almost the whole of the year 1965. The case took ninety days before Scarman J. (as he then was), from 8 February until 27 July, the main judgment was given on 1 November and the judgment on costs followed on 22 November. Peter Fuld's father Harry, had created one of the great industrial undertakings in Germany, Telef & Normalzeit A.G. He was a Jew who died during the Hitler period. His son Peter was in the Nazi sense "half-aryan". He spent the war years in England and Canada where he was naturalised, but returned to Europe after the war. He died in 1926 in Germany, divorced, and without issue. He left a will and four codicils, and in the result the court upheld the will and the first codicil, but pronounced against the others. This is not the place to discuss the intricate legal issues which arose both in England and in Germany.[68] In essense the case stemmed from a vicious attack by Peter's mother upon her son's friend and legal advisor, Philip Hartley, a London solicitor (who, originally, had made the elementary mistake of acting for himself, but whom I introduced to my friend Max Williams, a partner in Clifford Turner, a man of great ability and integrity) and from the intervention of a London medical practitioner, Dr Tarnesby, a German refugee formerly called Tarnowski, who, partly with the help of the mother, had assisted [110] in having the three impugned codicils executed which, incidentally, conferred substantial benefits upon him as the deceased's medical advisor. There were allegations of undue influence, of lack of testamentary capacity and of lack of due form (which involved grave problems of the conflict of laws and a very large amount of expert evidence on various aspects of German law) and much depended on Peter's domicile which in the lad the Judge held to be German. I acted for Peter's relations, who benefited substantially under the will and first codicil and who supported Hartley's case and opposed the mother and Tarnesby. Eighteen Counsel were engaged in the case, my team consisting of Tom Strangman, Mark Littman and John Wilmers. The picture of intrigue, envy and greed which the

---

66 (1957) 37 T.C. 493

67 The main case is reported (1966) 2 W.L.R. 717, but there were many interlocutory decisions which are reported elsewhere.

68 Two decisions of the Federal Supreme Court are reported, for instance, IP Rspr. 1966–1967 No. 168 and 1972 No. 124

148 Families

proceedings disclosed was quite fascinating, what was no less interesting was the fact that with a little bit of foresight and better legal advice much of the trouble could so easily have been avoided. As it developed, the case became an almost unique opportunity for lawyers to show the stuff of which they were made – and the mother's German lawyer was an unscrupulous man intent to promote litigation wherever possible. In these circumstances it was remarkable, but probably typical of the low quality of the majority of German lawyers that he failed to make a point which might have brought his client home and of which I was afraid throughout the case. Under certain decisions of the Federal Supreme Court (the effect of which has since then been much attenuated) a testamentary gift as a reward for past sexual relations was and to some extent still is *contra bonos mores.* Peter had conferred substantial benefits on four former girl friends, and although I do not know whether in fact the charge could have been supported it would have been in line with the conduct of the mother's German lawyer to make it and await events. How is it to be explained that he failed to do so? My own part went beyond the preparation of my own clients' case, for by arrangement with those on our side I undertook to do everything connected with the evidence on German law. This was a vital part of the case. The witnesses on our side were the late Dr. E.J. Cohn, Professor Kegel of the University of Cologne and Professor Firsching, then of the University of Munich. But our opponents were not lacking in talented experts. The principal one was Professor Coing of the University of Frankfurt and they also produced a high-ranking German judge. The English court dealt with the evidence on German law very summarily, but in this respect as well as in others it was probably impossible for Scarman to do full justice to the enormous amount of material which had been submitted to him and with which he had to cope. His judgment as reported is a master-piece of conciseness, though, as I remember clearly, when Tarnesby gave notice of appeal and the chances of the appeal were discussed, we would have wished for more detailed reasoning on a number of points. The appeal was not pursued in that a settlement was negotiated with Tarnesby which was clearly satisfactory to our side, yet far too favourable to him. The case as a whole makes a quite extraordinary story. I cannot tell it, particularly since I am writing now [111] without reference to the transcripts. Sybille Bedford was at one time interested in writing about the case, but never did so. Perhaps one day an imaginative author will make use of the material.

While the Fuld case was in progress, three persons came to meet me outside Scarman J.'s court. They were Miss Elisabeth Fay, Signor Pericoli and their Swiss lawyer. I subsequently saw them in the office, when they instructed me to act for them in *the estate of Sir Oliver Duncan deceased*, an affair which was occupy me for the next six years and involved innumerable trips to Rome, Monte Carlo, Geneva and elsewhere, including New York and Bermuda. Sir Oliver Duncan was an Englishman who long before the war went to live in Switzerland

Families 149

on the basis of the enormous fortune he had inherited from his mother, a member of the American Pfizer family. Sir Oliver who during the war was blacklisted by the English (I have no doubt for very good reasons) officially i.e. for the purpose of avoiding taxes, lived in an attic room of the Palace Hotel in Montreux, but in fact inhabited a chateau at Mies near Geneva. He must have been the greatest snobs, antisemites and good-for-nothings that ever lived. I say this, because I had the misfortune of reading through volumes of his correspondence to find material on the question of his status and thus obtained a very clear picture of his personality. He surrounded himself with people who, rightly or wrongly, had titles, – mostly members or alleged members of the Hungarian "nobility", hangers-on, frivolous members of the demi-mode, but apparently entitled to the title Princess or Count. He had a similarly grand house in Cannes and, in effect, lived from party to party, from lunch engagement to dinner engagement. He married only in the late 1950's when he was in his sixties, a Hungarian lady. He soon fell out with her and in circumstances which became very controversial, went to live in Rome. Suffering from Parkinson's disease he allowed himself to be cared for by Miss Fay, an old family friend. He died in Rome in 1964. He left a will made in Rome whereby he left the bulk of his fortune to Miss Fay. He had previously made two wills in Berne and Montreux respectively, under which the late H.S. Garfield, a partner of Herbert Oppenheimer, Nathan and Vandyk was the executor and which conferred large benefits upon the widow. Sir Oliver, of course, had acquired Liechtenstein nationality, – which other nationality would have been suitable for him? Proceedings for nullity of marriage which he had instituted in Liechtenstein were dismissed by a well-known decision of the Supreme Court. Divorce proceedings in Switzerland were still pending at the date of his death. Soon afterwards the executors of the Rome will, primarily Mr. Pericoli who had lived with Miss Fay for years settled with Lady Duncan by paying her several million of Swiss francs in what was believed to be a full settlement of all her claims. Yet at the same time Garfield was preparing proceedings in Monte Carlo, Nice and Lausanne to uphold the Swiss wills, and when in February 1965 Miss Fay, through other solicitors than myself, had obtained a grant of probate in England to recover the trifling sum of £17,000 in an English bank, he started proceedings to revoke the grant an the ground that the Rome will was null [112] and void on account of insanity, undue influence and lack of knowledge and approval. This is why I came to be instructed. After much deliberation and discussion among all the lawyers it was eventually decided that we would fight the principal action in England, where there were procedural advantages which Continental procedure failed to offer. The case was most bitterly fought and involved numerous interludes and events of the most atonishing character. Thus one of the executors of the Rome will, a Professor Biondi of the University of Florence, the holder of Machiavelli's chair, and an advocate in

Rome, produced shortly before his death a so-called diary for the year 1964 with entries design to show that Miss Fay had obtained the Rome will by threatening and pressurizing Sir Oliver. It will be obvious what a bombshell the production of this document constituted. But painstaking investigation, also by graphologists, soon established beyond any possibility of doubt that the "diary" was a forgery, that Biondi had written it up in the course of one afternoon on board his yacht with the object of enabling a woman friend to blackmail Miss Fay after his death, – it was a method of providing for her. In England we met with the most determined opposition and professional problems such as one is not used to. Thus the evidence of Sir Oliver's Rome medical advisor was taken in London on commission, but Counsel for our opponents did everything they could to turn it into a farce and sabotage it, with little success in the end. Many documents were withheld so that, in order to obtain obviously relevant documents, we had to appeal again an order of Ormrod J. and obtain them from the Court of Appeal. On the other hand, we did not appeal against Ormrod J.'s order holding legal professional privilege to extend communications with foreign lawyers,[69] nor did we appeal (no doubt wrongly) against an order of Ormrod J. rejecting our application to strike the proceedings out on the ground that they were champertous. Nor did we appeal against an order of Latey J. holding that a vicious article in the Evening Standard by Sam White, accusing Miss Fay inter alia of adultery with Sir Oliver, did not constitute contempt of court.[70] Eventually a date for trial was fixed and, moreover, it was arranged that the judge, Cummings-Bruce J. (as he then was) would take the evidence of certain witnesses in Rome, Montreal and Monte Carlo. It was at this point that the expected happened. The senior partner of Oppenheimer Nathan and Vandyk took over, changed Counsel and negotiated with me what was called a settlement, but what in fact was an unconditional surrender: the Rome will was recognised and all accusations and proceedings were withdrawn. Our only concession, a very substantial one, was that we did not insist on the payment of Miss Fay's enormous costs by her opponents. It was in June 1970 that the final document was signed at Geneva, but much remained to be done thereafter, particularly because Lady Duncan caused separate and new proceedings [113] to be instituted in Bermuda which, on the basis of the English decision we obtained pursuant to the compromise, were eventually dismissed. It was an extraordinary saga which thus came to an end and my only regret is that Signor Pericoli did not live to see our final success on all fronts. I could not help feeling that for once the defeat of the family, in this case Lady Duncan, was most satisfying outcome.

---

69 (1968) P. 306
70 Solicitors Journal 1969, 526 or 119 New Law Journal 508

Families                                                                                    **151**

In 1967 I became involved in a dispute which concerned what I can only describe as the most extraordinary family I ever came across. In July 1965 there had died in France one Nina Dyer. She had first been the wife of my old client Baron Heini Thyssen-Bornemisza and then of Prince Sadruddin Khan. Both marriges were dissolved, but left Miss Dyer an extremely rich woman. At her death two informal holograph documents were found which seemed to be wills and to leave the whole of her enormous estate to a friend, Miss Betty Esteves, a United States citizen, to use the estate for animal welfare. Miss Dyer had acquired Swiss nationality by marriage and was domiciled in either France or Switzerland, – in either case in a country in which a parent is entitled to a statutory portion of his child's estate. In these circumstances a Mr. Aldrich came forward and alleged that in June 1923 he was married to Elsie Edith Aldrich, that she left him in 1929 to live with Mr. Dyer, that Nina was born on 15 February 1930 and that she was his legitimate child. The Swiss courts were faced with a difficult problem of private international and English law and would have welcomed a decision by an English court. So Mr. Aldrich started proceedings for a declaration that he was validly married to Elsie Edith and that Nina was his legitimate child. Ormrod J. granted the former declaration,[71] but held that he had no jurisdiction to make the latter one. I acted for Miss Esteves and my Counsel, John Mortimer Q.C. leading Anthony Lincoln (as he then was) supported the proposition that the court could make a declaration for the enlightenment of the Swiss court. The effect of the judge's hold was that the Swiss courts were called upon to find the facts and this brought the parties to negotiate a settlement as a result of which Mr. Aldrich received a substantial part of the fortune which Nina's husbands had provided for her. So the rights of the family were vindicated.

Nothing I have said so far can be compared to the incredible bitterness with which during the years 1964 to 1971 the litigation relating to the affairs of Mauricio Hochschild was pursued. He was a German Jew who was a mining engineer, and before the first world war had emigrated to South America where he created a mining empire in Chile, Bolivia and Peru and vast industrial undertakings in other countries, including the United States and Europe. He married a Jewish lady from Mannheim who died in the 1920's leaving an only child, a son named Gerrardo or Gerald. The father later remarried a Belgian lady, a woman of a completely different calibre and background, who, so I always understood, hated her stepson and did everything she could to alienate his father. When Hitler [114] came to power in 1933 Mauricio went to Germany and made arrangements for about 150 Jewish refugees to emigrate to South America where he employed them in his various enterprises. He must have been very lucky in his choice, for there is no doubt that many of the young men to whom a new life was

---

71 *Aldrich v. Attorney-General*, (1968) P. 281

thus offered must have been very able. They made good and a certain group of them eventually became the real bosses of the empire, particularly during Mauricio's declining years. Gerald was much pushed around. I always understood that his father disliked him, that "the boys" were determined to exclude him from running and, in particular, from owning the empire. In short, Gerald became the victim of intrigues initiated partly by his step-mother (whom eventually the father divorced), partly by the father's collaborators. In the course of the 1950's the father at last seemed to be free to act independently and in accordance with his own wishes. In 1958 he created a Liechtenstein foundation to which all his interests were transferred and which conferred far-reaching rights upon the son "or his statutory or testamentary heirs". In particular, the son was to be given a leading position in the group. This incensed the collaborators who, with the help of an unscrupulous New York lawyer, caused the old man in 1960 to agree to the wholly illegal removal of all the assets from Liechtenstein and their transfer to a Bahamas trust of which they were trustees (together with the Trust Corporation of the Bahamas) and which conferred certain limited benefits on Gerald. He tried to attack what was one of the most shameful acts of robbery I have ever come across and brought proceedings in the Bahamas, New York and Liechtenstein, but, of course, did not possess the means to fight his immensely rich father and the latter's henchmen. So in June 1961 he agreed to give up all his rights against debentures totalling U.S.$ 3,300,000 and payable over a long number of years, – an altogether inadequate sum which no lawyer ought to have allowed him to accept in full settlement, but which his New York lawyers who had agreed a contingent fee with him most strongly advised him to accept. What was overlooked by all concerned was the question whether by reason of the words I quoted Gerald's children had independent rights not affected by the compromise. So the children started proceedings in Liechtenstein to recover a fortune estimated at some U.S. $ 125 million at 1961 values. The action was dismissed in the lower courts and at this stage, October 1964, I was consulted and instructed to take over the general conduct of the affairs of Gerald and his family.

At that time the appeal to the Supreme Court of Liechtenstein was pending and I was trying to make a contribution to its success. In fact it was lost. The case was heard by a tribunal consisting of Swiss and two Austrian Judges and a Liechtenstein school teacher and a farmer. It was argued by a Liechtenstein lawyer. The mistake which I made was that I had not found out that in special cases permission could be granted to foreign lawyers to argue a case in the Supreme Court. This was a special case indeed. The amount involved was vast, the interest of the infant plaintiff enormous. I think permission would have been granted. As it was, the argument by the Liechtenstein lawyers was wholly [115] inadequate, but in any case the sympathy of the court was against us, because the action was regarded as an attempt by the father to use his infant child to set aside

# Families

**153**

the compromise, but the result was probably correct[72] so we lost the case in this august tribunal.[73] Mauricio, of course in the company of one of his cronies, attended the hearing, but ignored his son and allowed an argument to be made in defence of a case designed to prejudice his grandchildren.

The next event was that early in 1965 I had a meeting in Paris with the father (who, of course, was again accompanied by one of his chaps) to see whether the whole dispute could not be settled and the family relationship re-established. I did not succeed, but I also received a clear impression of Mauricio. He was then more than eighty years old and, I felt sure, without any mind of his own. I was, therefore, not surprised to find that when he died on 12 June 1965 in Paris, his will ignored his family altogether, – his eldest grandson, also called Mauricio, did not even receive a watch or a pair of cufflinks.

I had, however, anticipated his death and calculated that for the funeral all his principal chaps, particularly the eight trustees, would be at the Hotel Meurice in Paris, where Mauricio had an apartment and his group used to stay. So in order to found an internationally recognisable jurisdiction I had them served on 15 June at the breakfast table with proceedings commenced in the French courts and claiming that by the law of France where we alleged Mauricio, then a Chilean subject, was "domiciled" Gerald was entitled to a statutory portion, a to have the Bahamas trust set aside.

We had hardly done this, when the French defendants started proceedings in England claiming an injunction to restrain Gerald from continuing the French proceedings. They applied by motion to Ungoed-Thomas J. for an interim injunction, Sir Milner Holland appearing for them and Mark Littman leading Peter Oliver (as he then was) and C.A. Brodie was instructed by me. Fortunately, the Judge dismissed the motion.[74] But, of course, the English proceedings were on foot and we saw the opportunity of an unexpected forum for a general attack. We required the plaintiffs to deliver a statement of claim and as soon as this was done delivered not only a defence, but also raised a counter-claim claiming damages for a general conspiracy to deprive Gerald of his rights. It was a most skilfully drawn document which had gone through numerous drafts. It must have come as a complete surprise and shock to these plaintiffs and should, incidently serve as a general warning: before proceedings are started in a foreign country, [116] think twice and check whether they will not enable the defendant to bring a counter-claim which otherwise could not be brought before any court.

---

72  because of their true construction the quoted words referred to Gerald's successorin – title in the event of his death rather than to his children as such

73  The decision is reported in Entscheidungen der Liechtensteinischen Gerichtshofe 1962–1966 page 170. The decision was rendered on 2nd December 1966, – long after the hearing and long after Mauricio's death.

74  *Settlement Corporation v Hochschild,* (1966) Ch. 10.

We then attacked on a third front. We applied in the Bahamas on behalf of Gerald's children for the appointment of a Receiver of the Bahamas trust. Tim Brodie obtained the order ex parte and at a full hearing attended by Sir Milner Holland and Peter Oliver it was confirmed.

I do not think that it would be of general interest to describe in detail the numerous steps which were taken in these various proceedings. Some of the English interlocutory orders are reported.[75] The result was that in 1971 all the proceedings were settled on terms which were not entirely unsatisfactory, yet were far from the success which Gerald and his children deserved.

But I must mention one feature which is of great general interest. In Paris the trustees pleaded to the jurisdiction of the French courts on the ground that Mauricio was not "domiciled" in France, but was "domiciled" – in the Bahamas of all places. Our evidence was very strong that the alleged Bahamas domicile was nothing but a fraudulent device designed to conceal the true domicile in France. But we lost in the Tribunal de grande instance and the Court of Appeal. The judgment of the latter court was quite particularly surprising in that it contained factual statements which were a pure invention on the part of the court and had no basis whatever in the record. Yet the French lawyers advised that nothing could be done about it. We lodged an appeal to the Cour ue Cassation, but the avocat instructed to present the case was so indolent and indifferent that there was no hope of success. It was a most disturbing experience sharpened by an almost tragical development: a few days after the decision of Court of Appeal we obtained irrefutable evidence that our opponents' case was, to put it at its lowest, factually wrong. The evidence consisted of copies of tax returns filed by Mauricio in New York and stating that he was not liable to tax, because he was resident in Paris. Again, the French lawyers advised that there was no method of bringing this conclusive material before the court and the French case, therefore, was decided on a basis which in vital respects was false. Perhaps the result would have been different if French law had something in the nature of the English institution of discovery of documents.

The Hochschild case as a whole remains for more than one reason a most challenging and also a most distasteful incident in my professional life. [117]

---

75 See, in particular, *Settlement Corporation v. Hochschild (No.2)*, (1960) 1 W.L.R. 1664

# Chapter 16 – Arbitration and Litigation

It is a wide-spread belief that arbitration is an institution of outstanding excellence that deserves unqualified support and is much to be preferred to litigation. In fact this is to a large extent a myth nurtured by interested persons, mainly the officials of the organisations, national and international, which, for business purposes, that is to say for the sake of their own positions, habitually sponsor and promote the idea as well as the organisation of arbitration.

Much depends on the composition of the arbitration tribunal, – it would, of course, be possible, to form a tribunal which would be superior to any national tribunal that could be created in any country. Much depends on the country if any in which, in the absence of an arbitration clause, the litigation would have to take place, – it is not difficult to think of countries whose judicial system is such that parties are anxious to exclude it. Much depends on the nature of the dispute. It is clear, therefore, that generalisations are not possible or that if one speaks in general terms qualifications must always be implied.

It is in this sense that I am bound to suggest that as a matter of experience wherever possible arbitration should be avoided. It is said that arbitration is quicker than litigation this is rarely so. If it is said that arbitration is cheaper than litigation that is never so, because arbitrators are invariably more expensive than judges. If it is said that arbitration takes place behind closed doors and the public is unaware of the dispute, this is frequently not so, because on far too many occasions applications to the court can and will be made either during the arbitration proceedings or after an award. If it is said (as it often is) that, contrary to litigation, arbitration in the end leaves both parties satisfied, such statements are nonsensical. We all know that a case may be won or lost, – and the loser will always be dissatisfied. If, on the other hand, arbitrators seek a solution which gives a bit to each party, no party will be satisfied, – the idea that the party which ought to have won will be ready to accept the compromise imposed upon it is totally unrealistic.

When parties enter into an agreement, they are usually very ready to agree to an arbitration clause, either because they feel compelled to avoid the courts of a certain country or because they are ignorant of the dangers and vicissitudes which arbitration may involve, that is to say, because they are led astray by propaganda which so many interested parties are in the habit of making in favour of arbitration. It is only when it comes to the point that disillusionment likely to occur, – and then it is too late.

I say all this on the basis of much practical experience. No doubt I have seen arbitrations which were acceptable, because justice was done and was seen to be done. No doubt in almost all those cases in which I was an arbitrator and sometimes a single arbitrator I firmly believed that I had done justice and that under my control justice was seen to be done. But speaking generally I am bound [118] to emphasise that most arbitrations in which I participated as Counsel were a disaster, – and this I propose to show in the course of the following pages in order to warn the naive and to counteract the invidious propaganda to which businessmen are continuously being exposed. Perhaps it will be answered that the fault lies with the arbitrators who purport to decide according to law and that all would be well or better if arbitrators were free to disregard the law, as to some extent they are allowed to do if they are given the power to decide as "amiable compositeurs" according to some mysterious "equity", fairness or "Billigkeit". My answer is that, when it comes to the point, this is the last thing that parties are prepared to put up with, for parties require a reasonable degree of certainty and foreseebility and they are therefore not prepared to submit voluntarily to a decision which almost by definition is and must be arbitrary. And if they have to submit, because they agreed to it nine out of ten in my intimate experience will deeply regret it.

Notwithstanding my dissillusionment by and my misgivings about arbitration I must make it clear that from a personal point of view I have derived very great pleasure from it, for where I represented a party I had the opportunity, so rare in the case of members of my profession to argue my own cases, and this always gave me great satisfaction and where I was arbitrator (as in recent years I have frequently been) I greatly enjoyed the task of conducting a case and giving what I hoped to be persuasive decision.

An instructive case was *Mechema Ltd. v. Mines, Minéraux et Métaux S.A.*, which led to a decision of the Brussels Cour d'Appel. Under a contract governed either by English or by Belgian law the English plaintiff company was appointed the Belgian company's sole distributor in Britain. The Belgian company duly terminated the contract and set up its own selling Organisation with personnel, formerly employed by my clients, the English company. The contract provided for arbitration under the procedure of the International Chamber of Commerce by three arbitrators who were to act as friendly arbitrators, i.e. as amiables compositeurs. The award was to be deposited with the Brussels tribunal de commerce. The three arbitrators who were sitting in Paris were Me. Gastambide

Arbitration and Litigation

of the Paris Bar as Chairman, Sir Francis Vallat Q.C. appointed by the Belgians and M. le Bâtonnier Dassesse of the Belgian Cour de Cassation. Amiable composition was at the time unknown to English[76] as well as Belgian law, but is well known in France. I was instructed well after the proceedings had been instituted. At first the case appeared to me quite hopeless, but after a while I began to see a line of approach which promised success. The difficulty was to persuade the arbitrators that on the one hand amiable composition was a procedure matter governed by French law as the law of the seat of the tribunal, the *lex arbitri*, rather than by Belgian or English law and that on the other hand compensation should be paid under Belgian substantive law, although if the contract was governed by English law none was due or simply as a matter of fairness. The tribunal accepted the first point. It went on to hold that, in [119] the absence of a clear choice of law by the parties the so-called *lex mercatoria* should be applied, and entitled my clients to reasonable compensation. They awarded me a sum of 1 mio Belgian Francs. The reference to the alleged lex mercatoria was, of course, futile and nonsensical, for French law permitted the arbitrators to act as amiables compositeurs, so that in any event they were entitled to act outside the law. The result was to my mind very satisfactory to my clients, although they had expected a much larger award, but the Belgian company attacked it in the Belgian courts;[77] – so much for the suggestion that arbitrators acting as amiables compositeurs will leave both parties satisfied.

Another, much more serious and, indeed, a disastrous case was *Societe des Grands Travaux de Marseille (S.G.T.M.) v. Republic of Bangladesh*, also a case proceeding under the auspices of the International Chamber of Commerce. S.G.T.M. had built a pipeline in Bangladesh. It claimed that a balance of more than 12 million French francs (about £1 million) was due to it for work done[78] from the contractor, a State corporation eventually called Bangladesh The contract, governed by the law of Pakistan, provided for arbitration under the rules of the International Chamber of Commerce in Geneva. Mr. Andrew Martin Q.C. was appointed as single arbitrator. The arbitration proceedings were initiated and continued for about two years. The final hearing was fixed for January 1973, but in October 1972 we were suddenly informed that the Bangladesh Industrial Development Corporation had been dissolved, its assets had been taken over by the Republic of Bangladesh and that the latter had reserved to itself the right to decide which liabilities it proposed to discharge "ex gratia". It was at that point that I was called in to deal with a case which had started as a wholly uninteresting building case. I came to the conclusion that the Republic of Bangladesh ought to

---

76 See

77

78 Industrial Development Corporation (B.I.D.C.)

be considered the universal successor of the Bangladesh Industrial Development Corporation and made an application to the arbitrator for the substitution of the Republic as a defendant. The hearing took place in Geneva in November 1972. R.A. McCrindle Q.C., instructed by Coward Chance & Co., appeared for the Republic under protest and argued their case. I appeared for S.G.T.M. and applied for an order of substitution. The arbitrator, having heard full argument for two days, and two experts on the law of Bangladesh, decided in favour of universal succession and made the order I had asked for. He held that on its true construction the Bangladesh decree transferred to the Republic not only the assests, but also the liabilities, that the Republic had reserved to itself only the right to decide upon the payment of debts for which as suc it had accepted liability and that in any event the taking of assets without liabilities was contrary to ordre public. So far so good. The Republic, however started proceedings in the Geneva courts in order to have the arbitrator's order set aside on the ground of lack of jurisdiction in respect of the Republic. It obtained a preliminary order for the suspension of the arbitration proceedings until final judgment. Eventually the case came before the Cour de Justice in [120] Geneva which after a long delay decided against us. We appealed to the Swiss Federal Tribunal against what was plainly an illogical and unjust decision, but in May, by a decision which was rendered by four votes against three, which adopted the views of the r a p - p o r t e u r, an auxiliary judge, M. Jolidon who was a practising lawyer in Berne, and which is open to the severest criticism, the Federal Tribunal upheld the lower court on the principal ground that the arbitrator was without jurisdiction.[79] A useful criticism of the decision was published by Professor Pierre Lalive,[80] and I discussed it in a German article.[81] Both contributions make the argument which I had asked S.G.T.M.'s Swiss Counsel, J.F. Lalive, the brother of Pierre, to put forward, but essential parts of which were omitted from an unduly long and diffuse brief submitted to the Federal Tribunal whose reasoning in a most important case is likely to become recognised as completely inadequate and, indeed, bungled. From my client's point of view, however, the decision had only academic interest, for the arbitrator very wisely decided to continue the arbitration notwithstanding the suspension order of the Geneva court. He took the

---

79 The decision is reported in BGE 102 Ia 574. The argument that there was lack of jurisdiction was surely wrong. The question whether a tribunal has jurisdiction is to be answered as at the date of commencement. If it exists it continues (principle of the perpetuation fori). The sole and short question for the court was whether Bangladesh was a universal successor. If noS.G.T.M. was bound to fail. If yes, it was bound to succeed. I have developed this and other criticism of the decision in a contribution to the Fetschrift für Konrad Zweigert under the title "Der konfiszierende Staat als Gesamtrechtsnachfolger".

80

81

## Arbitration and Litigation

view that the order was addressed to the parties rather than to himself, – a view which the International Chamber of Commerce shared. The proceedings, therefore, continued in January 1973 and after hearing of some four weeks, attended by one of my partners, but boycotted by the Republic of Bangladesh, we obtained an award of some 12 million French francs. It was recognised by the French Export Insurance Companywhich paid 90 % of the award, so that in substance my clients obtained satisfaction. The claim was, of course, assigned to the Insurers, i. e. in effect the French State. Whether it obtained any satisfaction from the Republic of Bangladesh or whether it made any international claim against Switzerland on the ground of a grave miscarriage and, indeed, a denial of justice on the part of the Federal Tribunal is unknown to me. This, therefore, is a case which does not involve any criticism of the arbitration proceedings, but of the courts which misapplied the law.

The last arbitration case which I would like to discuss is of a different kind altogether. In fact, it is unique in every conceivable respect. It is a telling example of the enormous risks which arbitration involves. At the same time, it proves in a striking fashion that if one of the parties or its lawyer are [121] unscrupulous and determined to obstruct, delay and undermine the arbitration they have ample opportunities. The case I am talking about is *Papierwerke Waldhof Aschaffenburg A.G. v. Black Clawson International Ltd.* which was pending for 1 years before an award was rendered. It should be instructive for many to hear the story in a little detail.

In the 1950's my clients, PWA, came into contact with a Mr. K.F. Landegger, an Austrian refugee who went to the United States and built up an international concern manufacturing paper-making machines. PWA bought from Landegger's English company, Black Clawson International Ltd., such a machine – an enormous animal of great length, size and complication – for some £1.5 million, one third of which was covered by bills of exchange payable over a number of years, while the rest was paid in cash. The machine was installed, but failed to function properly. So PWA consulted their German lawyer, my friend Dr. Zutt in Mannheim, who called me in, since the contract was, in the events which happened, governed by English law. This was in the spring of 1964, when it was still thought possible to reach a settlement. In order to familiarize myself with the issues I went to Germany and was shown the machine and the malfunctioning parts of which there were many and which were obvious even to the eye of a layman. We then had a meeting in Frankrurt with Sir Robert Clark, a director of Hill Samuel & Co. who were Mr. Landegger's advisors and a partner of Slaughter & May, my friend Geoffrey Williams, now a director of Henry J. Schroeder & Co. It was impossible to reach a settlement and, therefore, in the summer of 1965 arbitration proceedings were commenced. Under the contract they were subject to the procedural law of Zurich. The original artibtrators were Judge Trolle, of the

Danish Supreme Court as Chairman – he had been appointed by the International Chamber of Commerce, – Mr. Michael Kerr Q.C. (as he then was) nominated by me and a Montreal lawyer, Mr. Vineberg, appointed by Landegger and/ or BCI. We had a first hearing in the spring of 1966 in Copenhagen. It was intended to deal with formalities and future procedure. BCI was represented by New York lawyers, a Mr. Grouf and a Mr. Braunschweig, partners of Wachtel, Mannheim & Grouf, though Mr Williams was present without taking part in the proceedings, – in fact Slaughter & May dropped out of them. On this first occasion Mr. Grouf gave us a little introduction of the tactics he was to employ in the course of the succeeding years. At lunch with my clients in the famous Fiske Resturant in Copenhagen I said jokingly that Mr. Grouf was the type of lawyer with whom I found it almost impossible to get on. I vividly remember the consternation on the part of my clients who seemed to to lack a sense of humour. However, the poor opinion which they then formed of me changed completely as time went on.

It took more than two years, namely until December 1968, before pleadings were closed and discovery of documents was completed. At about that time it came to our notice that Mr. Vineberg had, unknown to us, for many years been the Canadian lawyer to the Landegger group and was, while the arbitration proceedings [122] were pending, actively engaged on behalf of Landegger in Canadian litigation which resulted in a reported decision. When we heard this, I wrote to Vineberg and asked for an answer to the question whether the facts as ascertained by us were true. He refused to answer. Further correspondence and some searching questions put by me failed to provoke any frank disclosure. The threat to apply to the Zurich courts for his removal equally failed to induce the learned arbitrator to make the facts known. This destroyed any residue of goodwill he possessed: had he frankly admitted his connection with Landegger it is by no means certain that he would not have accepted the position, for he seemed to be a perfectly reasonable and honourable man, but the complete lack of frankness was intolerable. We were therefore determined to apply to the court and take the risk of prolonged proceedings. In this state of affairs, a hearing in Zurich took place in October 1969, when Mr. Trolle stated that the case was too heavy for him and resigned and when Vineberg also decided at last to resign, – almost a year having been wasted.

Landegger then appointed a retired New York State Judge, Samuel Coleman, as his arbitrator, a man who was then approaching the age of eighty and thus was peculiarly qualified to act in a European arbitration. But over our protest the international Chamber of Commerce confirmed him. (Lesson: where the arbitration clause envisages arbitration in Europe, provide in it for the appointment of European arbitrators.) At about the same time the International Chamber of Commerce appointed as Chairman my friend Professor Frank Vischer, Basel.

Arbitration and Litigation

At the next session in July 1970 the tribunal decided that it would appoint its own expert, – a decision against which BCI appealed to the Zurich courts. Their appeal was finally rejected by a decision of 30 June 1971,[82] but as a result of the delay that had occurred the court's expert was appointed only in April 1972. His reports were rendered in January and October 1973. After a variety of further proceedings, the final argument was orally presented in February 1976 by which time Michael Kerr who had been appointed to the Bench was replaced by Dr. Anton Heini, a Zurich lawyer. There then began a number of manoeuvres to prevent the rendering of an award. As soon as Judge Coleman, now almost 90 years old, saw that his colleagues were about to render an award unfavourable to his appointors he, together with BCI's New York lawyers, set a variety of steps into motion with a view to obtaining the disqualification of Professor Vischer on the ground of partiality. Applications, founded on wholly baseless accusations and partly on facts deliberately provoked by the lawyers, were first made to and rejected by the International Chamber of Commerce and then repeated before the courts of Zurich and eventually the Federal Tribunal in Lausanne. It was only in November 1979 that the latter rendered its decision[83] rejecting the attack upon Professor Vischer's impartiality. The incident is remarkable, because one of the grounds upon which that attack was based was the fact that Professor Vischer had contributed an article to the [123] Festschrift dedicated to me on the occasion of my 70th birthday in 1977. The Federal Tribunal described this attack as remarkable and rejected it on the obvious ground that the relationship of the umpire with one of the parties' advocates cannot in the absence of special circumstances have a bearing upon his objectvity. Where would we end if a judge were not allowed to be on terms of friendship with a practising lawyer regularly appearing before him!

The award condemning Black Clawson International to pay a large sum of money to my clients was rendered shortly before the Federal Tribunal's decision. It was an unanimous award. Yet BCI immediately lodged a petition for nullity in the courts of Zurich. While I am writing its fate is still unknown.

While the arbitration proceedings thus summarised were pending, there were other battles fought on different fronts, namely in the ordinary courts of England and Germany. As I mentioned above, part of the purchase price was paid by bills of exchange drawn and accepted by my clients who, of course, had the greatest possible interest in avoiding payment before the publication of an award, for they realised only too well that they were unlikely to recover much if anything from BCI and therefore were anxious to retain the moneys payable in respect of the bills so as to be able to set off against at least part of the award. So bills had been

---

82 Reported in Zürcherische Rechtsprechung 70 (1971) Nr. 37.
83

discounted by Barclays Bank and the first set of proceedings involved an action by the Bank to recover the amount due under two bills. The defence was that the bank held the bills as trustee agent for BCI and that therefore PWA could set up the defence which it would have had in an action brought by BCI, namely the defectiveness of the machine. In order to prove the Bank's status in the action we required access to the documents evidencing the arrangements made with BCI. The Bank was suspiciously reluctant to disclose facts and we lost both before the Master and the Judge in Chambers. But when we came before the Court of Appeal (Lord Denning M.R., Harman and Salmon L.JJ) they were very puzzled by the fact that the available documents referred to a facility letter which the Bank refused to disclose. Counsel for the Bank (Mr Leonard Caplan Q.C.) then said that the Court could see certain parts of the letter and handed it up. These parts seemed to confiirm the Bank's case that it had purchased the bills without recourse. Salmon L.J. (as he then was), however was dissatisfied and asked whether the court could read the rest of the letter. Most reluctantly consent was given. It then became clear – and was in fact once admitted on behalf of the Bank – that in respect of some 27 % of the face value of the bills the Bank was trustee for BCI. The sensation was unforgettable and my readers can imagine my clients' indignation when the true facts so long withheld came to light. In the result the Court gave judgment for the Bank for 73 % and stayed the proceedings in respect of the 27 % for one year or the termination of the arbitration proceedings whichever was the shorter period. The Bank was ordered to pay the costs of the appeal.[84] We thus had a partial success, [124] but did not know whether we would not have been able to establish our case altogether if we had had full discovery and a trial with cross examination of the Bank's witnesses.

Always hoping that the arbitration proceedings might lead to an early award PWA did not pay the English judgment so that the Bank had to go to Germany to enforce it. In the German proceedings the defence was that under the English law of procedure a complete investigation of the facts was denied to PWA and that therefore the English judgment was contrary to German ordre public and also Art.6 of the European Convention on Human Rights, which guarantees to everyone "fair hearing" of his case. PWA lost in all courts. The case went through three courts, PWA lost in all of them. The decision of the Federal Supreme Court, although astonishingly it does not mention Art.6, is of fundamental significance. From the German point of view it is perhaps a little unexpected, because even in actions on bills of exchange German law provides for the possibility of a full hearing by a so-called "Nachverfahresn" and one would have thought that a German court might hold such a possibility to be essential to the recognition of a foreign judgment. However, the English practice under 0.14 which I had ex-

---

84 *Barclays Bank v. Aschaffenburger Zellstoffwerke A.G.*, 1 (1967) Ll.L.R. 387

# Arbitration and Litigation                                                                    **163**

plained as an expert to the court of first instance and to which the Federal Supreme Court refers in some detail did not strike the Federal Supreme Court as unacceptable.

Neverthelesswhen some further bills fell due the Bank dropped out of the picture and endorsed them back to BCI who after much delay brought proceedings against PWA in the German courts. In these proceedings PWA invoked as a defence the German statute of limitation which provided for a period of three years against the period of six years known to English law. PWA won in the first court[85] but the Munich Court of Appeal held the English period of six years to be applicable and gave judgment against PWA.[86] While a further appeal to the Federal Supreme Court was pending, BCI started proceedings on the same bills in England. We opposed under 0.11 on the ground that if the Munich judgment be affirmed proceedings in England were unnecessary and if the Munich judgment would be reversed the non-existence of BCI's claim would be res judicata in England. We won in the Court of Appeal[87] where Scarman L.J. (as he then was) delivered a particularly forceful judgment (about which he recently said to me that he still thought it to be right), but we lost in the House of Lords[88] over the dissent of Lord Diplock. Lord Reid delivered an opinion which I believe was the last one before he died and made his failing powers all too obvious. The other Law Lords [125] made the to my mind unforgivable mistake of looking beyond the tenor of the judgment which simply would read: "Action dismissed", and investigating the reasons for the dismissal; for the purpose of the recognition of a foreign judgment they are or should be irrelevant. Secondly the majority considered the German statute of limitation on which the dismissal of the action would be bar a procedural matter. They thus insisted on upholding the English classification and refused to follow the classification of German law on which the German judgment would be founded.

In the result, however, the English decision remained a dead letter, for shortly before the Federal Supreme Court was to hear the appeal against the judgment of the Munich Court of Appeal BCI suddenly and inexplicably agreed to a very satisfactory settlement: they agreed to refrain from enforcing their bills pending a dedision of the arbitration tribunal. This is really all we ever tried to achieve. Much effort and expense could have been saved to both parties if similar reasonableness had been displayed earlier by BCI and its lawyers.

The dispute between PWA and Black Clawson International was, of course, in every respect a unique case, – in fact, while I am writing it still is a case which

---

85 the author has not indicated where this footnote should go, and this seems the only appropriate place]

86 IPRspr. 1974 Nr. 26 (decision of 27 March 1974)

87 (1974) Q.B. 660

88 *Black Clawson International v. Papierwerke Waldhof Aschaffenburg*, [1975] A.C. 591

keeps me very busy. Nor have I described it in all its gruesome details. But it should be a warning to everyone and deter businessmen from arbitration. It is quite true that few parties are likely to meet such unscrupulous opponents as BCI or lawyers of the type which this English company found in New York. these are risks which no businessman should overlook. If he acts accordingly he will find that litigation, at any rate in English and probably German courts cannot be worse and will probably be much more effective.

I cannot conclude this chapter without recounting an indident which gave me quite particular pleasure. My firm was acting in an arbitration case of *Raytheon Ltd. v. Gregg and others.* The proceedings dragged on for years and eventually the partner in charge of the defendants' case decided that the point had been reached where in any civil proceedings the action would be dismissed from want of prosecution. Arbitrators acting in England did not at that time have power to make a similar order. So an application for an injunction was made to restrain the plaintiffs from proceeding with the arbitration. Both the judge and the Court of Appeal, the latter by a most elaborate judgment, granted the injunction. Our opponents had tried to butress their case by an extremely long and detailed affidavit sworn by the former Secretary General of the International Chamber of Commerce the short point of which was to suggest that arbitrations proceeding under the auspices of the ICC were not subject to the control by the ordinary courts and that the Rules of the ICC offered sufficient protection against undue dilatoriness. I swore an affidavit to refute these contentions the former of which was one of the ICC's favourite hobby-horses and was founded upon a legally unacceptable theory. The Court of Appeal did not find it necessary to deal [with] these points in any detail. But I had the satisfaction of reading Roskill L.J., [126] referring to me "whose experience in the field of international arbitration requires no endorsement from this court".

I cannot conclude this chapter without mentioning one type of case in which arbitration is the only available, though usually futile, remedy that is open to contracting parties. I am referrlng to contracts between States and aliens. In such cases a municipal tribunal will for obvious reasons not be agreed so that there is no alternative but to provide for arbitration, though it is rarely effective and at best leads to a poor settlement. This is what happened in the only case of this kind in which Iwas concerned, *British Petroleum Ltd. v. Republic of Libya.* The award had been published;[89] in fact many awards of the type have been published, though I fear improperly: the copyright, I should think, belongs to the parties, even if one of them does not participate in the proceedings, and the consent of the State party is unlikely ever to have been obtained, – I am certain that it was never obtained, so that publication is quite contrary to one of the principal purposes or

---

89 International Law Reports 53, 389.

Arbitration and Litigation **165**

at least implications of arbitration. However this may be, the *British Petroleum* case arose from the confiscation of the English company's assets valued at more than £300 million in Libya. We alleged the illegality and nullity of the confiscation. Libya failed to participate. So the President of the International Court of Justice appointed Judge Lagergren, a Swede, sole arbitrator. After several hearings in Copenhagen and an exchange of voluminous pleadings Judge Lagergren rendered a most unfortunate award. He held that the confiscation was a gross breach of international law, but denied the nullity in international law of acts which had been found to be illegal. The reason put forward by the learned Judge was that nullity would in effect amount to specific performance which, allegedly, is unknown to international law. The Judge committed the additional procedural mistake of refusing a declaration, the principal and, indeed, the only order for which, at the preliminary stage we had asked. He merely held the applicants entitled to damages to be assessed. That his principal propositions are bad, indeed very bad law appears from the award which in a similar case was rendered by Professor R.J. Dupuis a few years later.[90] I had in the meantime published a very full discussion of the problem in all its various aspects[91] and am inclined to hope that Judge Lagergren's views will be rejected. Professor Dupuy ordered specific performance which is, of course, as useless a remedy as the award of damages, – neither is capable of being enforced. The only effective order is a declaration of nullity, for it will enable and, indeed, compel municipal tribunals to treat property obtained by the State as a result of the illegality as belonging to the dispossessed owner. The *British Petroleum* case in which Lauterpacht Q.C. represented British Petroleum and I acted as Special Counsel was for many reasons most instructive. In particular it showed [127] once again how easily a silent tribunal can fall into substantive or procedural error, for Judge Lagergren did not open his mouth during the proceedings, while many misconceptions could easily have been cleared away if we had known what was troubling him.

This, however, is one of the great distinctions between Continental and Anglo-American procedure. I have no doubt where the advantage lies. A silent tribunal such as the Continental tribunal usually is constitutes a danger to litigants. Yet even where I was sole arbitrator in arbitrations to which the procedural law of a Continental country applied I have felt it necessary to be almost silent, for if a judge or arbitrator shows his hand he exposes bimself to applications for removal on the ground of partiality. This does not by any means always happen, but the difficulty of having a frank discussion in terms which cannot possibly give rise to

---

90  International Law Reports 53, 297.
91  British Yearbook of International Law 1976–1977, 1

such an application is considerable and the safest course, therefore, is to avoid it, however unfortunate and unhelpful such an attitude is likely to be. [128]

# Chapter 17 – Passing-off

Adrema Ltd. was the English subsidiary of a German company of the same name. The latter was to a large extent owned by the family of the well-known banker Jakob Goldschmidt. It was the sharpest competitor of the American-controlled company Addressograph. The English subsidiary was under the management of Mr. Kay Wolff, a very able and at the same time unusually demanding man who developed the company to such an extent as to make it one of the leading English companies in the field. Wolff and the company became clients in the late 1930s. They needed a lot of help and even at home Mr. Wolff was so often on the telephone that his name became a standing joke among my children, – he woud invariably ring at the most inconvenient moment. Already in 1945 I had a case for the company which Valentine Holmes leading Mr. R.T. Paget (later the Socialist Peer Lord Paget) won and the point of which may even today be of some interest, though the case seems to have been overlooked by modern scholars. The Divisional Court held that a change in the nature of the work which an employee is required to do at an unchanged remuneration but of an inferior type is not a termination of the employment (within the meaning of the Essential Work (General Provisions) No.2 Order 1942.[92] Today I fear any such direction given by an employer would provoke a strike.

But the great Adrema litigation began a little later and was not terminated during Mr. Wolff's lifetime. It began with an action brought by the German company against the Custodian of German Property in whom the English shares had become vested. The Custodian intended to sell the shares to Mr. Wolff and certain Associates of his. This caused the German company to apply for an injunction. We were not parties to, though vitally interested in this litigation the outcome of which was that a sale could not for some time take place.[93] But at a later date Wolff and his friends did acquire the shares and this caused the German company to set up a rival organisation in this country and led to the great action

---

92  *Adrema Ltd. v. Jenkinson,* [1945] 2 All E.R. 29
93  *Adrema Werke G.m.b.H. v. Custodian of Enemy Property*

of *Adrema Ltd. v. Adreme Werke G.m.b.H. and others*[94] which in June 1958 came before Mr. Justice Danckwerts for some ten days. Tom Strangman led J.G. Graham (as he then was) and Mark Littman for us and Sir Andrew Clark Q.C. and Mr. R.G. Lloyd were for the defendants. We had a complete victory, mainly because the defendants were shown to be dishonest. For me the successful outcome of the litigation was that the company which in the meantime had been acquired by American interests promptly left me and was never heard of again.

Another case which a relatively small company brought against a giant was *Rockwell Machine Tool Co. Ltd. v. E.P. Barrus (Concessionaires) Ltd*[95] where the real defendant was the enormous American company Rockwell Manufacturing [129] Company. Through Barrus they had imported goods into this country which we said constituted a passing-off of our trade name in the field of machine tools. The case in which Peter Oliver Q.C. (as he then was) appeared for the plaintiffs and Sir Lionel Heald Q.C. for the defendants was fought for many days until eventually the defendants submitted to judgment. In the course of the hearing it appeared that the defendants' discovery of documents was badly deficient, as we had suspected and alleged all along and this caused Mr. Justice Megarry to make an important pronouncement on the duty of parties to preserve documents required for the purposes of litigation.

A case of much greater general interest was *Peter Pan Manufacturing Corporation v. Corsets Silhouette Ltd.* which for three weeks was heard by Pennycuick J. in October 1962, Tom Strangman leading Mr. Brian Dillon (as he then was) and G.W. Tookey Q.C. and J.N.K. Whitford (as he then was) for the defendant. The case concerned confidential information in the manufacture of brassières which the defendants had obtained from the plaintiffs and is an early example of a doctrine which in later cases was more fully developed: confidence created a fiduciary relationship and anyone which exploits information obtained in confidence is accountable as a constructive trustee to the owner of the information. But the very important point which arose in the case was an entirely different one and was to play a considerable role much later. When we had won in principle, we decided on Tom Strangman's wise advice that we would claim, not damages, but an account of profits. I learned on that occasion that if you claim damages in such cases you have to prove your loss which would probably be calculated on a royalty basis, – what would the plaintiff be entitled to if he had granted a licence and negotiated a royalty? But if you claim an account of profits you get much more, namely the difference between the cost of manufacturing the article incorporating the offending material and the sal price obtained for it. This the defendants vigourously opposed, but the judge granted the order in the terms

---

94 (1958) R.P.C. 323
95 [1968] 2 All E.R. 98

Passing-off                                                                    **169**

suggested by us and there was no appeal. A few years later we lost the important case of *General Tire Corporation v. Firestone Tire & Rubber Co.*[96] a patent case of very great importance which related to tire threads made with synthetic rubber and to which I shall have to revert in a different context.[97] We were amazed and overjoyed, when after the judgment the plaintiffs, advised by Sir Lionel Heald Q.C. and Mr. Stephen Gratwick opted for damages rather than an account of profits. On the latter basis they would have been entitled to an enormous sum. On the former both the judge and the Court of Appeal awarded them an enormous sum, but the House of Lords re-established the traditional law of damages, i.e. the principle of proven loss and awarded the plaintiffs about £150,000, less than a seventh of what they had recovered under the orders of the lower courts.[98] Where they, unconsciously, trying to undo the tactical mistake which the plaintiffs and their advisors had been making? [130]

The saddest experience I had in this field of litigation was the case of *Parker Knoll Ltd. v. Knoll International Ltd.*,[99] which I lost in the House of Lords by the votes of Lord Morris, Hodson and Guest against the powerful minority of Lords Denning and Devlin. Wilhelm Knoll was a furniture manufacturer in Stuttgart. In 1930 he granted a licence for a patent in respect of a particular chair to Frederick Parker & Sons Ltd., furniture manufacturers in England, who in 1942 adapted the name of Parker-Knoll. A nephew of Wilhelm, Hans Knoll, went to the United States after the war and together with his wife set up a business for modern furniture and textile under the style of Knoll International Ltd. when this company intended to open business in England, Parker-Knoll started proceedings which they won in all courts. The decision of the House of Lords is now the leading case on passing-off in a case in which the defendant honestly uses his genuine own name. I have re-read the decision of both the majority and minority and realise, of course, that even after so many years I cannot (and do not) have an objective view, but I must confess that the result reached in that case still strikes me as very unsatisfactory and inviting reform. The decision means that a man is allowed to use his name for business purposes, but he must not use it as a trade name if this would be liable to lead to confusion with the established name of another trader's goods: Hans Knoll could carry on business under the name of Knoll International, but he cannot describe his goods as Knoll International chairs if people may be led to infer from this user an association with Parker-Knoll Ltd's goods. The distinction in fact proved illusory, as subsequent proceedings clearly established.[100] The effect was that Knoll International were ex-

---

96 Reports of Patent Cases
97 Below p.
98 *General Tire & Rubber Co. v. Firestone Tyre & Rubber Co.* [1975] 2 All E.R. 173
99 R.P.C. 1962, 265
100

cluded from the English market. This seems to me an unacceptable result. Fraud, that is to say the intention to deceive, to appropriate another's goodwill is, of course, an entirely different matter and nothing must be done that could facilitate it. One can even discuss whether the honest use of a man's own genuine name should not be forbidden, where there is identity with the trade name of another: if Parker-Knoll had proved the use of, and confusion with, the name Knoll simpliciter Hans Knoll might have been required to use a distinguishing word. But the breadth of the decision in this case of the judge, of two out of three judges in the Court of Appeal and of three out of five judges in the House of Lords is such as to require further consideration. [131]

## Chapter 18 – Commercial Cases

Commercial cases are the lifeblood of every litigation lawyer, but few are worthy of remembering. Most of them are glorified debt collecting, – the inevitable by-product of any lawyer's practice. It is a type of work which is far from profitable and which one would normally refuse to do, but one has to do it for established clients and for foreign lawyers. In my life there was, however one special type of ordinary commercial cases which had a peculiar character and was a continuous source of interest. Since the early 1950's I have been acting for Sotheby's and, although in more recent years we no longer did their ordinary debt collecting work, we did the rest of their litigation. Most of it we succeeded in keeping out of court by reaching a compromise, but this does not mean that the legal and factual problems were not frequently most intriguing, for in the course of their work Sotheby's in their various departments come across the most unusual situations. Items offered for sale or actually sold are said to be stolen, forged or wrongly attributed or described. Others are said to be exported without licence or subject to charges. Such allegations frequently involve the law of foreign countries and many difficult questions of private international law. In fact there has for years been practically no day in my professional life, when a member of my firm did not come to me with some such problem arising in the course of Sotheby's business. The cases may have been small, but the problems were frequently great.

The first commercial case which came into court and about which I wish to say something concerns an entirely different client. I mention the case here only because I learned such a lot from it and perhaps others will do so too. This was the case of the late Karl Halle, a man who at the time, about 1947 or 1948, had a small factory which he sold partly for cash, partly against bills of exchange which fell due on 1st April. A few days before he received a letter from some solicitors stating that the bills would not be met, because the purchasers had been induced by fraud to acquire the factory. So Karl Halle came to me. He was in a state of the utmost indignation about having been accused of fraud and instructed me to start proceedings immediately. And he added the words which one expects an honest man to use "You are going to fight this case, irrespective of expense and without looking right or left. There will never be any question of compromise. I am not compromising where I am accused of fraud. I want judgment." So I went ahead. We sued on the bills. The defendants, having put forward a defence of fraud, obtained leave to defend. We obtained an order for a speedy trial and pressed with all possible energy for an early date. We succeeded in obtaining a date for about the 20th July. I instructed Gilbert Beyfus Q.C. leading Mark Littman. On the day of the trial which was to come before Birkett J. the other side applied for an adjournment on the ground that they were not ready; at the same time they approached Beyfus for a settlement [132] which was rejected out of hand. There was no doubt in our minds that the Judge would refuse an adjournment. But Beyfus gave very good advice: he agreed to the adjournment on condition that the whole of the balance of the purchase price plus interest and an estimated amount of costs be brought into court. This had to be accepted by our opponents and was complied with. The hearing was adjourned to some date in the following October. The case came before Streatfield J. and continued for about nine days. My client was under cross-examination by Mr. Berryman Q.C. who on the ninth day came back at 2 o'clock and without any warning to us said to the Judge that he had given certain advice to his clients as a result of which they were submitting to judgment. Whereupon the Judge let his pencil drop and with tears running down his face said: "At last, – for most of the nine days I have been waiting for this to happen." It was the only time in my life that I saw a judge so moved as to cry. But he was so impressed by my client's transparent honesty and by the defendants' wickedness that I can well understand his reaction. My client, as result of Mr. Beyfus' excellent advice, was not only rehabilitated, but also received every penny that was due to him.

Mr. Halle's case was for what at the time was and perhaps even today is or should be a substantial sum, about £50,000 (though some of my partners are now hardly prepared to look at anything involving less than a million), but another case of that period, the case of Baroness *Rausch von Traubenberg against Davies Turner & Co.*,[101] the forwarding agents, was for a mere £493. Reading the report today I marvel at the fact that we fought it through two courts and did so with prominent leaders (John Foster in the first, H. Glyn-Jones, as he was then, in the second court, with Mark Littman as a junior). Baroness von Traubenberg was, in Hitler's sense, of non-aryan origin. She was married to an "Aryan", a professor at the University at Kiel, I believe. One day the Gestapo called to send her to a concentration camp. Her husband prevented it, but as a result of the excitement he suffered a heart attack and eventually died. Immediately after his death she was sent to Theresienstadt concentration camp, where she was liberated by the Russians and sent to this country where her son-in-law was a professor for

---

101 (1951) 2 Ll.L.R. 179, 462.

mathematics at Liverpool University. Before she was taken away she deposited a case with silver heirlooms with a friend who at her request sent it to England in 1948. The forwarding agents in London, Davies, Turner & Co., duly received and then dispatched it by rail from Euston to Liverpool. In the course of this journey it disappeared, it was no doubt stolen. The question before the court was whether it was the duty of the forwarding agents to insure it or to obtain instructions as to insurance or to send it at company's risk at a certain declared value. The defendants, without further enquiry, sent it at owner's risk, although they knew that the case contained old silver. McNair J. held that they were not negligent, the Court of Appeal (Somervel, Jenkins and [133] Hodson L.JJ.) disagreed and held the defendants liable for £493: before deciding on the type of contract to be made with the railways the forwarding ought to have obtained the plaintiff's instructions. It was probably a clear case, for this is how it strikes me today, when I look at it again. Yet it seems to me that I had a lot of courage both when I started the case and, in particular, when I took it to appeal, – in great style, and, I seem to remember, without legal aid.

From the point of view of financial interest, the decision of the Privy Council in *Linz v. Electric Wire Company of Palestine Ltd.*[102] is even more astonishing. The plaintiff claimed £775, – she lost in two courts in Palestine and then took the case to the Privy Council where Sir Valentine Holmes and Mr. Denys Buckley (later Buckley L.J.) argued the case before a Board presided over and dominated by Lord Simonds. The plaintiff's case was that, having paid the money for certain preference shares the issue of which was ultra vires the company and therefore null and void, she was entitled to a refund of the money. If one now reads the decision rejecting the appeal it appears to be entirely convincing: having been registered as a member, the plaintiff then sold her shares and received the full price for them. How could she now claim that the consideration had wholly failed and she was entitled to a refund from the company of which she no longer was a member? Yet on reflection one is bound to ask oneself whether the case is really so simple and whether Sir Valentine Holmes' view was not the better one. The sale of a non-existing chose in action cannot easily be said to deprive the seller of the purely personal claim which he has on account of the nullity of the shares and, therefore, the failure of the consideration. She may or may not be liable to her buyer. Why should this be material as between the seller and the company? If I buy a car which is stolen and title of which I do not acquire have I lost rights against the seller by reason of the fact that I re-sold the car for value? Surely the answer must be in the negative and it does not matter whether the car is in the hands of my buyer or myself or the true owner. Lord Simonds seems to think that total failure of consideration presupposes that the plaintiff is still in possession of

---

102 [1948] A.C. 371

**174**                                                                Commercial Cases

the car or the shares. Is this really correct? Perhaps the case would have been decided differently if the Board had included a single common lawyer.

It was shortly after this case had been decided that I became involved in a whole series of company law cases. At the time I acted for a man who made it his business to take an interest in special and unusual situations and if necessary to make himself the guardian of shareholders' rights. I remember some litigation about the reconstruction of the Peruvian Corporation as well of a certain South American public utility company, but there was also a case against Henry J. Schroeder as trustees of the Potash Syndicate Loan, – litigation which [134] was far from popular in the City, for it involved an allegation of breach of trust committed by the failure to enforce the security for the Potash Syndicate's indebtedness. One of this group of cases, however, *Re Old Silkstone Collieries Ltd.*[103] was reported and became a case of some importance. The company petitioned the court for the confirmation of a reduction of capital. A group of shareholders, led by my client, opposed on the ground that the preference shareholders had certain "special rights" within the meaning of the Articles of Association and that in general it would be unfair to sanction the proposed reduction of capital. We lost before Vaisey J., but in the Court of Appeal the opposing shareholders, represented by Tom Strangman Q.C. and Peter Oliver (later Oliver L.J.) succeeded. The judgments dealing with the first point are of a somewhat technical character and of little interest in the present context. But the second point is more interesting, because the case is one of the extremely few in which the court actually exercised its power to refuse confirmation of a reduction of capital on the ground that it was unfair and inequitable, – usually the court rubber-stamps resolutions which have been passed. In this case a special feature was provided by a circular which mentioned that certain important City Organisations had recommended the scheme. In fact it turned out that these organisations had hardly any interest in the shares and since such references are frequent in circulars it is important to remember Lord Eversheds' warning that such a statement "does have so important an effect on the mind of the ordinary individual shareholder that the use of such argument in a circular is undesirable, prima facie, without sufficient explanation to give it its true significance." It is by reason of the discussion of these aspects of company law that the case has become a great one.

Many years later I acted for Henry Ansbacher & Co. in a bid to take over Oriental Telephone and Electric Co. Ltd. This led to a dispute with the Commissioners of Inland Revenue over the liability of a guarantee to stamp duty in the princely sum of £1875. Believe it or not, my clients, acting more in general than in their own interest, took the matter to appeal and won before Danckwerts

---

103 [1954] Ch. 169

Commercial Cases **175**

J., but the Revenue appealed to the Court of Appeal and the House of Lords.[104] Fortunately my clients, represented by R.E. Megarry Q.C. (later Vice-Chancellor Sir Robert Megarry) and Brian Dillon (later Dillon J.) were successful. I believe it was the first case in which Lord Dilhorne as Lord Chancellor presided. My clients could have afforded to lose, but it is horrifying to think of the costs which a private individual would have had to pay had he lost on a point of such little financial importance.

From this point of view I confess to be staggered by re-reading the [135] decision of the Court of Appeal in *Jones v. Herxheimer*.[105] This was a case in which in the County Court the landlord was awarded the sum of £36 for dilapidations against the tenant for whom I acted and who appealed to the Court of Appeal in order to be relieved of so large a liability. He seemed to have a good case. The £36 was the cost of the repairs, but s.18(1) of the Landlord and Tenant Act 1927 provides that such damages shall not exceed the amount by which the value of the reversion is diminished. The County Court Judge equiparated the £36 to the damage to the reversion. This process had been disapproved by earlier decisions which had made it clear that the two types of losses were quite different. But now the Court of Appeal held that the cost of the repair represented the diminution in the value of the reversion. Since then this has been the law and it may well be that s.18 (l) of the 1927 Act is now to a large extent a dead letter. However, why and how the tenant came to take this case to the Court of Appeal appears inexplicable. There must have been some reason, but I have forgotten it. The case is probably the smallest I was ever concerned with.

I am hardly less astonished when I look at a quarrel between two commodity traders in the City about £553, *Charles H. Windschugl Ltd. v. Alexander Pickering & Co. Ltd.*,[106] a case the importance of which is, I believe, not sufficiently appreciated. The plaintiffs had bought goods "subject to licence". Devlin J. held that these words were different from "subject to contract", and imported a condition into a contract which was binding, that in the circumstances the sellers had to use their best endeavours to obtain a licence and that it was for the sellers to prove that any application was "foredoomed to failure", a burden which could not be discharged so long as there was a possibility that a licence might be granted.

In this case I had my usual team, John Foster leading Mark Littman, whose opponent was Alan Mocatta, then a junior. I do not know why in the much more substantial and important case of *Trans Trust S.P.R.L. v. Danubian Trading Co. Ltd.*,[107] I changed my team and instructed Alan Mocatta, by then a silk, and T.G.

---

104  [1963] A.C. 191
105  [1950] 1 All E.R. 323
106  84 (1950) Lloyds L.R. 89
107  (1952) 2 Q.B. 297

**176**                                                                                    Commercial Cases

Roche as a junior. In the action the buyers, my clients, claimed damages for loss of profits on the ground that the defendant sellers had failed to open a letter of credit. The action succeeded both before McNair J and in the Court of Appeal, where Denning L.J., concurring with Somervell L.J. made some important statements which are worth being revived. He dealt with the phrase "subject to letter of credit" and held that in certain cases it could be a condition precedent similar to "subject to contract", but in this case it was "a condition which is an essential term of the contract." Secondly, the price of the goods, i.e. steel, had steadily risen and therefore, so Denning L.J. said, the damages would have been nominal if the claim had been for failure to accept [136] delivery or for repudiation of the contract. But it was "a claim for damages for not providing a letter of credit". Such an obligation is different from the obligation to pay a price. "A banker's confirmed credit is a different thing from payment". Another point of monetary law established by the case is that there may be a claim for damages for failure to pay and the creditor's remedy is not limited to interest. So damages were awarded, but the Court of Appeal refused to sanction the very sensible practice of granting a declaration for an indemnity against damages due to the sellers' suppliers for failure to accept. This requires a separate action.

*Kores Manufacturing Co. Ltd. v. Kolok Manufacturing Co. Ltd.*,[108] was a case of importance and novelty. The two companies, strong competitors and neighbours had entered into an agreement whereby either would employ anyone who during the preceding five years had been an employee of the other. We believed that in this case of agreements between two companies the parties were the only judges of what was a reasonable restraint of trade, subject of course to the restraint also being reasonable in the interest of the public. But notwithstanding a most persuasive argument by Charles Russell Q.C. (later Lord Russell of Killown) and Peter Oliver (later Oliver L.J.) the Court of Appeal held that "the mere fact that parties dealing on equal terms have entered into an agreement subjecting themselves to restraints of trade does not preclude the court from holding the agreement dead when the restraints are clearly unreasonable in the interests of the parties." This was, I believe, a new departure by Jenkins, Romer and Ormerod L.JJ. and it is surprising that it seems to have been accepted by legal writers without criticism, for it involved a limitation upon freedom of contract between persons of equal bargaining power, which was not only new, but also far from compelling. The court may have been influenced by the fact that, as it was inclined to think, but did not hold, that the agreement also had the effect of imposing a restraint upon the relationship of employer and employee, i.e. it restricted a man's opportunity of finding work. This is undeniable, but here again there had never before been a case extending the protection of potential em-

---

108  [1959] Ch. 108

Commercial Cases **177**

ployees by disallowing an agreement of this type between employers. The force of the court's reasoning cannot be denied, but its novelty was and remains striking.

This case indicates very clearly how "policy", i.e. "legal policy" influences the outcome of a case, – in another period legal policy might well have demanded a different result. There can be no doubt that at present we live in a time in which the merits of a case and judicial policy determine the result. The remaining cases to which I wish to draw attention will confirm this view.

Perhaps I may first mention the case of *Rockwell Machine Tool Co. Ltd. v. Handley Page Ltd.,*[109] in which the court had to interpret the words "the person by whom it (i.e. the import deposit) was paid." That person was entitled to the [137] refund of the import deposit. If it was paid by Handley Page Ltd. that company's Receiver, in other words, its debenture holders, would receive the payment. If my clients, Rockwell received it they would obtain a refund of what they doubtless had disbursed. The point was that Handley Page Ltd. argued the money had been paid on its behalf, because it was in the last resort responsible for it, while Rockwell argued that it had made the payment out of its own resources. Both Mocatta J. and the Court of Appeal, accepting a brilliant argument by Michael Kerr Q.C. (later Kerr L.J.), held in Rockwell's favour. The case is of some interest on the question of drawing the line between acting on one's own account and acting as agent of another, but its real significance lies in the astuteness of the judges in avoiding a result which would have deprived the meritorious party of the fruits of its fairly conducted business.

In the early 1970s I was involved in numerous pieces of partly very heavy litigation arising out of the activities of the former manager of the London branch of the Central Bank of India, one Patel who, together with certain others, was subsequently convicted at the Old Bailey for, I believe, fraud or forgery. I acted for a number of German banks, in particular Bank für Gemeinwirtschaft in proceedings against the Central Bank of India. These were ultimately settled and their only remarkable aspect is that Counsel would have been prepared, and indeed was most anxious, to settle for £250,000, but very much against his advice and opposition we held out and obtained three times that sum in settlement of a claim for about a million pounds. Only one of the cases connected with this litigation reached the Law Reports. This is the decision of the Court of Appeal in *Bank für Gemeinwirtschaft v. City of London Garages Ltd.*[110] It is of great importance to the law relating to bills of exchange and has done much to preserve the protection of holders in due course, for it establishes two propositions designed to secure the international status of bills of exchange. The first is of a substantive kind and is to the effect that where earlier parties to a bill have a

---

109 [1971] Lloyds L.R. 298
110 [1971] 1 All E.R. 541

**178**                                                                                    Commercial Cases

fraudulent intent or pursue an illegal purpose this does not affect, or prejudice, the title and rights of a subsequent holder in due course who takes the bill in good faith and for value. The second is procedural: if in an action on a bill of exchange the defendant alleges fraud or illegality this does not entitle him to leave to defend in a case in which the plaintiff can show by clear and unchallenged evidence that he or his predecessor in title took the bill in good faith and for value. We had relied on documentary evidence of great detail and cogency to show that the plaintiffs had discounted the bills in the normal course of business. This evidence was not challenged by the defendants and the court described it as almost un-challengeable. So we had a great success. Fortunately a case which arose out of the same set of facts and a little later came before a different Court of Appeal presided over by Lord Salmon and in which leave to defend was given was not reported and is therefore unlikely to influence the development of the law. I have forgotten the details, but I remember that the defendant had made an attack on the good faith of the plaintiff bank. It was entirely unsubstantiated and lacking in particulars, but the court thought it sufficient to disentitle the bank to summary judgment. Although the facts were different, the second decision undoubtedly made an inroad upon the strength and significance of the first.

Another action on a bill of exchange had many repurcussions and shows up some serious defects in the judicial process. My clients *Nova (Jersey) Knit Ltd.* had in the year 1970 formed a German limited partnership together with another German textile industry, *Kammgarnspinnerei GmbH*. The partnership agree-ment included an arbitration clause covering all disputes arising from the partnership relationship. In fact very bitterly fought arbitration proceedings were between 1974 and 1978 pending in Germany which on numerous occasions compelled me to go to Munich to argue the case and which eventually were settled on terms that amounted to an almost complete success for my clients. In 1972 they had sold twelve textile machines to Kammgarnspinnerei GmbH. The price was payable by twenty bills of exchange of which six were paid. The others were dishonoured. In 1974 we started proceedings in respect of four bills which had by that time matured. We took the view that the bills were governed by English law and started proceedings in England. The German defendants entered an un-conditional appearance, but applied for a stay on the ground that the arbitration clause in the partnership agreement extended to the bills of exchange. Both parties filed extensive evidence on German law. The defendants' case was that they had a claim for damages which permitted a set-off against the bills. The claims arose from the fact that allegedly some of the twelve machines were not new and that my clients had participated in and profited from the alleged mis-management of the German limited partnership which in the meantime had been forced to cease to trade. Both the Master and the Judge rejected the defendents' appiication, but much to my amazement it succeeded in the Court of Appeal

Commercial Cases                                                              **179**

(Lord Denning M.R., Stephenson and Bridge L.JJ.). The judgment is fortunately
not reported. My recollection is that it took a very broad view to the effect the
whole complex of disputes fell within the jurisdiction of the arbitration tribunal.
It is very likely that, as so often, the Court of Appeal was influenced by some
insinuations to the effect that the plaintiffs had been guilty of fraud, – a completely unsupported and unparticularised allegation of which nothing further
was heard, but which did great harm in the Court of Appeal. The worst was that
the Court of Appeal refused leave to appeal. So we petitioned for leave and were
lucky to obtain it. When in December 1976 we came before the House[111] there was
a welcome tendency to consider the case from a strictly legal point of view. We
took two principal points, viz. that the arbitration clause in the partnership
agreement did not extend to the claims [139] under the bills of exchange and that
as to these claims there was no "dispute" within the meaning of s.1 (1) of the
Arbitration Act 1975. The first point depended on German law and the House of
Lords preferred our evidence which, with much help given by me, had been
provided by my old friend Dr. Jaques, another refugee lawyer who, unfortunately,
died soon after the termination of this case. But we also won on the second point
and this is a matter of some importance to English law: unliquidated cross-claims
intended as a set-off against bills of exchange do not create a dispute in respect of
claims under the bills. If it were otherwise the character of bills as deferred cash
would be gravely prejudiced. My dear old friend Sir John Foster Q.C.who argued
this case on all occasions was splendidly vindicated and we had created a precedent which has done much for the continued predominance of an English bill of
exchange.

The decision of the House of Lords, however, was by no means the end of the
affair. The defendants no longer took part in the further proceedings. So we
obtained judgment by default not only in respect of the bills of exchange, but also
for damages for libel which we had included in one set of proceedings. The libel
was contained in a letter which the defendants' German lawyer had written to
Barclays Bank to justify non-payment of the bills. Barclays Bank, unfortunately
never allowed us to see the letter, but we knew its essential terms and I had the
claim included in the writ against the strong views of Counsel who thought such
joinder unwise and improper. But eventually we recovered no less than £6,000
damages for libel in the course of assessment proceedings before Master Jacob.

We then had to enforce the English default judgment in Germany where we
were met with many objections, the principal one being to the effect that by
entering an unconditional appearance and thereafter applying for a stay the
defendants had taken steps which precluded a voluntary submission to English
jurisdiction. The German courts were supplied with numerous opinions, from Sir

---

111  [1977] 1 W.L.R. 713

Otto Kahn-Freund, from Mr. David Donaldson, from Professor Böckstiegel, from me on the one side and from Dr. Graupner, Mr. Mance, Mr. Anthony Walton Q.C. on the other side. I went twice to Stuttgart and took part in the argument before the Court of Appeal. Much to my relief in December 1978 we won the case[112] and a further appeal to the Federal Supreme Court was filed, but withdrawn, so that by the spring of 1979 we had achieved total victory. I felt convinced that we had been right all along the line, but also very lucky, because the defendants had made many and serious mistakes which led to their defeat. I had had some anxious moments, both in the Court of Appeal in England and in Stuttgart and in the course of the hearing for leave to appeal to the House of Lords and I frequently wondered whether at my advanced age I would be able to stand the pace of this litigation upon the outcome of which much depended for my clients. In the end my relief was very great and today I look back with some pride upon this litigation which I believe was fought with a certain amount of forethought [140] and technical skill. I confess that the libel damages gave me particular pleasure. Curiously enough, the decision which deals with a remote point of German law and also clarifies some important points of the English law of arbitration and bills of exchange failed to attract the attention of academic lawyers in either country. In view of my connection with the case I felt, in accordance with my usual practice, precluded from writing about it.

The last case which belongs to the present chapter is the great case *Cassell & Co. Ltd. v. Broome*,[113] the case about the PQ 17. Towards the end of 1970 a New York lawyer introduced to me an American publishing House which had recently bought all the shares in the well-known London publishers Cassell & Co. Ltd. They had a few months earlier been involved in a jury trial about a book "The Destruction of Convoy PQ 17"; at the end of which the jury found that the book had libelled Captain Jack Broome and awarded him compensatory damages of £15,000 and exemplary (or punitive) damages of £25,000. I was asked to act in the appeal.

The plaintiff's allegation, accepted by judge and jury, was that three passages in the book accused the plaintiff of cowardice in escaping from German ships and allowing the convoy PQ 17 to be destroyed by enemy action. I never understood how the three passages in question could be so read as to be capable of bearing the meaning alleged by the plaintiff. Many knowledgeable people whom I asked to read them agreed with me. But Roger Parker Q.C. (now Parker J) whom, together with Robert Alexander I instructed on the appeal, strongly disagreed and in accordance with his advice we decided only to attack the award of £25,000 punitive damages on the ground that, firstly, the judge's summing on the point was

---

112 Reported A W D 1980
113 [1972] A.C. 1027

not in harmony with the directions given by the House of Lords in *Rookes v. Barnard*[114] and, secondly, the amount was excessive. The case which had taken 17 days in the first court took 9 days in the Court of Appeal, for there the plaintiff's argument was that the principles of *Rookes v. Barnard* could and should for a variety of reasons, be disregarded. The Court of Appeal so decided and dismissed the appeal. We decided to appeal to the House of Lords. On account of the importance of the case we came before a Committee of seven law lords. The case was argued for 16 days. Roger Parker's advocacy was most impressive, for he had to overcome marked hostility before he achieved a quiet and judicious hearing on the important questions of law that arose. In the result we lost by four (Lord Hailsham L.J., Lord Reid, Lord Morris and Lord Kilbrandon) against three votes (Lord Dilhorn, Lord Wilberforce and Lord Diplock). All seven held that the principles relating to the award of punitive damages had been correctly and exhaustively laid down by *Rookes v. Barnard*, [141] but only three held that the summing-up offended against that case and that in any event the damages were excessive. It was the narrowest possible defeat and the disappointment was great, nevertheless in view of the difficulties we had to face during the first two days of the argument it was a great achievement and we all felt that the defeat was an honourable one. Even my American clients and their New York lawyer agreed, although three years later they were to throw me over board, when they had to settle a hopeless case on unfavourable terms.

The decision of the House of Lords led to two incidents which are worth recording.

The print of the opinions was handed to us at 9.45 a.m. in the morning, 45 minutes before the law lords assembled in the Chamber to record their votes. That print extended to some 70 pages. We had just sufficient time to ascertain the result, but an assessment of the judgment and its consequences was impossible. We undoubtedly ought to have applied to defer a decision on the question of costs, but, frankly, we did not think of it, because we read Lord Hailsham's words "that costs should follow the event." Yet, when I studied the opinions in peace, I came to the conclusion that on the issue which took most of the time, viz. the continued validity of *Rookes v. Barnard*, we had won and since we had not at any time done anything even to raise that issue it seemed very unfair that we should be responsible for all the costs. I went to see Roger Parker and Robert Alexander. They did not think anything could be done. I communicated with the Judicial Office of the House of Lords and learned that there existed some precedent for petitioning the House of Lords before its Order was final. I arranged for the Order being held up. I literally compelled my Counsel to settle a petition on the ground that we had nothing to lose except a small sum in costs. Eventually, in May our

---

114 [1964] A.C. 1129

petition came before the same seven law lords.[115] Roger Parker had no hope of success at all, but he presented a strong and persuasive argument. I was immensely pleased and relieved, when we had a great success: Broome was awarded only one half of his costs in the Court of Appeal and the House of Lords. So he lost the greater part of his £25,000 which I always thought were undeserved, – more undeserved than the rest which, as I have said, I believed to be unjustly awarded on the ground that there had never been any defamation.

The second incident is not without interest. All the law lords expressed the view that the damages awarded by the jury were excessive, though four of them felt it impossible to interfere with the jury's verdict. I advised my clients to apply to the European Commission for Human Rights on the ground that the award of punitive damages of £25,000 constituted an excessive punishment within the meaning of Art. [...] of the European Human Hights Convention. At first [142] my clients gave me their enthusiastic support. But a well-known figure of the English establishment was very close to them and very stupidly persuaded them that it was just not done to apply to Strasbourg against a decision of the House of Lords. Accordingly, the idea was abandoned, – in my view foolishly. This, then, was the end of one of the greatest cases it was ever my privilege to fight, a case of far-reaching importance to the law, but also a case which was characterised at every stage by an enormous amount of prejudice in favour of a gallant Captain of the Royal Navy who, singlehanded, undertook to fight a well-known and, presumably, wealthy firm of publishers. The destruction of the convoy PQ 17 with the immense loss of lives and material was one of the great naval disasters of the Second World War. Captain Broome was a participant in and a victim of great tragedy for which the First Sea Lord was responsible. I am convinced that no member of a jury nor few of the eleven judges who were concerned in the case were able to approach the case against Cassell & Co. with that complete detachment and coolness which in circumstances less burdened with emotion would prevail. [143]

---

115 [1972] A.C. 1136

# Chapter 19 – Conflicts about Conflicts of Law

A very great part of my academic work was concerned with the Conflict of Laws. The first article of any importance which I published in England in 1937 in the British Year Book of International Law dealt with a serious problem of the private international law of contracts. My publications in the field which have appeared since then would fill a volume. The astonishing thing is that at the same time an equally important part of my professional work related to the same subject. I say "astonishing", because I have always wondered what was cause and what was effect: did I get the work on account of my writings or did I write on account of my work? With one single exception, namely the *Zeiss* case (which is a very special matter and about which I shall have something to say presently) I have never written about any of my cases while they were pending and even after their termination I have refrained from any comment other than purely incidental remarks or references. Nor have I written about pending problems so as to attract work from those who were involved in them. I thus feel compelled to conclude that there was no connection at all between my academic and my professional work, – but who knows? This is only one of the many aspects of the mysterious and unanswerable question: how does one get practice?

In no case were the circumstances of my involvement more puzzling than in the case of *Callwood v. Callwood* which in the year 1960 came before the Judicial Committee of the Privy Council consisting of Lords Tucker, Jenkins and Morris of Borth-y-Gest.[116] It was an appeal from the Federal Supreme Court of the West Indies. Why it came to me I have never been able to find out, mainly because I never met my client. All that happened was that one fine day the telephone rang and the operator said to me: "There is a call from the Virgin Islands for you." It was a Mr. Callwood who spoke from St. Thomas and asked me whether I was prepared to represent him in an appeal to the Privy Council. It was with delight that I answered in the affirmative and in due course I received the papers, but never any explanation of his introduction to me. The case was picturesque. It

---

116 [1960] A.C. 659

concerned the ownership of Great Thatch Island in the British West Indies. Richard Edward Clifford Callwood and his wife Elsie Callwood, the plaintiff in the action, were domiciled in St. Thomas, then a Danish colony which in 1917 was sold by Denmark to the United States of America. In St. Thomas the Danish system of community of property prevailed and, put very shortly, the question was whether this community comprised Great Thatch Island, property situate in British territory and subject to British law. The plaintiff so contended, the defendant, her son and my client, denied it. The only evidence on Danish law was a reported case in the United States Court of Appeal for the Third Circuit between the same parties, where the Danish law on community of property was expounded in a different context and with reference to an entirely [144] different question. The argument before the Privy Council was that there was no evidence on the question whether by Danish law the community of property extended to immovables situate in foreign territory and that even if there had been such evidence and it had been in the affirmative English law would not have recognised it, but would have refused to allow Danish law to regulate title to English immovables. Here were problems after my own heart as well as the heart of my Counsel, John Foster Q.C., Mark Littman and C.A. (Tim) Brodie. They involved a close consideration of a famous case in private international law, *Nicols v. Curlier*,[117] but unfortunately the Board decided the case on the narrowest possible ground: it decided that there was no evidence before the court on the relevant question of Danish law. But, in addition, their Lordships did "strongly deprecate" the method of providing evidence on foreign law by reference to an American case concerned with a different type of question, – we had saved at least something of a little general interest. So Mr. Callwood jr. won, – I had a satisfied client, but one whom I never saw and of whom I knew nothing. Nor do I know what has become of Great Thatch Island, – perhaps it has become a centre of modern tourism.

Contrariwise in the Greek bond litigation which occupied me between 1955 and 1970 and went four times to the House of Lords I knew perrectly well how this came to me. It is interesting to tell the story in a little detail, for its outcome is quite remarkable. In 1927 the National Mortgage Bank of Greece had issued sterling bonds guaranteed by the National Bank of Greece. In 1953 the latter bank and the Bank of Athens were amalgamated into a new entity then called the National Bank of Greece and Athens. It took over and carried on the London branch of the Bank of Athens which had been carrying on business in England for many years. The bonds were due for repayment in 1957, but in 1955 the National Mortgage Bank of Greece made an offer to its bondholders: they proposed to pay one half of the principal debt; the interest from 1941 to 1954 was to be waived,

---

117 [1900] 2 Ch. 410

Conflicts about Conflicts of Law

thereafter interest was to be paid at the rate of instead of 7 % p.a. At this point an old client, a banker in the City, asked me on the telephone whether he and certain clients of his should accept the offer. He was most surprised when I told him that l had to see the original bond before I could advise him. Eventually one such bond was sent to me. I studied it and came to the conclusion that it was clearly governed by English law and that therefore Greek legislation which included a moratorium covering foreign debts was inapplicable. I searched the file at the Companies Office and found that there was a branch of the National Bank of Greece, which had resulted from the amalgamation with the Bank of Athens, as recorded in the files. So I advised that the offer should not be accepted, but that proceedings for the full [145] amount of the interest and, in due course, the capital should be instituted against the guarantor in its new emanation. This was duly done and on 12 July 1956 (an important date) Sellers J gave judgment. John Foster and Mark Littman appeared for the plaintiff (as they did in all subsequent litigation) and Mr. Harold Lever (now Lord Lever) appeared for the defendants, as he did on all subsequent occasions, though sometimes he was led by T.G. Roche Q.C. The great question argued before the judge was whether English law applied. He decided this point in our favour. It was never raised again during the ensuing fifteen years. But there was a second and much more formidable argument: was the new entity liable for the debts of the constituent predecessor companies whose assets it had taken over? The judge heard much evidence on Greek law and much argument on the private international law relating to the status of foreign corporations in England. In an unreported judgment he decided in our favour, except that he allowed us interest only for six years on the ground that interest for the earlier years was not payable under the terms of the bond, a decision which, as will appear, was unfortunately not appealed by us and which I am convinced was wrong. The appeal came before Denning. Romer and Parker L.JJ.[118] and their decision affirming the judgment is one of those cases which, on account of a subsequent decision by the House of Lords is liable to be overlooked, but deserves to be remembered, for it has some useful remarks on public policy and the distinction between confiscation and amalgamation. There is also an interesting observation by Denning L.J. on the nature of universal succession or rather the necessity of allowing liabilities to follow assets, – a point which years later I was to take up after I had learned something of the French doctrine of the "patrimoine", its antecedents and its implications.[119] The decision of the House of Lords[120] (Viscount Simonds, Lords Morton, Tucker Keith and Somervell was much more

---

118 [1957] 2 Q.B. 33
119 Der konfiszierende Staat als Gesamtrechtsnachfolger, in Festschrift fur Konrad Zweigert (1981) p.
120 [1958] A.C. 509

pedestrian in character. I remember an interesting feature of the oral argument: Lord Somervell from the beginning took a lively part in it. His questions indicated at a very early stage that it struck him as absurd that the new company should claim and own all the assets and liabilities of the two old companies, but disclaim liability for these English debts, – yet it was Lord Somervell who did not deliver a separate opinion at all, but simply concurred with Viscount Simonds. The one sentence that appears in print cannot give an impression of the leading part he took in the oral argument. The argument in the House has also stuck in my memory for another reason. In the course of his address Mr. Roche relied on the decision of the House of Lords in the case of *Kahler v. Midland Bank*.[121] Lord Simonds interrupted him and said "You know this case has come in for a lot of academic criticism." (It was in fact subject to such criticism, mainly in various publications of mine.) Whereupon Mr. Roche made the typical and for the English legal system characteristic reply: "My Lord, I do not know, because I never read the stuff." I have always told this [146] incident to my students, because it illustrates the average English lawyer's view of academic law.

After this great success achieved by a single plaintiff, Mr. Cyril Metliss, then a partner of Stoy Hayward & Co., the Accountants, there were various other actions brought by altogether some 400 plaintiffs asking for the same relief. The new proceedings involved a different issue: on 16 July 1956, i. e. a mere four days after the judgment of Sellers J. in the Metliss action, the Greeks passed a further decree whereby the 1953 decree providing for amalgamation was retrospectively amended so as to exempt from the universal succession obligations arising from bonds expressed in non-Greek currency. We did not know this until the decree was pleaded as a defence in the second action, which was accompanied by an-other, much improved, yet still wholly unsatisfactory offer. Numerous plaintiffs, in particular the most powerful one, the Prudential Assurance Company, ac-cepted it, but a substantial group led by a Mr. Adams carried on the fight which in March 1958 came before Diplock J. (as he then was).

We argued three points: In the first place we said that, although the 1956 decree purported to effect the status of a foreign corporation, in substance it was a law discharging it from liabilities and was therefore ineffective in regard to contracts governed by English law; secondly we relied on an old line of cases holding that succession could not retrospectively be altered, – my particular hobby horse; thirdly we said that in the circumstances in which it was promulgated the 1956 decree was discriminatory and contary to public policy. The judgment of Diplock J.[122] should receive the special attention of scholars, for it makes it very clear that the case involved one of the most famous problems in private international law,

---

121 *Kahler v. Midland Bank* [1950] A.C. 24
122 [1958] 2 Q.B. 59

# Conflicts about Conflicts of Law 187

the problem of classification, and solves it with great elegance and clarity. Certainly, the point was made clear by the House of Lords too, but Diplock J.'s statement of the law will forever retain its peculiar value.

We won before him, but in the Court of Appeal[123] (Jenkins, Morris and Ormerod L.JJ.) disaster befell us. The appeal was allowed and the action was dismissed. I never doubted for one moment that the decision was wrong in that the Court had failed to grasp the somewhat abstruse problem of private international law which the case involved: they thought that if the Greek legislator says "this is a law of amalgamation applying to all Greek companies" a foreign court is bound to stick the same label to it. I immediately decided to appeal and fortunately my clients went along. We had a relatively easy run when in April 1960 we came before Viscount Simonds, Lords Reid, Radcliffe, Tucker and Denning.[124] We won without difficulty and, again, it should be emphasised [147] (for most scholars have overlooked it) that Viscount Simonds' speech contains a most striking and, indeed, exemplary solution of the classification problem: whatever its label, the law of 1956 purported to do to an English contract what it could not do viz., to discharge a measure reserved to the proper law of contract. But the House of Lords also sanctioned the old rule about the retrospective alteration of the rules of succession, a rule which years earlier I had attacked in an article in the British Year Book of International Law,[125] but which the Greek Bank's advisors were unable to displace or which, in accordance with Mr. Roche's views, they did not cite and probably did not find.

In due course we had the pleasure of a third trip to the House of Lords. The Greek bank purported to deduct income tax from the payments of interest even where the coupons were presented by non-residents. So an action was brought by Westminster Bank Executor and Trustee Co. (Channel Islands) Ltd. to claim the amount of the tax payable to a Jersey trust whose settlor and beneficiaries were non-residents and valuable clients of mine. In July 1968 Donaldson J.[126] and in June 1969 the Court of Appeal (Lord Denning M.R., Sachs and Karminski L.JJ.) decided in our favour and in November 1970 the House of Lords (Lord Hailsham, Viscount Dilhorne, Lords Upjohn, Donovan and Pearson) dismissed the appeal. The House held that, although the proper law of the bonds was English and interest was payable and paid in England where the Bank had a branch, the source of the income was foreign, so that in casu income tax could not be deducted; and the non-resident plaintiff was, of course, not subject to tax on income arising abroad. The decision was a great success and of fundamental importance for

---

123 [1960] 1 Q.B. 64
124 [1961] A.C. 255
125
126

foreign holders of bonds issued and payable by foreign issuers in England. The English capital market would have been gravely prejudiced if the decision had gone the other way. It was, in fact, one of the few cases in which the Crown, invited to argue the case as amicus curiae, took the sensible course of suggesting that tax was not deductible. But the National Bank of Greece and their lawyers were even more annoyed with me than they had been before: they were made to pay for clarifying a point of law which was of little importance to them, but was of great importance to the general public and the Revenue.

We had thus been very lucky in most interesting litigation. But there was an interlude to which I must now turn and in the course of which luck failed me for reasons for which I feel responsible and from which I have learned so much that today the same misfortune would not occur and, I trust, will not occur to such of my readers as will follow me with attention.

I mentioned that by his first judgment in 1953 Sellers J. denied us the interest represented by the coupons, which fell due for payment more than six years before the date of the writ and that we did not appeal against this ruling. The point rested on a clause in the bond to the effect that coupons not presented for payment within six years of the date of payment would become void. Our argument was that the clause presupposed the company's willingness and readiness to pay and that where this was missing presentation would not only have been a mere formality which must have been intended to be dispensed with, but would also have meant that the statute of limitations would have begun to run from the date of nonpayment, so that bondholders' rights could only be protected by futile and expensive actions. By 1962 one company owning a substantial amount of bonds, U.G.S. Finance Ltd., had so many unpaid coupons that it was worth its while to start fresh proceedings to test the point. But they did something else. They circularised other bondholders, bought their unpaid coupons for a nominal amount and extended the proceedings to the coupons so acquired. The action came before McNair J. He held that there was no basis in law for dispensing with the six-year clause, but he also held that the plaintiffs were not entitled to sue in respect of the coupons detached from bonds they did not own and acquired by them for a nominal consideration. The reason was that, in spite of an enormous amount of evidence we called, he held that coupons bearable to bearer were not negotiable instruments. One of the reasons no doubt was that he intensely disliked the plaintiff's "immoral" attempt to enrich themselves by buying up coupons for a song and claiming the full amount from the defendants. The decision is not reported, – this no doubt is unfortunate, for there has not been an English decision on negotiability of bearer instruments for many years and McNair J.'s unsatisfactory decision would have given some impetus to the law, even if only for the purpose of exposing its unsatisfactory character. We appealed, but the Court of Appeal (Lord Denning,M.R., Harman and Pearson L.JJ.) dismissed our appeal.

The decision as reported[127] does not let it appear how hostile the Court's attitude was towards a claim which was believed to be unmeritorious.

On the issue of negotiability which was argued first John Foster Q.C.was stopped, – which meant that the Court was in our favour on this point, but this does not appear from the report. Our case on the substance of the matter was put in three ways all of which were rejected. In the first place we suggested that the six-years clause, on its true construction, applied only if, and presupposed that, the defendants were ready and willing to pay; in my view this was the strongest argument, but the court rejected it, as it did reject the argument based on waiver or fundamental breach. The Court, having taken so unfavourable a view of the merits, refused leave to appeal and our petition for leave was also dismissed, – again, as became quite clear, mainly because we were thought to be without such merits as would justify the House of Lords to become involved in the case. [149]

Two most important lessons are conveyed by this case. In the first place insufficient research was done with the result that three Canadian cases were not brought to the court's notice, in which it had been held that where a company is not ready and willing to pay interest coupons, presentation would be an "idle gesture" which by law was dispensed with;[128] was years later that I came across these cases which might have made all the difference. The six-years-clause was at the time a typical one in the case of international bearer bonds and it was as a result of the Court of Appeal's decision which bought to the attention of the Association of Issuing Houses and other City organisations that bonds floated in London now include a different clause which is to the effect that the six years began to run from the date when the paying agents are put into funds to pay the interest. So the mischief which the decision of the Court of Appeal did nothing to eliminate is in practice unlikely to recur, and in this sense the case with all its lack of persuasiveness will have led to a satisfactory development of the law or at least of practice.

Secondly, however, it is clear to me that the action was brought by the wrong plaintiff. In the present climate a finance company is suspect and subject to prejudice, including judicial prejudice. What we should have done was something entirely different. We should have first started proceedings on behalf of a widow somewhere in, say, Northumberland who, preferably suing as a legally aided person, would have claimed the arrears of interest due in respect of the period prior to the last six years. She would have had the sympathy of the court and I have no doubt a way could and would have been found to allow her claim. Thereafter we should have started a second set of proceedings on behalf of, say, a

---

127 [1964] 1 Ll.L.R. 446

128 *Montreal Trust Co. V Abitibi Power and Paper Co. Ltd.*, [1944] Ontario Reports 515 at p.523 with reference to earlier decisions.

**190**                                                    Conflicts about Conflicts of Law

respectable bank to claim the coupons purchased for a nominal sum from third parties; in this case only the question of negotiability would have been decided, if, as I firmly believe, the Northumberland widow's case would have been decided in our favour. So the lesson is: if you have a doubtful claim start, where you can, on behalf of a poor widow with a minimal claim and defer the larger one until you have won on her behalf. I am saying all this with great seriousness: in a period when cases are so often decided, not by strictly legal rules, but by virtue of what one may call the philosophy of merits choose your plaintiff so that he or she will enjoy the sympathy of the court and arouse its willingness to help.

The next case about which I would like to say something has nothing in common with the Greek bank litigation except that on three occasions it went to the House of Lords for leave to appeal which on the last occasion was granted in singular circumstances. I am referring to the case of *Buttes Gas & Oil Company v. Dr Armand Hammer and Occidental Petroleum Corporation.* It is a [150] romantic story and the trial would be fascinating. The essence of the case was that as long ago as the the 5th October 1970 Dr. Armand Hammer, the Chairman of Occidental Petroleum Company and a colourful figure in the world of finance, oil production, art and East-West relations, gave a press conference in London in the course of which he alleged that Buttes, a close competitor, had used "improper means" to procure the Ruler of Sharjah not only to extend its territorial waters for 12 miles, but also to back-date the decree so as to invalidate a concession granted to Occidental by the neighbouring Ruler of Umm Al Quaiwain. Immediately afterwards Buttes started proceedings against Dr Hammer and Occidental for damages for slander. We first tried to have the order for service outside the jurisdiction set aside, mainly on the ground that actions between the same parties, both Californian companies carrying on business in Los Angeles, were already pending in the United States and that it was therefore inconvenient and uneconomical to have the same issues tried in England once more. We won before the Judge in Chambers, but the Court of Appeal (Lord Denning M.R., Phillimore and Negan L.J.J.) reversed him[129] and our application to the House of Lords for leave to appeal failed, so we were forced to deliver a defence in the English action. Once again the foreign plaintiff learned to its great chagrin that if he sues in England he exposes himself to counterclaims of any kind and possibly wholly unconnected with the claim.[130] What we did was to plead by way of justification all the facts on which the American proceedings were bases and to add a counterclaim for conspiracy based on the same facts. This must have caused great consternation in our opponents' camp, for it put into issue all the facts which, by means of the defence of act of state they were trying to suppress in the United

---

129  [1971] 3 All E.R. 1025.
130  Above p.

Conflicts about Conflicts of Law **191**

States. So Buttes tried their American tactics in England: they applied to strike out our defence and counterclaim on the ground that they involved a foreign act of state. They had considerable success before the Judge in Chambers, but in December 1974 the appeal came before Lord Denning M.R., Roskill L.J. and Sir John Pennyuick; John Foster had by that time returned to the Bar and he was once again instructed by me, together with Eli Lauterpacht and Colin Ross-Munro. After an elaborate argument our appeal succeeded.[131] The court made some important pronouncements on the scope of the doctrine of act of state in England; they were particularly welcome to me, for as early as 1943 I had drawn attention to the dangers and the unsatisfactory nature of the American doctrine which in certain English cases had been repeated somewhat uncritically.[132] In particular the court held that we could not be restricted in our defence against the claim for slander. This being so, it was clearly illogical and contrary to [151] principle to refuse to allow the same facts to be the basis of a counterclaim for damages for conspiracy. The decision of the Court of Appeal must have come as a great blow to Buttes and its advisors, for they applied to the House of Lords for leave to appeal. So we again marched to the Judicial Committee, where an elaborate argument took place, but in the end the application was dismissed.

We then came to discovery and this entailed a further trip to the Court of Appeal by which time it was 1980, almost ten years after the utterance of the alleged slander. In the summer of 1979 McNeill J. had allowed us certain documents, but in respect of the bulk of them he held that they were privileged. The Court of Appeal dismissed the appeal on grounds which in the events that happened are no longer of interest. For when we applied to the House of Lords for leave to appeal Buttes made a similar application in that they applied for a second time for leave to appeal against the judgment of the Court of Appeal of 1974. To my amazement the House of Lords granted an application which six years ago it had rejected, and it also grauted our application. This unheard of, unique and probably wholly unconstitutional order was made by Lords Wilberforce, Keith and Bridge. These three were also sitting with Lords Russell and Bridge, when the appeals came to be argued. In the result our appeal was dismissed and on the application of Buttes all proceedings were stayed,[133] the application having been made for the first time in the House of Lords and, accordingly, not having been heard by any lower court. These extraordinary procedural orders were accompanied by an equally novel reason for the decision. It was said that in illdefined circumstances which apparently have something to

---

131 [1975] 2 All E.R. 51
132 "The Sacrosanctity of the Foreign Act of State", 59 (1943) L.Q.R. 42, 155 or Studies in International Law p. 420
133 [1980] A.C.

**192**
Conflicts about Conflicts of Law

do with "transactions" between sovereigns the English courts are entitled in the exercise of "judicial restraint" to decline to adjudicate upon the rights and wrongs of two private parties. No such doctrine had ever been announced before. It constitutes a complete rejection of earlier English practice according to which on facts of State the courts were bound to accept a certificate of the Executive, but without asking for it could not simply abstain from fulfilling their duty. I am deeply sorry that I have to some extent been instrumental in bringing about a decision which is likely to discredit the English legal system. To add insult to injury only one opinion was delivered, namely by Lord Wilberforce. In a case of such fundamental importance, such unusual character and such far-reaching consequences for the law this in itself is a fact inviting regret and criticism.

Before I come to a discussion of the case which is the centrepiece of this chapter I must, with great shame and embarassment, refer to one of the most unfortunate incidents of my career, namely the case of *Ascherberg Hopwood & Crew v Case Musicale Sonzohno and others.*[134] It concerned the United Kingdom copyright in Pietro Mascagni's works Cavalleria Rusticana and L'Amigo Fritz. The action started in the 1950's when the case was introduced to me by my late friend Tullio [152] Ascarelli, then Professor of Comparative Law in the University of Rome and one of the leading Italian lawyers. The question was whether the copyright belonged to Mascagni's heirs or his Italian publisher Sonzogno. There was no real dispute with the English agents, the plaintiffs in the action: the question was to whom they had to account. At the time I instructed Deny, Buckley, later Buckley L.J to settle the defence and after he went to the Bench Peter Oliver (as he then was) and when he took silk E.P. Skone James were the juniors. I repeat all these names in order to provide the background for what happened in the end. The action took so long, because there were proceedings between Mascagni and Sonzogno pending in Italy and their outcome was, so we all thought, decisive for the English proceedings, because they would establish whether and to what extent Sonzogno had acquired copyright. Eventually there was a decision of the Italian Corte di Cassazione. Accordingly, we prepared for trial in England. All the Italian documents had, of course, been disclosed by both parties. Translations were available and we obtained the assistance of an Italian Copyright specialist whom we intended to call as an expert witness. A few days before the trial, however, the plaintiffs told us that they would resist any evidence on Italian law being called, because Italian law had not been pleaded! This was correct. It was an omission for which every single junior Counsel concerned in the case was responsible, – and they certainly were among the most distinguished. And I felt equally responsible, for I should have spotted the point years before, and blamed myself bitterly for it. I felt equally bitter about the plaintiffs who all

---

134 [1971] 3 All E.R. 38

# Conflicts about Conflicts of Law

along had known our position and who relied on what was in my view a mere technicality. However, they presisted in their attitude when the case came before Ungoed-Thomas J. We applied for an adjournment to amend our pleadings and after a long debate this was allowed on uniquely stringent terms, on terms which were almost punitive in character and imposed a heavy financial burden on my poor Italian clients.[135] We appealed to the Court of Appeal, but Peter Oliver, then a Q.C., failed to persuade Russell and Karminski L.JJ. and Sir Gordon Willmer that the order was unduly harsh.[136] The result was that we had to settle the action on very unsatisfactory terms, but they left one ray of hope in that they were without prejudice to any rights which Mascagni's heirs might assert against Sonzogno in Italy. I have often wondered how it was that this disaster occurred. How was it that such experienced pleaders as were from time to time engaged in the case, had pleaded the Italian agreements in great detail and advised on evidence had failed to invoke the Italian law which plainly governed them? Since that time English law has developed so that Counsel could have been held responsible in law for the damage which the Mascagni heirs suffered, but could anyone visualize proceedings against an active judge for a mistake he made [153] as a junior? I have told the sad story in some little details for it should be a warning to everyone concerned with litigation involving foreign rights.

A much more satisfactory case was *Pick v. Manufacturers Life Insurance Company*[137] which involved the sum of £250, a small sum even by the standard of 1958. Dr. Pick was a German lawyer who was living and practising in Dusseldorf. During the war he lived in what then was Palestine and, while there, took out a sterling endowment insurance policy with the defendants whose head office is in Canada. The question was whether the policy monies were payable in what by 1958 had become the State of Israel only or elsewhere, in Canada or England. In the former case the payments would become subject to Israeli exchange control regulations and would in effect be lost to the plaintiff in Germany. The point depended on the proper law of the contract which the defendants said was Israeli (they did not plead Art.VIII (2)(b) of the Bretton Woods Agreement). The judge, Diplock J. (as he then was), had no difficulty in finding that the law of the contract was Canadian and that the place of payment was London or Toronto, at any rate not exclusively in Israel. Accordingly judgment was given for the plaintiff. The judgment is not very elaborate. It would have been interesting to know whether on the footing of Ontario law being applicable a place of payment in Israel would have been the exclusive one or whether it would have been merely optional or subsidiary. The function of the place of payment is a problem that in many ways

---

135 [1971] 1 W.L.R. 173.
136 [1971] 1 W.L.R. 1128
137 [1958] 2 Ll.L.R. 93

**194** Conflicts about Conflicts of Law

is unexplored, but will one day have to be discussed in depth; in the fourth edition of my book on Money I have added a few remarks on it, which I hope will one day induce someone to work on the problem on a broad comparative basis.

Another case which had a bearing on the law of money and which happened to come before my dear friend Kerr J. was *Lively v. City of Munich.*[138] Long before the war the City of Munich had issued bonds on the London market, – they were unquestioningly governed by English Law. Their terms were altered in pursuance of the London debt settlement of 1952/3. As a result, the principal fell due for repayment on 1 December 1973. The bonds provided for payment in sterling on the basis of a dollar clause. The question to be decided was whether for the calculation of the due amount the rate current on 1 December 1973 or the par value rate as declared to the International Monetary Fund applied. This depended on Art. 15 of the London Debt Settlement Agreement and, more particularly, on the question whether the par value rate was "in force". I had no doubt whatever that in view of the events of 15 August 1971, when President Nixon declared the dollar to be inconvertible into gold, the par value system had broken down and that, whatever remnants were still in operation for internal bookkeeping and other purposes of the International Monetary Fund, [154] the par value was in no realistic sense in force. But all this had to be proved to the court. After a great deal of trouble we found an expert of the highest standing, the late Professor Fred Hirsch, though the Judge later said and quite rightly that the evidence of experts (the defendants called my friend Professor James Fawcett, a former Legal Advisor to the Fund) was of little value for the purpose of construing the IMF Articles of Agreement. The Judge gave a very full judgment in which he analysed the Agreement in detail and agreed that in no commercially acceptable sense could the par value be said to be in force.

The outstanding, indeed the unique piece of litigation which I have to discuss in the context of the present chapter is the case of *Carl Zeiss Stiftung*, one of the most famous of Germany's industrial undertakings. In about February 1964 I was in New York. On a Saturday afternoon I was standing in the lobby of my hotel, the San Regis Hotel, waiting for a friend who was expected to call on me. Suddenly someone stormed across the hall towards me, shouting with great excitement: "Here you are, I have been telephoning all over Europe to get hold of you". It was an old friend, Walter Derenberg, then a Professor for Industrial Property Law at New York University and a partner in a firm of lawyers. This is what happened: the Carl Zeiss Stiftung of Heidenheim in West Germany for whom Derenberg acted in the United States had lost its English case which had been decided by Cross J.;[139] they had decided to appeal, but were dissatisfied with their team and

---

138 [1976] 1 W.L.R. 1004
139 [1964] R.P.C. 299

wished to instruct other lawyers; they had decided to approach me, but had been unable to get hold of me, – my office had said I was in New York but the foolish girl at the switchboard did not know my address and failed to put them through to my secretary, my wife could not be reached by telephone, the University of Bonn did not know where I was, and so forth. He had come to the San Regis to meet a friend, – and saw me, the man he had tried to reach. It was as a result of this meeting that I was instructed to take over the case in England. In due course I received all the papers. I was amazed how badly it had been conducted, mainly because no internationalist had ever been concerned with it. The witness on German, for instance, was a well-known patent law specialist in Dusseldorf. The case at that stage raised no more than a preliminary point: did the East German "Carl Zeiss Stiftung" exist as a legal entity so as to be able to give instructions to English solicitors or had "the" Carl Zeiss Stiftung the original, genuine entity been validly transferred to Heidenheim? Before Cross J. Sir Milner Holland who appeared for my clients and whose conduct of the case was far from impressive had expressly abandoned any contention to the effect that the "German Democratic Republic" was not recognised as a State or government by Britain and that therefore its legislation could not have any [155] effect in Britain. It seemed to me that this was the central point, for if East German legislation could not be recognised, if decisions of the so called East German Supreme Court were no valid precedent in England and if the only admissible German law was West German law, including the decision of the Federal Supreme Court on the very point to be decided in the English case then we had a chance of success. So the view I formed was that in the first place we had to seek a method of bringing before the court the whole of the international law point which in the first court had been thrown away. I instructed Mark Littman Q.C. who studied the papers during the vacation at Easter 1964 and eventually we decided to move the Court of Appeal to put questions on the status of East Germany to the Foreign Office. The application came before Lord Denning M.R., Pearson and Salmon L.JJ. in July 1964 and succeeded.[140] The Court, in the face of strong opposition, held that the status of 'the "German Democratic Republic" was a matter of public policy and could be put in issue in the Court of Appeal, although it had not been raised before the judge of first instance. So far so good.

In due course we received the answers of the Foreign Office. They made it clear that the German Democratic Republic enjoyed no measure of recognition. On the authorities there was therefore a strong case for arguing that the laws of an unrecognised State were without effect. The Court of Appeal (Harman, Danckwerts and Diplock L.JJ.) in fact so held.[141] Its judgment is clear, free from tortuous

---

140 [1964] 3 All England Reports 326
141 [1965] Ch. 596.

reasoning and wholly in line with the traditional tendency of English decisions. The judgment of Diplock L.J. (as he then was) still seems to me particularly clear and persuasive and in judging subsequent events should not be overlooked.

In the House of Lords[142] the case took an entirely new and wholly unexpected turn. It became clear at a very early stage of the argument for the appellants (for whom Guy Aldous Q.C. appeared) that the House found it unpalatable to reach a decision which would prevent the appellants from asserting and pursuing their alleged rights in England and which, would preclude any discussion of true merits of the case. Another point was that the House was aware of trade relations with East Germany and felt that a decision denying the existence of the "German Democratic Republic" would prejudice them. The attitude could not have been more different from that adopted by the courts in the Russian bank cases, – the non-existence of the Russian companies and the personal liability of the solicitors acting for them never caused a moment's hesitation. It was Lord Reid who threw the thought into the debate that the "German Democratic Republic" was [156] a subordinate organ of the Soviet Union, – a thought which cannot have been very welcome to the appellants, because the "German Democratic Republic" was keen to assert its own, independent existence. Yet their Counsel took it up with alacrity and eventually the House decided the case on this extraordinary ground. This was not, of course, possible without a good deal of tortuous reasoning of which, in fact, the opinions display an unusual amount. It is even more apparent, when the House came to deal with the effects of the German judgment and with the argument that, whatever the status of the "German Democratic Republic", in England the Federal Republic and its organs, including its events, were alone entitled to speak for Germany.

This is not the place to enter upon a detailed discussion of a decision which, as its almost contemptuous rejection by courts in the United States shows, is one of the most unfortunate and unrealistic in the history of English law. It remains a mystery to me how men like Lords Upjohn, Hodson, Guest and Wilberforce could allow themselves to be misled by Lord Reid's dominating and domineering influence. But if I am asked today where the fundamental mistake lay, I would say` that the House plainly failed in its elementary duty when on two separate and distinct occasions it refused to ask the Foreign Office for further guidance and clarification. The reason undoubtedly was that the House knew it would be given an answer which it would dislike and which would render a decision in favour of the appellants impossible. This, again, was contrary to tradition: the courts have always been anxious and indeed proclaimed their wish not to speak with voices different from that in the Sovereign in foreign affairs, a principle subsequently applied by the House of Lords in remarkable circumstances, but pushed aside in

---

142 [1967] 1 A.C. 853

the *Zeiss* case. This is not the place to discuss in detail the legal reasons which prove the decision of the House of Lords inconsistent with English law and practice, – I have written an article about it which appeared both in English and in German.[143] I reread it recently and am bound to say its reasoning still seems to me irresistible and conclusively exposes the flaws in the House of Lords' odd theory. I remember that the article was originally a lecture which I gave under the auspices of the British Institute of International and Comparative Law. Cross J. was in the audience and in the course of the discussion he asked me whether the consequence of holding the East German regime to be internationally null and void would not be a complete anarchy. I was amazed at the question asked by a distinguished judge. The international invalidity does not mean that internally there does not exist an effective system of government: when the Soviet government was unrecognised internationally, there was yet a government [157] inside the Soviet Union. Nullity in law does not mean non-existence in fact. In any event, to hold the Soviet Union to be the "sovereign" in Germany was wholly contrary to every international arrangement made after the war and, of course, the true meaning of the Foreign Office certificate.

For the House of Lords I had instructed Michael Kerr Q.C. as a second leader, for I could not take the risk that my first Leader, Mark Littman, might not fall ill in the course of a hearing extending over four weeks or so. It was a splendid team and everything possible was done to change the law lords minds which seemed to be closed to any argument put forward by our side; some of them, indeed, received with a degree of hostility arguments or suggestions which might prevent them from deciding as they wished and were determined to decide. Looking back upon the experience I am bound to say that Mark was too polite: when applying for further answers from the Foreign Office, he ought to have said to the House that they would not like the answers and that for this reason they were hesitating to request them, but that it was their judicial duty to do so. In a situation when all is lost, such brutal frankness is often the only method of remedying a lost cause. But it is not Mark's style. It is easy to be wise after the event.

While the decision of the House of Lords remains a blot on British jurisprudence, the American case went forward and was decided both by Judge Mansfield and by the Court of Appeal of the 2nd Circuit in an exemplary manner and the Supreme Court refused certiorari. The West German Carl Zeiss Stiftung had the complete victory which it deserved and which in view of the facts and the law was a matter of elementary justice. After the decision of the House of Lords it became necessary for me to prepare the main case on the merits and for this

---

143 Germany's Present Legal Status Revisted, International and Comparative Law Quarterly 1967, 760 or Studies in International Law (1973) 660. In German: Juristenzeitung 1967, 585, 617.

**198**                                                          Conflicts about Conflicts of Law

purpose close co-operation with New York was necessary. My clients were represented by William Jackson and Jacob Shapiro of Millbank, Tweed, Hadley and McCloy and a close and lasting friendship developed which I valued highly. We helped each other to the best of our ability, selflessly and effectively, and, as I have said, with complete success in the United States.

In England we had a less satisfactory result. Initially things went well. The East made two grave mistakes. In the first place they brought an action against Herbert Smith & Co. They made the extraordinary claim that we were liable to account to them for the moneys received or to be received by us in respect of costs and disbursements. The reason was that we were said to know from the pleadings in the rnain action that the monies paid to us were trust monies belonging to the Eastern Foundation and that we were committing a breach of trust in accepting them. We applied immediately for an issue to be tried, viz. whether in law the point pleased against us was a good one. The judge refused to make such an order, but the Court of Appeal allowed an appeal and clarified the law which had become very muddled.[144] This action itself was dismissed both by Pennycuick J. and by the Court of Appeal[145] [158] (Danckwerts, Sachs and Edmund Davies L.JJ.) and the judgment is now a leading case on fiduciary duties of solicitors, though when it was started and came upon us out of the blue it seemed to be a threat primarily directed against me and might have deterred many less resolute and determined men than my partners and myself. The second favourable development was that the East applied to Buckley J. (as he then was) to strike out part of our defence, mainly on the ground that as the result of the decision of the House and of courts on Pakistan and India the issues were *res judicata*. The application failed[146] and there was no appeal, but it gave great trouble to my team (Michael Kerr Q.C., Christopher Slade Q.C. and Brian Davenport).

Eventually early in 1970 the main trial began before Megarry J. It had all the trimmings of a monster trial. The case was expected to take 9 to 12 months. There were three leaders and two juniors on our side, and four leaders and two juniors on the plaintiffs' side. The court was filled with papers and books. Special cupboards had been put up. We had hired a consultation room in which we had not only our papers, but at Michael Kerr's request also a coffee machine. John Arnold Q.C. (as he then was) opened the case for the plaintiffs, – if I am entitled to use the word "opened". It was the most unusual and inadequate opening I have ever heard and I admired the patience of the judge who during days and days hardly opened his mouth. For during these days Arnold simply read documents, without ever explaining the issues or, accordingly, the relevance of the docu-

---

144  [1969] 1 Ch. 93
145  [1969] 2 Ch. 276
146  [1969] All E.R.

ments or the legal nature of his case. He read and read, interspersed with snide remarks about my client or about me or about whoever else he thought fit to attack, such as the German courts or any German lawyer who had ever said anything unfavourable to his case. At this rate the case threatened to go on endlessly and my Counsel began to talk about a possible settlement. Some of my clients' directors were very receptive to such suggestion, because Carl Zeiss Stiftung in Heidenheim was going through a difficult phase commercially and financially, the costs threatened to become astronomical and the time of leading personnel was taken up by the case to an enormous extent. The net result was that after some weeks of the most pointless reading of documents we did settle the case on unfavourable terms: the world was divided up between East and West. Where final decisions had been reached (Germany, U.S.A., Holland, Switzerland, Italy and some other countries) they remained unaffected. In other countries, including Britain, both sides were free to compete. Perhaps it was a commercially sensible result. From a legal point of view, it was unsatisfactory for two reasons. The East German confiscations were allowed a large measure of [159] extra-territorial effect, – contrary to all principles recognised in the civilised world to which East Germany does not belong. And innumerable untruths alleged by the East in numerous proceedings, particularly before Cross J. in England remained unrefuted. I give a single example: Cross J. held that my clients' legal advisor, Dr. Walter David, had lied when he said that he made a secret trip to Jena and entered into an oral agreement with the head of the rump organisation in the East about the re-creation of the Carl Zeiss Stiftung in the West. Before Cross J. it was denied that any such trip ever took place and the judge so held. At the trial we would have been able to call an entirely independent witness who could support Dr. David's story. It was very painful that such and very many similar matters could not be brought out into the open and that Arnold's vituperation could not be answered. Our chances, I was convinced, were at least as good as in the United States, but the outcome was a stalemate both in fact and in law and for me it left forever a bad taste caused by which I can only describe as the quixotic decision of the House of Lords.

I always thought that *Carl Zeiss* would be the last of my great cases in the international field, but very late in my career President Carter provided me unexpectedly with a new problem of immense size and difficulty. His Proclamation of 14 November 1979 blocking Iranian assets led to great litigation by Iranian banks against American banks in London. One of my partners acted for Manufacturers Hanover and I acted for Irving Trust Company (and a third one for the Continental banks against which no proceedings were brought). The problems raised by these cases were far-reaching. [160]

# Chapter 20 – International Advocay

All my life, as I have said more than once, it has been a matter of the deepest regret that I have been unable to argue my own cases. On many occasions I asked myself whether I should not change over to the Bar. I rejected the idea mainly because I could have afforded the change only towards the end of my career but at that point it would not have been fair towards my partners to leave them. Nor was I certain whether I would be given silk, for the idea of spending my time doing paper work did not appeal to me. I know that what at an earlier stage was a serious obstacle, namely my foreign accent, would not have mattered in the type of case I would have tried to specialise in. Or was it perhaps my notorious lack of decisiveness in my own affairs, my natural indolence, my inclination to leave things as they are that prevented me from making the change? I cannot myself give judgment on the point, but I can say one thing which played a certain role. I am referring to the fact that, curiously enough, even as a solicitor, I again and again did find opportunities of arguing cases of considerable importance, although normally members of my profession do not engage in advocacy except in minor matters which never came my way. These opportunities arose in four contexts (if I disregard the occasional German case which, accompanied by a local German lawyer, I could argue before a German court, – if what takes place in a German court can fairly be called an argument). Each of these groups of cases were international in character.

The first arose from international commercial arbitration. This I have related earlier in these pages.

A second type of international advocacy came my way, when, as a concomitant of restitution, supreme courts of appeal were established in Germany. As a rule I did not accept restitution cases and without exception I refused to accept compensation cases, – to do this type of work would either have killed my general practice or required the creation of a large separate organisation which would probably have brought great wealth (as it did in the case of many other lawyers of German origin), but would also have had to take care of many cases of a somewhat unattractive flavour. But to argue an appeal on a point of law before the highest tribunal in charge of restitution case, – this was something entirely different. I argued some such cases before the highest Restitution Court in the British zone of occupation, the so-called Board of Review. There was, in particular, (on September 15, 1953, the day of my father's death) the case of *Blank v. Kassenarztliche Vereinigung*[147] which laid down the important principle that, although Capital Flight Tax was introduced long before Hitler, namely in 1931, its application after 1933 in the case of Jewish emigrants was a measure of persecution. Another case before the Supreme Restitution Court of the America Zone sitting at Nurernberg involved the gravest miscarriage of justice I have ever come across in my own career. It was such a scandal that even now I am liable [161] to burst a blood-vessel, when writing about it, and I feel in duty bound to tell the story in all detail so that posterity will know what injustice justice can do. Dr. Walter Kahn was the owner of an extremely valuable building in the principal shopping street at Wiesbaden. In 1936 he had to sell it to Mr. and Mrs. Zapp for a mere RM 100,000 less than half of which the purchaser paid so as to make it freely available to him, the balance was paid to the State. Restitution proceedings were started for the account of Dr. Kahn's former wife to whom the property was allocated in the course of a divorce settlement. She was living in England, was almost penniless and represented by me. She did not and, indeed, could not make any payment to me except for my out-of-pocket expenses. Both the District Court and the Court of Appeal at Frankfurt dismissed the claim on the ground that Dr. Kahn had emigrated to Israel in 1932, i.e. before Hitler, and was therefore not protected by the Restitution Law. Other points which would have arisen had the preliminary point been decided in Dr. Kahn's favour were hardly touched upon by either court. We appealed to the Supreme Court. In the summer of 1954 I went to Nuremberg and argued the important point of law before a bench whose members should for all times be identified: they were Justice Marc J. Robinson as Chairman and Justices Frank Flammger and Fred J. Harris. When I had concluded my argument on the preliminary point of law and was about to address myself to the remaining point, the Chairman interrupted me and said: "Since the courts below did not really investigate these points, would it not be the fair solution for us to send the case back to the Court of Appeal if we should decide the first point in your favour?" I replied immediately that the suggestion was not unexpected and seemed to me eminently fair. The Chairman then turned to my opponent and asked whether he agreed. When he received an affirmative answer, the Chairman said: "So be it". (At this point I probably made a mistake for which I have always blamed myself, but which is entirely excusable: I should have insisted on a formal record, order or note being made.) My opponent replied on the preliminary point, but again did not deal with the merits. My few concluding

---

147  Decisions of the Board of Review, Para. 19 p. 124.

remarks were also confined to it. I returned home and during the next *two* years or so I wrote every few weeks or months to the Registrar enquiring about a decision. The answer invariably was that it would be rendered in due course. On the 29th June 1956 a decision was published. The appeal was dismissed. The preliminary point of law was decided in my favour, but the court proceeded to deal with the merits (which I could have shown to be entirely on my client's side) and decided them against me.[148] The decision was rendered by a reconstituted court whose members should also be identified so that their names will for ever be known: they were Mr. Hans Gram Bechmann as President (I believe he is or was a Scandinavian lawyer), Justices Flammger and Harris [162] (who had participated in the year 1954), Dr. Hans Wilden (a new German Judge) and Justice Hardy C. Lee, an American who had been appointed on April 22, 1956. When I had recovered from the shock, I applied for re-argument. My principal reason was that the decision was a nullity, or that it was at least fair to hear re-argument, because it had been rendered in disregard of the order made at the hearing and, in addition, because only two out of the five judges who were responsible for it had participated in the oral hearing, heard my argument and were parties to the order then made. My application was summarily dismissed. How was such a disaster possible? Had there been foul play at work during the two years of gestation? And if a genuine mistake had been made would not the court or an honest court have been only too anxious to hear re-argument or do something else to prevent a grave miscarriage of justice?

I know no answers to these questions. What I did do was to apply against the Federal Republic of Germany to the European Commission for Human Rights in Strasbourg for an order that the judgment be set aside, alternatively that Germany be liable to pay damages. The Commission, presided over by Sir Humphrey Waldock, gave me at least a hearing. My application alleged a violation of Art.6 of the Convention which guarantees a "fair hearing", but the argument was limited to the question whether the Federal Republic was in law responsible for what it alleged to be an American or an international tribunal sitting in Germany, but exempt from its jurisdiction or control. On June 10, 1958 in a frequently quoted and frequently criticised decision the Commission held my application "manifestly unfounded" and dismissed it on the ground of lack of jurisdiction without investigating the merits[149]. My written and oral arguments had failed. All my efforts on behalf of poor Mrs. Kahn had been in vain. Justice had not been vindicated.

---

148 *Kahn v. Zapp*, Decisions of the Supreme Restitution Court (Third Division) Volume VI (1955–1956) p. 258.

149 Yearbook of the European Commission of Human Rigfhts II, 288: International Law Reports 25 (1958i) 190 (Case 235/56)

**204**  International Advocacy

Yet I made two additional efforts. I tried to induce the Federal Republic to make an *ex gratia* payment. They refused on the ground that if they accepted responsibility for the mistakes made by the Americans in Germany there would be no end to claims for compensation. I also tried to persuade the Foreign Office in London to afford diplomatic protection to Mrs. Kahn, a British subject, against the United States of America which should be liable for the denial of justice caused by Messrs. Robinson, Flammger and Harris. The Foreign Office, however, not surprisingly refused to intervene.

The affair of Mrs. Kahn thus came to an end, though it continues to live on my mind as a bad dream.

My appearance in Strasbourg was the third type of international advocacy [163] I engaged in. Two later occasions are worth recalling, although there was no advocacy, for without granting a hearing the Commission thought it right to dismiss my application as "manifestly ill-founded", a decision which may not have been entirely free from harshness.

The first of these cases was *Booth & Co. against the Federal Republic of Germany.*[150] Booth & Co. had sold goods to a South German firm at a certain price. When the goods were delivered and an invoice was sent, the clerk made a mistake and the invoice was issued for an amount which represented about a third of the purchase price. It was promptly paid. Some months later the auditors of the sellers discovered the mistake and an invoice for the unpaid balance was sent. The buyer refused to pay. We started proceedings, but to our amazement the action was dismissed on the ground that as a result of the first invoice we were stopped from claiming the balance. We appealed to the Court of Appeal at Stuttgart. The court clearly indicated that the reasoning of the first judge was nonsense. Yet a few weeks later our appeal was dismissed on a ground which I have forgotten, but which was equally nonsensical and – what is more – which had not been mentioned by anyone, but which, had we known it, we could very easily have refuted. The amount was too small for a further appeal to the Supreme Court. My own remedy was an application to Strasbourg on the ground of a Violation of Art.6 of the Convention which guarantees a fair hearing. I argued that under the law of all civilised states a fair hearing presupposed giving the parties an opportunity of dealing with any point considered relevant by the court. I relied, for instance, on the predecessor of Art. 16 of the French Code de procédure civile: "Aucun moyen, même d'ordre public, non soulevé par les parties, ne pourra être examiné d'office sans que celles-ci aient été appleés à présenter leurs obervations à cet égard". The Commission, however, dismissed my application on the ground that the principle was jura novit curia, and it added that 'allowance had to be made as regards the existence of different legal systems in

---

150 Yearbook of the European Convention of Human Rights 1968, 608.

International Advocay **205**

interpreting the concept of "fair hearing"'. The practice of German courts in denying to the parties the opportunity of dealing with a point of law – which is an extremely doubtful and probably unfounded statement – was not contrary to Art.6. I leave it to the reader to decide whether even assuming the German practice to be what the Commission alleged it to be this is a convincing decision. Was the apploication really "manifestly ill-founded"?

The second case was *Firestone Tyre & Rubber Co. Ltd. v. the United Kingdom.*[151] In patent proceedings in which Firestone was a defendant it raised a separate defence in regard to two claims, namely lack of novelty for a particular reason. [164] If this defence had succeeded, s.62 of the Patent Act would have applied and the plaintiffs would have had to prove that the invalid claims were framed in good faith and with reasonable skill and knowledge, before the court could award any damages for the infringement of any valid claim. Neither the judge nor the Court of Appeal dealt with this defence in any way, – why they failed to do so has never been clarified and has remained a matter of great anxiety to Firestone and its advisors. The House of Lords, somewhat surprisingly, refused leave to appeal. There was nothing left but an application to Strasbourg. But the application was dismissed as "manifestly ill-founded". The Commission held that although the point had been fully argued, the special character of the separate defence (which, of course, had been pleased) had not been made clear to the courts and that the applicants "have <u>not</u> shown…that the courts were *not* justified…in giving <u>little or no</u> weight to the separate defence in their judgments".[152] Is this not very odd? You plead a defence, you argue it fully before the court. If the court ignores it altogether you have yet had a fair hearing, because you have failed to emphasise the "special character" (whatever this may mean) of the defence, so that the court was entitled to give "little or no weight" to it. One wonders what a lawyer has to do in order to make "the special character" of a defence clear and so to obtain the court's ruling upon it. What does fairness of a hearing require?

The fourth opportunity for advocacy came, when to my immense satisfaction I was instructed to appear in truly international tribunals. In 1966 I suddenly received an invitation from the Belgian company Sofina to come to Brussels for an interview with their Chief Counsel, Professor Henri Rolin, in the case which Belguim had instituted against Spain in the International Court of Justice in The Hague which concerned *Barcelona Traction & Power Co.*, a Canadian company controlled by Sofina. Rolin, so he later told me, had read the course of lectures on The Doctrine of Jurisdiction in International Law which in 1964 I had given at the Hague Academy of International Law,[153] and thought that I might be a useful

---

151 Yearbook of the European Convention of Human Rights 1973, 152.
152 Yearbook of the European Convention on Human Rights 1973, 152.
153 Rec. (1964i) 1.

addition to his team. The result of that first interview was that I became deeply involved in the preparation of the case, attended the oral hearing from February to July 1969 and presented orally the Belgian argument on two parts of its case, namely abuse of administrative discretion and excess of jurisdiction.[154] In February 1970 Belgium's application was dismissed by a judgment[155] which, for reasons I shall develop, is one of the most disappointing and, I am tempted to say, shameful documents in the history of international litigation.

Barcelona Traction was a Canadian holding company which had no office, no business, no [165] assets, no activity in Spain. It owned all the shares of another Canadian company, Ebro, which had a registered branch in Spain and there carried on a large enterprise that supplied all the electricity in the northern part of Spain. The shares in Ebro which, as I just said, were owned by Barcelona Traction were in fact held by a Canadian Trustee as security for certain bonds issued by Barcelona Traction on the London Stock Exchange. On 12 February 1948 the judge in the little Catalonian town Reus, on the application of two henchmen of Franco's financier Juan March, one of the great criminals of the Franco regime, issued a bankruptcy order against Barcelona Traction in remote Toronto and ordered the seizure of all its assets. Next day a trustee in bankruptcy, another henchman of March, took control of Ebro's offices in Barcelona and elsewhere. The Reus order was never served upon Barcelona Traction nor was it ever given a chance of presenting its case and showing that there was no basis on which any court, not bribed by March, could make it bankrupt. During the following years innumerable proceedings followed which resulted in some 3000 judicial orders and judgments, – all of them, without exception, unfavourable to Barcelona Traction. Eventually the trustee in Bankruptcy caused new share certificates in Ebro to be printed, used them to "transfer" Ebro to Spain, to "hispanize" it and sold them in the course of a mock auction to March. This is the broadest of outlines of a long, complicated and sad story which post-Franco Spain has done nothing to undo and the details of which have often been told, for instance, in two excellent articles which in May 1979 appeared in the New Yorker and were written by John Brooks. When all hope of obtaining satisfaction in Spain had been exhausted, Belgium started in September 1958 proceedings against Spain in the Hague. Spain denied the Court's jurisdiction and also Belgimn's *jus standi*, i. e. its right to exercise diplomatic protection on behalf of Barcelona Traction, a Canadian company. While these proceedings were pending, the Spanish Ambassador in Paris approached Belgium and suggested meetings with March to discuss a settlement. He stated, however, that Spain's pride and March's mentality required the previous withdrawal of the proceedings. In view of assurances

---

154 See two volumes of oral argument published by the International Court of Justice.
155 Reports of the International Court of Justice 1970, 3.

given by the Ambassador Belgium in fact withdrew them in April 1961. A meeting with March took place in the South of France, but it became at once obvious that he had no genuine wish to settle and that the whole manoeuvre was nothing but a trap. So Belgium started a fresh set of proceedings in the Hague. Spain raised the same preliminary objections and added a new one, viz. the withdrawal of the earlier proceedings which was alleged to be a withdrawal of the claim. By a judgment rendered in 1964 the Court rejected the last-mentioned objection, declared to have jurisdiction to hear the case and ordered the question of the *jus standi* to be heard together with the merits.[156] So the parties spent some four years in exchanging voluminous pleadings and submitting many thousands of documents, opinions on Spanish law, affidavits by potential witnesses, and [166] preparing the oral argument. March is said to have had some 200 lawyers of all nationalities working on the case. He certainly procured opinions from innumerable lawyers of the first rank, – frequently mainly for the purpose of preventing Belgium from employing them. The Belgian case was fought on a much more modest scale. Henri Rolin was the undisputed leader of the team, he was a wonderful man, lawyer and advocate who had a perfect command of the facts and the law and who was excellent in organising the work of his colleagues and their assistants. Many, somewhat formal meetings took place in the great conference room in the Sofina building, when special problems of particular importance, mainly tactical problems, were discussed. The effect was that we were well prepared and in good heart, when on 4 February 1969 we entered the great hall of the Peace Palace in The Hague and started the hearing with a long introductory speech by Rolin who had been in almost every earlier case before the Court and enjoyed the respect of friend and enemy alike. It was a great occasion. As time wore on, the interest of the public diminished, because the facts and the law became technical and difficult. I did not, of course, attend all the hearings, particularly when it was Spain's turn to make its submissions. I stayed away and on occasions went back to London, partly to work on the case, partly to look after the rest of my work, but I was, of course, in The Hague, when the parts falling within my responsibility were argued.

While the hearing proceeded, we began to feel that the Court was leaning towards the Spanish side. All sorts of rumours reached us. They may have been engineered by the Spanish team, but there is reason to think that they emanated from the Spanish judge *ad hoc*, the Uruguyan [...] who in February 1970 was to be responsible for the result of the decision in all its details being known some three or four days before the promulgation of the judgment. The Spanish side was wholly unscrupulous, not only in its allegations, irrelevant and unsupported by evidence though they were, but also in the way they conducted the hearing and

---

156 I.C.J. Reports 1964, 6.

the argument. The essential facts were so simple and so indefensible that their hope lay in confusion, and this technique they practised to an amazing extent. It was, therefore, very satisfactory to read the rebuke, mild though it was, which in the last paragraph of its judgment the Court expressed.

In the course of the many months, as the Belgian team worked together, we naturally discussed again and again how the Court was likely to decide, on what ground it was likely to decide etc. Speculation of such kind is the normal topic of lawyers' conversation. On one point we were all agreed: none of us considered it likely or even possible that the Court would deny Belgium's *jus standi*, for this ground was open to the Court in 1964, it did not employ it to dismiss the application, and joining it to the merits could only mean that the [199] point depended on the facts of the case, – and these were clearly in Belgium's favour. We considered it therefore almost scandalous that on 4 February 1970 the Court delivered a judgment denying Belgium's *jus standi* on grounds which without exception were open to it in 1964, which had nothing whatever to do with the facts of the case and which were as abstract, academic, arid and dogmatic as a pan-adectist of the 19th century could have wished. Millions of dollars, thousands of working days were spent in vain. All the arguments presented in 1969 were ignored, none of the facts were explored or even mentioned. The judgment of the Court does not even once mention the bankruptcy and its essential features, which was at the root of the case. A Court capable of rendering this judgment (and incidentally the later judgment in *Nuclear Test* case between Australia and France) has lost all claim to respect and it is not surprising that this is now a Court witn very little work, – how could one have any faith in its ability to decide according to law?

A year or so later Professor Briggs who was one of the advisors of the Spanish side analysed the judgment in an article in the American Journal of International Law.[157] This gave me the opportunity of publishing in the same Journal my analysis and to show what the Court had failed to do or, to put it differently, what extraordinary propositions the Court must be taken to have sanctioned.[158] I am glad that I was given the opportunity of propounding this analysis, for it exposes the true character of the Court's judgment.

There was, however, one piece of satisfaction which I had. In a separate judgment which Sir Gerald Fitzmaurice delivered he did deal with the merits to a considerable extent. He not only condemned sharply the Spanish illegalities, but also stated that if there had been a *jus standi* he would have denied Spanish jurisdiction over Barcelona Traction, – in other words he accepted my argument

---

157  American Journal of International Law 1971, 327.
158  American Journal of International Law 1971, 259.

International Advocay 209

on the point. His pronouncements on it retain much general importance, though they tend to be overlooked by scholars.

In the circumstances the case of *Barcelona Traction* was a unique professional experience, but also a unique disappointment. No layman can appreciate the bitterness of the pill which a lawyer has to swallow if the plainest possible injustice, committed with unsurpassed effrontery and legalised by the bribed judiciary of a fascist regime, is perpetuated by an institution which calls itself a Court and professes to be helpless or unwilling to undo a wrong. Where law and justice part company one becomes the witness of a tragedy.

I was in many ways much luckier in my last and certainly my most satisfactory international case. At the same time it was the height of my career and it is, therefore, fitting to end with it this part of my report. [168]

In 1979 the government of the Federal Republic of Germany approached me with the request to appear as their "leading counsel", that is to say, to undertake the argument in a case which had been brought against it by Belgium, France, the United Kingdom, the United States of America and Switzerland before an international Arbitration Tribunal which had been constituted under the London Debt Settlement Agreement of 1952. The case related to the question of the extent if any to which Germany's liability under the Young Loan of 1930 had been affected by the two German revaluations of 1961 and 1969. A clause in the treaty of 1952 provided that in the event of a change of more than 5 % in rate of exchange prevailing in 1952 the amounts payable in respect of the Young Loan would be brought into line with the rate of exchange for "the least depreciated currency" or in German "die Währung mit der geringsten Abwertung". Did this clause come into operation as a result of the appreciation or devaluation of the German currency?

I accepted the offer with alacrity, although the fee offered to me was ridiculously low: the amount involved was a minimum of about 50 million DM, i.e. about £12½ million, my fee was DM 50,000 plus part of my expenses or about £12,500. Of course one accepted that governments pay badly, but this seemed to me an extraordinary degree of meanness which was surpassed only by an incident that is so extreme that it is funny and worth recording: In the course of the preparatory stage I was once called to Bonn and attended a meeting at the Foreign Office. At 11 o'clock a trolley with coffee and sandwiches came around. I took a cup and one of the most attractive sandwiches. A few minutes later a lady came to collect the price: 60 Pfennigs. My clients, and hosts allowed me to pay!

The case involved the interpretation of some seven lines of print. When I was instructed the written pleadiags had been closed. I read the Memorial, the Reply, the Duplique and the Rejoinder. I read them twice. At the end I understood nothing. What was worse, I found it wholly impossible to think of an argument in support of my client's case. I was in despair. Later I learned that some of the judges felt similarly, for the written pleadings, particularly those of the Federal Republic, were so bad that they left the reader in a state of mind of the most complete confusion. It was in this situation that in the summer of 1978 I went to Gstaad and decided to think the case through myself, unaided by any of the available pleadings, by any literature or documentary evidence. It was this process of a completely independent review of my own, that saved me. I returned to London with a clear picture of the argument I had to present.

The oral hearings started on 4 March 1979 in the Great Conference Room of the Foreign Office in Bonn. The President was Professor Castren, a Finnish international lawyer whom I knew well from the meetings of the Institut de Droit [169] International, the judges were Mr. Maurice Bathurst Q.C. (United Kingdom), my old friend[159] Mr. Mark Robinson (United States), M. [...] (France), a retired President of the Cour de Cassation, Professor Arndt, Mrs. Hedwig Maier, Professor Kewenig (Germany). I had numerous opponents, in particular Sir Francis Vallat Q.C. for the United Kingdom, Mr. Kearney for the United States, Professor Gianviti of the University of Paris for France and Belgium. On my side I had my old friend Professor Hahn of the University Wurzburg with me. The hearings extended throughout March. Some eight witnesses on the origin of the clause in the London Debt Settlement Agreement were heard and very detailed arguments were presented. The tribunal was almost completely silent and at the end of the oral hearings it was impossible to obtain any impression of its views. We had to wait an unusually long time for the decision. It was rendered only on 16 May 1980, when the Federal Republic won by four votes against three, – by the votes of the German judges and the Finnish Chairman.[160]

I think that in all modesty I can say that I won this case with my argument, – for this is what several of the judges and of my opponents told me. The majority judgment itself is based on narrow reasoning of treaty interpretation and, unfortunately, does little or nothing to discuss and clarify the monetary law which arose in this case. Its essential aspects were twofold: in 1952, in the heyday of the Bretton Woods system, there could be no depreciation which was not a devaluation or "Abwertung" and the indirect depreciation which a currency suffers as a result of another currency being revalued or appreciated is not an event against which any protective clause is designed to guard. Of course, where continuing equivalence is intended this can be achieved, but is entirely different from the scheme applicable to the Young Loan.

These aspects of monetary law, though not properly discussed, at least become apparent to the attentive reader. But two other matters are not mentioned at all. Evidence was taken at considerable length to ascertain the "intentions" of

---

159 See above p.
160 International Law Reports 59, 499.

International Advocay                                                    **211**

those participating in the London Conference of 1952. This gave rise to the question what the term "travaux préparatoires" really means and to what extent it admits material other than documents available to all members of the Conference or oral statements made otherwlse than by or with the authority of the Head of Delegations. In this case the clause was drafted by a Committee on which the German Delegation was not represented. It was shown to the Head of the German Delegation, Dr. Abs, by Sir Otto Niemeyer and accepted by the former in the lift going from the ground floor to the fifth floor of Lancaster House in London. I protested against the admissibility of evidence about events which occurred in the absence of a German representative. I also protested against the evidence of witnesses who had not previously submitted an affidavit or a [170] written statement and the point of whose testimony had not previously been disclosed. These are serious questions relating to the procedure by international tribunals, on which very little if any material is available. It is a matter of regret that the tribunal did nothing to clarify them. I hope that one day I shall be able to discuss them in the course of an academic contribution.

At the time I thought it very odd that the German Government did not invite me to attend the promulgation of the judgment. Nor did they officially inform me for some four weeks, when they sent me the texts of the majority and minority opinions, so that I would have remained in ignorance of the result had not Hahn telephoned me in the evening of the Friday and had not the English Foreign Office telephoned me in the morning of the following Monday to express its congratulations. Only in July the German Foreign Minister wrote me a very formal letter and in the autumn of 1980 the President of the Federal Republic decided to confer [...]

One of the most interesting bye-products of this great case was my acquaintance and, indeed, friendship with Hermann Joseph Abs, the former President of the Deutsche Bank. Our relationship did not start off well. In the course of one of the conferences preceding the hearing I explained to him that he would be subject to cross-examination if he had to give oral evidence in amplification of an affidavit which he had submitted and which had been incredibly badly drafted by the German Foreign Office. He replied: "I have learned so much in my life, – if it comes to that I shall get two Jewish lawyers from Chicago to teach me how to behave in the course of cross-examination." I asked him why the Chicago lawyers had to be Jewish, but did not receive an answer, as another participant in the conference quickly intervened. Nevertheless during the hearing we became friendly. He seemed to have a certain admiration for my achievement in the case, but I had the most real admiration for his immense contribution to the reconstruction of the German economy after the war. He undoubtedly is one of the architects of Germany's post-war revival and since he met all prominent people of his period he was full of the most interesting stories about some of them. [171]

# Part III: Paralegomena

If at the end of the road I try to summarise the lessons I have learned and the experiences I have gathered I must begin by emphasising the grace that was conferred upon me by the combination of academic and professional activity, by the double life that I have been able to lead and trying to describe. In both spheres the gods have been kind to me. Neither would, I am convinced, have flourished without the other. Many intereting cases would not have reached me had I not done some academic work in the field. Such academic work would not have been conceived or done without the background of stimulating practical experience; indeed, if I had been only an academic, free from pressure and surrounded by the leisure and narrowness of University life and politics, I fear I would have been wholly sterile.

This is so, although I have made it a rule, and adhered to it with very few exceptions, not to write about the case in which I have been involved partisan publications under the guise of academic objectivity such as occur only too frequently in Continental countries, particularly in such fields as labour or tax law, must be avoided and will, I trust never be tolerated in England. The exceptions, I believe the only ones, were my article on Barcelona Traction,[161] – it was necessary in order not to leave Professor Briggs' article unanswered – and my articles on the status of Germany in general and *Zeiss* in particular[162] – they were necessary to fit the unfortunate decision of the House of Lords into the background of public international law and to show how paradoxical that decision was bound to be as a result of the two refusals of the House to ask the Foreign Office for guidance.

When I say that practically the whole of my academic work was provoked by practical experience, I am not by any means referring only to my own cases. It was case law in general that provided the impulse. This can best be shown by the origin of my book on *The Legal Aspect of Money*. There were in the 1930s on the one hand some important cases decided by the House of Lords and the Privy Council which invited analysis, often in the light of the wealth of material accumulated by Germany's unhappy monetary history. There was on the other

---

161 Above p.
162 Above p.

hand my daily concern between 1933 and 1939 with the implications of German exchange control. It was from these sources that the book took shape and as time went on and it reached a third edition in 1971 and a fourth one in 1982 the book became the only one in the world on the subject, since Nussbaum's work which had appeared in 1952 was not carried on. And it became influential. The landmark decision of the House of Lords in the case of *Miliangos v. George Frank (Textiles) Ltd.*[163] might not have been rendered without the teachings of the book and there are many other cases in which its effect is noticeable even [172] if it is not expressly or only incidentally mentioned. The same applies to some other writings, the most sensational yet the least generously recognised instance being my article on *The present Validity of Nazi Nationality Laws*[164] add the outcome of the case of *Oppenheimer v.Cattermole.*[165] The question in that case vas whether Mr. Oppenheimer, a Jewish refugee from Germany, was still a German national, notwithstanding his expatriation by Hitler in 1941 and his naturalisation in England in 1948. The Court of Appeal had answered in the negative, primarily for reasons which interested me jurisprudentially: the Court took the view that, however obnoxious Hitler's decree had been, it constituted German law at the time and must therefore be given effect. I did not know that the case was going to the House of Lords, for the Court of Appeal had refused leave to appeal. So I wrote my article in which I discussed the whole problem. Shortly before it was published, I met Lord Hodson at a reception. He began to talk about the case which, I was amazed to hear, the House of Lords had just heard. He said that he had written his judgment and gave me the clear impression that the decision of the Court of Appeal was going to be reversed. A few days later my article appeared. I then heard that the House had ordered the case to be re-argued and, as appears from the report, it was sent back to the Special Commissioners and after receipt of their findings again argued with the result that the appeal was dismissed. Lord Salmon, so he told me later, had read my article as soon as it appeared, drawn his colleagues' attention to it and in reliance on it advocated a reversal of the decision previously reached. The report discloses very little of this unusual, perhaps unique swing of the judicial pendulum to which I later had occasion to refer,[166] when quite independently the German Constitutional Court formed almost the same view as the House of Lords.[167]

These incidents among many others establish that the old rule according to which a living author could not be cited to or by a court is now obsolete. Con-

---

163 [1976] A.C. 443
164 (1973) 89 L.Q.R. 194
165 [1976] A.C. 249
166 97 (1981) L.Q.R. 220
167 That decision of the Constitutional Court seemed to me open to grave doubts and I discussed and criticised it in an article contributed to the Festschrift für Coing (1982).

tinental lawyers have always treated the old rule with hilarity. But it was by no means devoid of a measure of wisdom. If one knows the partisan nature of much of the literature published in Continental periodicals, if one realises how many articles are written by interested lawyers for a specific purpose some scepticism is not out of place. In a German case I had, a lawyer who was not [173] on the record, but who advised one of the parties published an article on the legal point involved in proceedings to which his clients were a party, and this article was then cited to the court as an authority. In another case certain German lawyers asked me for an opinion on a point of monetary law on condition that my opinion for which they would, of course, pay a fee would be published by me in a legal periodical without an indication of the origin of the article. I sent them home.

\* \* \*

There is another general point to be made about publishing legal work. It is nothing should ever be published except where the author has something new to say and can say it in such smple and clear language that all readers can understand it.

Occasionally, it is true, articles of a descriptive nature or articles summarising the existing law serve a useful purpose and are therefore worthy of publication. But such work should as a rule be done by beginners, – it is the type of work with which an academic reputation may be started, but hardly established or maintained. The language problem is much more serious. The utmost care is required in order to avoid unnecessary words, and to find expressions which convey the thought readily and without a second reading. For the English lawyer this should be easier than for most, for he is being brought up on cases which are usually written in exemplary style. There are, of course, differences and the quality of a judge is indicated by his style, so that the attentive student can appreciate distinctive features and qualities.

Style, it is to be feared, will to an increasing extent deteriorate. This is due to the mechanical side which breed indifference and neglect. I pride myself that I can discover from reading a letter whether it was spoken into a dictaphone or dictated to a secretary or drafted by hand. It is long winded and repetitive in the first case, it is much better in the second and most precise in the third. The great Valentine Holmes wrote every pleading, every opinion by hand, – the clarity and conciseness was incomparable. I am used to dictating to a secretary and have often been complimented on my letters but all my writings destined for publication were first sketched roughly in handwriting and then typed and often retyped once, twice or three times by myself. This technique I learned from Martin Wolf and he certainly was a master of language. From him I also learned my concern for language, my sensitiveness about it.

If I had to mention an English lawyer whose style is outstanding, I would mention Lord Denning. He has a command of the language, a felicity and simplicity of expression and at the same time a precision of formulation which [174] is most instructive and singularly persuasive. But the short, somewhat clipped sentences which in recent years he has come to prefer are so characteristic that they should not be imitated too readily: the imitation would be too obvious and style being a peculiar quality of a person no-one should adopt a style which does not come naturally.

* * *

I have spoken about the quality of judges, – as if not every judge had the same quality! This may be so in theory. The facts are different and very mysterious. They constitute one of those oddities of English law which exist and play a great role in real life, but are nowhere discussed, analysed or taught. In theory all judges are equal, but the fact is that the authority of a judge depends on his personality, intelligence, experience, judiciousness, influence and reputation. Judgments by judges in England are, to start with, very much like statements by textbook-writers on the Continent: they are expressions of opinion. Whether they are or become authoritative depends on the standing of the judge. I am not, of course, talking about unanimous decisions on a clearly defined point. Nor am I speaking about such facts as the binding character of precedent on lower courts. I am primarily thinking of dicta and obiter dicta and suggesting that their effect depends on the authority of the person who expressed them. And that person is to an English lawyer a living person. He has made (or failed to make) his reputation at the Bar, he comes to the Bench with the goodwill (or the indifference) which his standing at the Bar has created, his progress is being critically observed, he becomes a good or a bad, a popular or a disagreeable judge, a broad-minded man or a stickler, an able author of judgments or a muddle-headed or verbose writer or a superficial sprinter. In short as a personality, as a lawyer, a man, a character he lives while he is alive and forever after, for his judgments speak for him and the traditional view is passed on. And when it comes to the citation of authority one will find that it is only on rare occasions that every speech made in the House of Lords or every judgment of the Court of Appeal in a particular case is being read, – you confine yourself to the speech which by common consent is the most authoritative; you sometimes take a particular passage out of another speech, or you read a speech made by a law lord whom, as you know, your judge respects specially, – always it is the particular person who speaks, influences, persuades. And with experience, but not from books, you learn how to evaluate the voices speaking from the past.

Although in theory all judges are equal, in fact, therefore, the differences are striking. You know that for Lord Goddard L.C.J. the judgments of Channel J. were almost sacrosanct. You know that Viscount Simonds would much prefer Lord Tomlin to Lord Atkin, – surely one of the greatest judges of this century, but [175] for some reason no favourite of Lord Simonds. You know that Lord Denning who assuredly will in years to come carry the greatest authority was so much out of favour with the House of Lords of the 1970's and 1980's that to have his decisions on your side was almost a guarantee for having them disregarded or reversed. You knew that Lord Wright was a first-class advocate, but that his judgments were liable to be muddled. You know that Lord Reid was a wonderful presiding judge, but that his written work was by no means up to his true intellectual standard and that his judgments were at times much overrated, and are likely in the future to be considered uneven and full of defective reasoning.

And so I could go on, I could not add to the point I would like to make. It is most vividly illustrated by an incident I remember well. Some years ago when entering Lord Denning's Court, the woman reporter who had covered his court for many years asked me about the case I was going to have. She then said to me: "There are two grounds of appeal in this court. One is: 'This is an appeal against a judgment of Mr. Justice X'; the other is: 'This is an appeal against a judgment of Mr. Justice Y'". The former is now a Lord Justice. He has not improved. Nor will his standing in the eyes of lawyers change. And in some mysterious way, without a textbook, even without oral instruction the intelligent and interested members of future generations of English lawyers will know too. The personality of a judge lives, continues to live and is always liable to be evaluated.

\* \* \*

This brings ae to what I believe to be the essential feature of the legal system in the Anglo-Saxon world. I have often been asked about it and found it easy to say where it is not to be found. It is not the absence of codification that is the fundamental characteristic. On the one hand codification on the Continent has failed in the sense that it is not more than an extraordinarily meagre skeleton that cannot be understood, implemented or developed without the thousands and thousands of decisions which have changed and frequently revolutionised it and will, in another hundred years or so, make it almost unrecognisable. On the other hand it would not be difficult to cast English law into a number of so-called rules which would correspond to the Articles of a Code. Dicey's *Conflict of Laws* has shown the way. Jenks succeeded in putting the common law into rules which, roughly, correspond to the sections of the German Civil Code. Much statute law is available. Codification or non-codification is something entirely external and superficial. Nor is it the principle of precedent that is essential, although it is sometimes so described. It is a technique rather than a principle. Admittedly a judge of first instance is bound by a decision of the Court of Appeal or the House of Lords. Certainly the Court of Appeal is bound by its own decisions as well as by the decisions of the House of Lords. But there are very few decisions which a trained mind [176] cannot avoid by a process of "distinguishing", whether it be intellectually honest or dishonest. On the other hand, while technically there is on the Continent nothing like a "binding" precedent in law, in fact decisions of the higher courts and, most certainly, of the highest court are being followed. Again the difference is one of degree rather than principle.

I suggest that the real difference lies in the Anglo-Saxon principle of the personal responsibility of the Judge as opposed to the Continental principle of judicial anonymity. On the Continent you speak of a decision of the Chambre Civile of the Cour de Cassation or of the Cour d'Orléans. In Germany you speak of the Third Chamber of the Federal Supreme Court or the Court of Appeal at Hamburg or the 22nd Civil Chamber of the District Court at Munich. The names of the judges, the lawyers and the parties are unidentified in Germany, though not altogether in France. In England every single decision is given by named judges who accept towards history a personal responsibility for it. (In addition, of course, the parties and the lawyers and, frequently, their arguments are known and available for scrutiny.) I believe that these differences are of an absolutely fundamental character. They are so fundamental that one is even entitled to ask whether decisions rendered under the Hitler regime would have been the same if the judge had not been able to hide behind the anonymity of the Chamber of Senate and the lawyers had had to disclose their identity. The historical responsibility which on point of law an English judge carries is, I believe, a matter that weighs heavily upon him and is in the forefront of his consciousness. At any rate in the House of Lords (where the argument is regularly reported) Counsel, to my knowledge, is very much alive to the judgment that his peers, present and future, are likely to pass upon the character and range of his argument.

There is another aspect that is both essential and peculiar to part of the English legal system, yet is not the one outstanding characteristic. I am referring to the principle of the single, continuous and completely oral hearing of a case. In civil cases several hearings, each taking a little bite at the cherry, are quite usual on the Continent. The idea of the single hearing which continues until the case is completed is entirely unknown in civil matters. So is the total orality of a hearing. Numerous and lengthy "briefs", as the Americans call them, are being exchanged with the result that in civil cases the oral hearing is usually only formal. This fascinating and most important and, I believe, most beneficial aspect of English civil procedure deserves to be underlined, but the reason why it cannot be regarded as the primary characteristic of the English legal system is that in criminal cases Continental and English procedure is the same: there is on the Continent, as

Paralegomena

in England, a single, continuous and oral hearing in criminal matters. What is remarkably different in civil matters only cannot be considered a feature of the legal system as a [177] whole.

There is another aspect of the English legal system which distinguishes it from those on the Continent, but to which I would not attribute pride of place, because it applies to points of law only and has nothing to do with fact finding and therefore again does not comprise the judicial process as a whole. I am referring to the fact that the principle of *jura novit curia* does not apply in England. On the Continent advocates need not, and in some courts are not expected to, make submissions on the law. It is for the judge find and apply it. It is only in the highest courts of appeal which are exclusively concerned with points of law that the lawyers argue them, – usually in writing. In England, on the other hand, law is being "submitted" by Counsel. The judge is not expected to know or to search for it. Sometimes he does carry on his own research but in that event he is expected to put the result to Counsel in order to enable them to make submissions on it and to prevent surprise. In principle, however, and in normal practice, the judge does not have to know or deal with any case that has not been cited to him. In this respect the differences are striking indeed, but I do not think that they have paramount significance, because they relate only to part of the judicial function, viz. the decision on a point of law.

\* \* \*

If one looks for the outstanding characteristic, not of the English legal system, but of the English polity as a whole, there can be only one answer: England is a country without a Constitution. The English doctrine and belief, it is true, is that the country does have a Constitution: it has a Parliament consisting of the House of Commons and the House of Lords, it has a Monarchy, a government, a judiciary, it has a substantial number of substantive rules which relate, for instance, to such matters as the privilege of Parliament, the enactment of legislation, the independence of the judges, the control of executive acts by the courts, the immunity of the Crown and so forth. Many books have been written about Britain's constitutional law. Judicial decisions mention its existence. Lawyers and political scientists distinguish between it and constitutional conventions. Yet constitutional law in England is not more than an illusion. England is a country without a Constitution, for the essence of a Constitution is the existence of checks and balances, of firmly fixed rules which are either unalterable or capable of alteration only in very special conditions the observance of which is subject to some sort of judicial control. In England, on the other hand, a vote by the House of Commons with a majority of one only can, subject to a mere delaying power of the House of Lords, completely change the whole system, for instance, by abolishing the House of Lords or the Monarchy, even the House of Commons itself or, of course, any rule of law. [178] This doctrine of the sovereignty, i. e. the omnipotence of Parliament involves the negation of a Constitution, and to speak of constitutional law is mere eyewash, – dangerous eyewash, because people are liable to put their faith in it and to become at some time greatly disappointed.

All my life I have been oppressed by the state of affairs I have indicated. In more recent years I have become almost terrified, because it has become obvious that there are very strong forces in the country which would be only too readily prepared to exploit the real legal situation for the purpose of imposing an alien system of government upon a naive and unsuspecting country.

In the last resort it is this political danger which has induced me to favour the adoption of a Bill of Rights, possibly in the form of the European Convention on Human Rights.[168] My determination was reinforced, when I had to learn that it was the left which opposes a Bill or Rights, – that is to say, the very political wing which stands ready to exploit to the fullest possible extent the absence of a Constitution or the doctrine of the sovereignty of Parliament. The very people whom one would expect to be in favour of human rights, freedom and liberalism fear the restrictions upon parliamentary dictatorship which, so they hope, will enable them to carry through their "unconstitutional", their revolutionary designs. It is instructive to read the evidence which in 1977/1978 was given to a Select Committee of the House of Lords on a Bill of Rights. If one reads between the lines, if one looks through the fine words, if one analyses the real motives of most of those on the left who spoke, their opposition, so contrary to the radical tradition, particularly in the 18th century, and to the original idea of the Fabians, is firmly derived from their hope that the present system if unchanged facilitates a bloodless, but comprehensive revolution.

In the circumstances it is pleasing to report that to an increasing extent informed opinion has come to promote the idea of a Bill of Rights. Lord Scarman has long been an adherent, but Lord Denning and Lord Salmon have more recently joined the bandwaggon, and even Lord Wilberforce has spoken of the need for a reformed Constitution, albeit in Israel only.[169] Lord Hailsham of St. Marylebone is certainly no opponent, though I am not certain about the intensity of any support from him. I can only hope that by the time these lines are being read real progress will have been achieved.

A Bill of Rights, so congenial to the English tradition, would render it possible to abandon the Strasbourg set-up and thus to get rid of the wholly unacceptable philosophy and practice of the European Court of Justice which I [179] have

---

168 See my article "Britain's Bill of Rights" 94 (1978) L.Q.R. 512 and a number of subsequent contributions.
169 Israel Law Review 14 (1979) 269

Paralegomena

criticised on numerous occasions, but cannot discuss in the present context,[170] and would substitute for it the control by English judges from whom, until a short time ago, I would have expected a saner and sounder approach. I have become somewhat sceptical as a result of certain recent, retrograde decisions and, in particular, of the disastrous decision of the majority of House of Lord in the case of *Rossminster Ltd. v. Inland Revenue*,[171] probably the most regrettable decision of this century, a decision which has caused more despair than any other known to me and which one could not reasonably expect to be rendered in a democratic England. The reasons why it must be regarded as wrong in strict law as well as in legal policy are indicated in a note I wrote with a heavy heart.[172] Since the decision was clearly contrary to the European Convention on Human Rights, it would surely have been contrary to any Bill of Rights, howsoever framed, and it is for this reason that it had to be mentioned in the present context as a most serious incident requiring an English Constitution in the true sense of the word, since without it there is now no guarantee against arbitrariness and abuse. The case, it will be remembered, arose from s.20C of the Taxes Management Act 1970 according to which if "the appropriate judicial authority is satisfied ... that ... there is reasonable ground for suspecting" a tax fraud it may issue a warrant authorising a search of premises and the removal of documents. What happened was that, suspecting a tax fraud committed by the plaintiffs a large number of Inland Revenue officials, accompanied by police officers were held to be entitled to enter private premises at 7 o'clock in the morning and, without disclosing any particulars, to collect and remove documents of the most varied character, including, for instance, children's school reports. In fact nothing further was heard about a prosecution or even a tax case.

Another branch of the law, among many others, which only a Constitution can tame is labour law, and this may well be the reason why the left stands in such fear of a Constitution. English labour law has reached a state which one can only describe as absurd: there are in England two groups entitled to immunity, the Queen and the trade unions. Once again the House of Lords, in a wholly unconvincing, almost paradoxical decision,[173] has quite unnecessarily aggravated the position to an extent which strikes one as almost masochistic. And the Conservative government has approached the problem in so faint-hearted a manner as to defend the closed shop even in Strasbourg, when it had a splendid opportunity of showing that the idea of freedom had not entirely disappeared in England.[174] Freedom, – it is odd how this word is being abused by the left [180]

---

170 See, e.g., [no text]
171 [1980] A.C. 952
172 96 (1980) Law Quarterly Review 201
173
174

**222** Paralegomena

when talking about trade unions. As if their activities were carried on in defence of freedom and did not involve a gross abuse of monopoly power! Monopolies and restrictive practices on the part of enterprises are subject to strict supervision, but are sacrosanct when emanating from trade unions. It is difficult to believe that any sane person with a minimum of detachment and objectivity could support and defend the English system which has brought the country to the brink of ruin. Yet there are many intelligent people who find specious arguments in favour of it. In fact the responsibility of the intelligentsia, particularly in the Universities and the Law Faculties in defending the indefensible is enormous. How can it be changed? I believe that a Bill of Rights may provide the only, albeit faint, hope. If it should prove an ineffective remedy then it is only a complete economic collapse which can save England, – a collapse followed by sensible reconstruction. The alternative will be totalitarianism from the right or the left, and this can hardly be described as a saviour.

I do not by any means wish to suggest that the two examples I have discussed are the sole or even the main reason why I am so much in favour of an English Constitution in general and a Bill of Rights in particular. I selected two which at the moment of writing came into my mind. There are much more important freedoms which deserve and need a guarantee and which are threatened, when 1984 arrives. But I do not propose to embark upon a long political dissertation which can be of no interest to anyone. Rather it is my purpose to propound a few reflections which trouble me as a practical lawyer.

\* \* \*

In my own life there have been few things which I have valued as highly as freedom, – both academic and professional freedom.

I have never been able to understand how anyone who had the choice should prefer the life of a civil servant or an executive in a large enterprise. And in my own firm I have continuously warned against "institutionalisation", against the spirit of the civil service which is ruled by administrative instructions, commands from above, fears of the superior, decisions made by others.

The great attraction of the professional man's life is his independence, and even a large firm with almost fifty partners and almost 400 members of the staff should consist of professional men practising independently, though, of course, responsibly. Independence means that you follow your own judgment rather than that imposed from above. It also means that you follow your own standards. But you cannot be truly independent, unless you are in a position to say No, where such an answer is required. This, indeed, is one of the tests: the intellectual and moral ability to refuse to act or to do what the client requires [181] is an asset which even a poor man must possess if he desires to be a professional man. The temptation of a surgeon to operate upon a rich patient and to charge a high fee for an unnecessary operation must be high. Similarly the temptation for a lawyer to fight profitable proceedings which have no reasonable chance of success or to defend a case with vigour (possibly under the protection of legal aid), when there is no real defence, – such a temptation probably exists, but it is vital to resist it, to remember, to practise and to teach resistance, conscious resistance, even at the risk of losing a client. Sometimes it is not easy to draw the line: the lawyer has to carry out the client's instructions and, in principle, there is nothing wrong in that, – on the contrary it is a duty. But it is different if the client's instructions are unreasonable or perhaps even indefensible and if he rejects advice clearly and honestly given then you should withdraw rather than continue to act, notwithstanding the absence of that complete confidence which must exist between lawyer and client as it must exist between doctor and patient.

What I have said is no doubt platitudinous, but it cannot be said often enough, for there are far too many who abuse their independence or who are unaware of the responsibility which their profession imposes upon them. There is no doubt in my mind that during the fifty years of my professional life standards have gravely deteriorated outside the small number of large and well-established firms of solicitors and that the Law Society has sadly failed to enforce professional behaviour of high quality. I realise that this may be due to the inferiority of the average solicitor and to the Law Society's lack of concern for the enforcement of standards. Whatever the explanation may be, the fact remains but should disappear.

The academic freedom which I was allowed to enjoy has been no less a blessing than the professional freedom. Fortunately, I never wanted anything from anyone. Except on one occasion I never applied for a Chair. I never wanted an honorary doctorate. I never wanted any appointment, nomination or honour. I was always free to write or to say what I thought or felt and did not have to look right or left. I could be entirely honest and I hope that I acted accordingly. In academic life this, I believe, is rare. Most scholars, for one reason or another, have to consider others. They must not give offence to people who are very sensitive and regard disagreement as something personal. They cannot even criticize, for they may not be forgiven by their elders and betters. In judging academic work it is frequently necessary to ask whether there were perhaps special reasons, unconnected with the issue which required a certain lack or reduction of intellectual independence or, on the contrary, a measure of hostility. Such considerations, of course, are evidence of dishonesty. My suggestion is that they should be alien to academic life and [182] activity, but are unfortunately being practised by many who are or believe to be bound to have regard to extraneous matters.

This is particularly so in the case of book reviews. I have always felt free to speak my mind, to be completely frank. If I am asked to review a book people will know what I think. I know that I have made enemies in this way, but I have also acquired respect. The odd thing, though, is that as I grew older fewer books have been offered to me for review. Neither the Law Quarterly Review nor the Modern Law Review with which I used to be so closely connected have for many years sent me any books for review. It seems that this is a business which editors prefer to have done by younger authors. I do not complain, because in most cases reviewing is a bore. I merely state what seems to be a paradox.

\* \* \*

The academic freedom allowed to me in England was, of course, complete, for I never was inside any academic group or organisation, and while I have from time to time given lectures at the International Law Club or similar bodies in Oxford and Cambridge, I have never had the opportunity of teaching. I think it is a defect of the English Universities that they forego the great advantages which Contineutal Universities derive from honorary professor – or lectureship, that is to say, from the appointment of outsiders such as practising lawyers, judges or others (to mention only candidates in the field of law) who sacrifice part of their time to give courses or lectures, holding seminars or discussion groups. Is it the damnable idea of the closed shop which in England precludes the opening of the doors of the Universities to outside teachers?

Whatever the answer may be, in my case post-war Germany most generously afforded me the opportunities of teaching which England had denied. I have already referred to this part of my life as it developed from 1959 onwards, but at this point I feel I should pay tribute not only to the extraordinary generosity and decency shown by the Federal Republic to Hitler's victims, but also to the sanity and strength of a country which 35 years ago was prostrate and gave the impression of remaining so for decades.

It was not only the legislator who assumed immense liabilities towards the victims of Nazi persecution. It was also the judiciary which, in a quite unique manner, succeeded in mastering the injustices of the Hitlerian years. Thus, the Federal Supreme Court developed the theory of the absolute injustice, of the non-law which, irrespective of its legislative origin, was not at any time part of the true German law. It was a theory wholly opposed to the positivism and literalism of most English judges, a theory which met with far too little recognition or even study outside Germany and which, I am convinced, is expressive of the natural law origin of all true law. It led to the criminal [183] and tortious liability of persons who believed to be and in fact were acting in strict accordance with Hitler's "laws" (which were not law). Or as late as 1979 it led to the great decision of the Federal Supreme Court which, in view of the special history of Jews in Germany, recognised every German Jew as entitled to demand an injunction against anyone who denies the murder of millions of Jews during the Hitler period, – the defence that an attack upon a group is not a libel upon any one member of the group was held to be inapplicable.[175] A State the judiciary of which is so true to the judicial ethos stands on firm foundations. In fact the whole of the Federal Republic's history, with the great wealth it has created and the impressive health of its industrial relations, proves its inner soundness which strikes the observer with particular sadness when he thinks of England's sickness predominantly created by her trade unions, their incredible stupidity, their irresponsibility which seems to be almost designed to lead the country to ruin such as their masters in Moscow desire it. Take one single example: while I am writing these lines the workers in the British steel industry are on strike. They do not receive any payments from their unions. They live on social security payments provided by the very State against which the strike is directed and the economy of which is bound to be severly damaged. In Germany the State makes such payments only in very special conditions and then by way of loan which is being recovered on the resumption of work by way of deduction from wages. Where does sanity, where does madness lie?

I seem to remember that there is not a word about all this in the Donovan Report, one of the most negative, uninformed and useless documents ever produced. As we now know from the Diaries of Richard Crossman and Barbara Castle, two of the most illuminating books that appeared in England for many decades, not even the Labour Government of the day derived any help from a document which might have been written by and for trade unions, when the whole point was to bring them under control. The Labour Government of the day was too weak to achieve [it]. The Parliamentary Labour Party was too dishonest to support the Heath Government in enacting and enforcing the Industrial Relations Act 1971 which to a large extent did no more than Donovan and later Mrs. Castle's *In Place of Strife* had prescribed. And many lawyers teaching labour law found the legal arguments which allegedly made it inevitable to have a government by trade unions for trade unions, a State within a State.

My dear friend Sir Otto Kahn-Freund was unfortunately one of those who carry a very large share of the responsibility for the intolerable conditions which have underminded England's strength. I can say this without disloyalty to the memory of one whom I loved dearly, for I have often argued the matter with him, – without success, though at the very end of his life when even [184] Mr. Callaghan's Government began to see and warn against the dangers which Mr. Callaghan's interventions in 1968 so prominently increased and extended, he seemed slightly to change his tune. He wrote a large part of the Donovan Report with its main policy of "hands off the unions". He had much to do with the very

---

175 BGHZ 75, 160 = NJW 1980, 45.

careful selection of the foreign experiences which the Report used or mentioned. He argued against the idea of learning from foreign experiences in his Chorley lecture. He wrote a book on *Labour and the Law* which in far too many contexts was a wholly destructive criticism of the Industrial Relations Act 1971. He discovered much of the intellectual foundations which were intended to clothe an unjustifiable development with legal respectability. He was in this sense a guilty man, – but it will take many years and events of great bitterness for the general body of intelligent observers and lawyers to appreciate his unfortunate influence. Yet I repeat: he was a dear friend, a great lawyer and a remarkable personality.

\* \* \*

When speaking about the German doctrine of "non-law" I referred to the English lawyer's addiction to literalism and positivism and have given two examples which I could easily multiply. Yet there is another strand of thought in much of modern English law which cannot be left out of account. This is what I may call the philosophy of merit. I believe that at the end of a case a judge stands back and asks himself: Who deserves to win? Who has the merits? He then proceeds to find the legal reasons to support the result intuitively arrived at, – I say intuitively, but realises, of course, that intuition is not merely a hunch, but is derived from experience, from surveying the whole of the facts and inspecting what is behind the external facade. If this is correct then law is largely a lie: it is no more than words made to support a result extraneously reached.

I believe that in the large majority of cases the judicial reasoning proceeds as indicated. The judge is not always conscious of his process of reasoning. But this does not alter the facts. The judge who is fully conscious of the process and who in fact practices it with great persistence is Lord Denning, and his influence on this aspect too has been enormous, for since the Second World War his approach has, consciously or more probably unconsciously, been followed by most. The cold, logical, strictly legal method of reasoning and reaching results has gone out of fashion. It is a broad assessment of merits that is decisive. I am far from suggesting that this is always so or that every case permits a process of reasoning such as I have indicated. Nor can I positively prove my point. But I am speaking about the majority of cases and my judgment is based not only on experience, feeling, instinct, but also to some extent on remarks which are liable to be and have in my hearing been made during [185] the course of the argument. Hence it has become my invariable practice to look for the objective merits, when I get a new case. I greatly regret this development, for it does involve a measure of arbitrariness. I once talked to Lord Denning about it. I had lost a case before him and shortly afterwards, when I met him, he said to me: "There was no merit in your man's case". I argued with him and said that it was wrong to assess merit as a guide to decision without having heard argument on the pros and cons, but that this very subject was not permitted to be argued, since, allegedly, it was irrelevant to any issue. The great man's answer was: "We see through all this – we do not need an argument on merit". Since then I have always instructed my Counsel somehow to make the points necessary to show that we had some "merit", something of that elusive quality that might appeal to the Court's sense of justice.

The result is that a case which is intrinsically sound but against which a technical defence may be raised will in all probability succeed, – the court will find a way of letting it succeed. A good example is *Adams v. National Bank of Greece*.[176] Conversely, a case which has or may be said to have no merit will fail, however weak the defence may be. An example is *U.G.S. Finance Co. Ltd. v. National Bank of Greece*.[177] To the latter type of case there is only one exception to which lawyers should give much closer attention: the case should be brought by a widow in, say, Northumberland who preferably is legally aided. Where such remedial action is taken a balance is established which will compensate for the lack of merit.

What I have said here about the philosophy of merit may strike some readers as cynical. It must, however, be accepted as a fact of legal life. The odd thing is that those concerned with jurisprudence have preferred to continue their interminable battle of words and neglected the realities. Is there not more to be said for or against the philosophy of merit? If, as I believe, it ought to have no place in the law how is to be eradicated? The first step, surely, is to be aware of its existence and its force, – and for this reason I have always drawn my students' attention to its operation. But what is the next step? How do we get rid of an attitude of mind which, if followed by lesser men than Lord Denning, constitutes a great danger?

It should not be thought that the attitude I am discussing is confined to England. I am sure it also operates in Germany. The best example is a decision of the Federal Supreme Court.[178] In the words of a close friend, Jews in post-war Germany are protected like ancient monuments. In the case in question a Jewish refugee claimed repayment of a loan of zloty granted by her [186] before the war, which in strict law had become worthless. The Supreme Court adopted a solution which allowed her a substantial measure of satisfaction, but which in law was in my view unjustifiable. I attacked the decision in a lengthy note in a German periodical.[179] When the Official Reports appeared, the case started with the words: "The plaintiff, a Jewess..." The fact that the plaintiff was Jewish had

---

176 Above p.
177 Above p.
178 BGHZ 43, 162.
179 Juristenzeitung 1965, 448.

nothing whatever to do with the legal issues before the court. But it explained the decision in the most striking manner.

A few sentences earlier I mentioned legal aid. This reminded me of the necessity for a few words about professionalism.

In my youth in Germany legal aid did not exist. Lawyers were allocated to poor persons according to a rota and had to do the work without remuneration. My father used to tell me that poor persons' cases were a *nobile officium* and had to be handled with special care. I was brought up to regard this as characteristic of the professional man's sense of propriety. Accordingly, I was greatly shocked when later I worked for a time in a large lawyers' office in Munich and on enquiry was told that it was their custom to find ways and means to avoid poor persons cases.

In England legal aid is paid for by the State. Yet there are big firms which refuse to do it. This seems entirely wrong to me. Even if it were true that legally aided cases do not pay sufficiently for those firms whose overheads in times of inflation are enormous, even if legal aid were a sacrifice a professional man should accept every case that falls within the scope of his activity in general. But the existence of such a principle is a matter of continuous argument in the large firms.

On the one hand it is said that, in view of the expense of maintaining an accounting- and computer system the mere opening of a new file costs £30, and that therefore one cannot afford small or otherwise unprofitable cases. On the other hand it is my experience that every client brings a second one, that every case means that there will be another one from the same client or a third one introduced by him. Admittedly, it is necessary and unobjectionable to refuse County Court work or criminal cases. But even there an exception is called for. One should never reject work introduced by foreign lawyers. Contact with lawyers, particularly foreign lawyers is one of the most important ingredients of one's goodwill and very much on a par with the preeminently valuable connection with banks.

Speaking generally, every lawyer will find it easy to lose his goodwill. It is very difficult to create it. At the same time it is the essence of a profession as opposed to an institution that one must not ever take the [187] continued existence of one's goodwill for granted. Young lawyers brought up in a large firm are liable to be unaware of, or to forget, this elementary lesson. It is one of the functions of a senior partner in a large firm to teach the elements of the true professional spirit.

Another, and much more important, element of it is that the interest of the client must always be paramount. This is what distinguishes a professional man from a business man such as a merchant banker. Your own financial advantage, your convenience, your ulterior interests have no place in your process of arriving at decisions, rendering advice or taking action, if you belong to a profession and wish to be true to it. The conduct is in every respect an entirely

# Paralegomena

fiduciary one. The point is so important that it cannot be exaggerated: in a well-run firm it should be the rule that no partner should hold any shares in a client company so as to eliminate the danger of the personal interest interfering with the protection of the client company's interest.

The considerations which I have indicated are the reason why I have come to look so critically at the activities of merchant banks as they have developed since the Second World War. Merchant banks render advice for which they usually charge wholly exorbitant fees and which could just as well, though much more cheaply, be given by stockbrokers, lawyers and accountants. Sorne of the merchant banks even purport to advise on law, tax or accountancy. One day the courts will be called upon to decide whether and to what extent these advisory activities impose fiduciary duties upon banks. It is to be hoped that the courts will be very strict. I believe, however, that banks are conscious of the danger and will not allow the point to be decided. At any rate it is my experience that, probably for the reason I have mentioned, they prefer generous settlements to litigation! The fees which they charge for the advisory work is so unjustifiably high, particularly in relation to the fees of the professional man, that that part of a merchant bank's income must not be jeopardised.

A further ingredient of the professional man's attitude is his absolute duty of observing confidentiallty. Nobody will deny the principle. But its application may give rise to doubts. Are you allowed, while in company of others, to tell a story without mentioning names? The answer must be in the negative, for there might be someone who knows the persons referred to. I have known occasions, when it was good or necessary policy even to ignore a client in the company of others, so as to prevent the conclusion that he knows me, possibly professionally. I remember many years ago a divorce case I had for a friend of ours. Naturally I did not mention it at home. One fine day Eleonore met my client and, so it appeared, was about the only one of her friends and acquaintances who was unaware of the pending proceedings. The greatest sinners against the principle of confidentiality are members of the Bar. There is [188] in my experience no greater hot-bed of talk than the Temple or Lincoln's Inn. Nothing remains unknown in this small and narrow world. At the same time, oddly enough, secrets are never abused. Thus I would have no hesitation to instruct a barrister in Chambers to which the opposing party's barrister also belongs, – provided the Chambers are one of the renowned ones. Most lay clients, all foreign clients find this unacceptable, but in Chambers of the type I am thinking of no I member would ever read another member's papers.

Having mentioned what some may regard as the shackles of professionalism I would like to conclude by emphasising again its great attraction: this is the independence which a member of a profession enjoys or ought to enjoy. He is not subject to directions. He does not want to obtain anything from anyone. He does

**230**                                                                    Paralegomena

not care about popularity, recognition, decoration. This, it is true, is a picture of the ideal world which a beginner often finds it difficult to live up to. But he should persevere. If he does his reward is bound to come. He will succeed, he will be respected and sometimes even loved. His unwillingness to compromise, to deviate from the highest standards even when it is difficult to observe them, – these are great assets which will bear fruit in every sense of the term.

* * *

The relationship between a barrister and his solicitor is normally one of subordination. The barrister is supposed and believed to know the law, the solicitor is ignorant and carries out, as a rule uncritically, what he is told to do. Some years ago I wrote an article on the problem of fusion of the professions. In my first draft I had some very outspoken comments on the average solicitor's lack of quality and knowledge. I toned them down considerably, but here I am free to speak my mind. I am convinced that the standard of solicitors should not be judged by that of the very few large and prominent firms which enjoy a wide reputation. The average is quite different and, I am convinced, infinitely lower with the result that the relationship between the average barrister and the average solicitor is much more that of teacher and pupil than that of equals. I have come across a barrister, curiously enough a member of a first class set of Chambers, who invariably in his opinions issued commands: "my solicitors will do this or that", "my solicitors are to…etc.". This may be typical.

I confess, however, that my own experience has been entirely different. In the first place almost all barristers with whom I worked were or became friends, – I am thinking, in particular, of such close friends as John Foster, Tom Strangman and Mark Littman, – not to mention many others, particularly Michael Kerr, who belong to a different category. Secondly, I have been [189] exceedingly careful in the selection of barristers and always took the view that the best were just good enough. The result has been that a disproportionate number of those whom I used to instruct became judges and, indeed reached the highest positions. Lord Wilberforce, Lord Russell of Killowen, Lord Simon of Glaisdale, Lord Justices Megaw, Templeman, Oliver, Griffiths, Kerr, Mr. Justice Parker, Dillon, Milmo, Lloyd, Lincoln, Mocatta, Comyn, – these are the principal ones with whom I worked while they were at the Bar. Quinton Hogg advised me in an important matter a few hours before he became Lord Chancellor. In 1940 I consulted Lord Denning on a point connected with the Trading with the Enemy Act – Mrs. Beaumont-Thomas, an English woman, was in France on holiday when she became insane and was detained in an institution. Was she "resident" in enemy territory so that her property became subject to the control of the Custodian of

Enemy Property? Denning K.C. gave me an opinion telling the Custodian off in no uncertain terms.

Is it conceited if I say that the high quality of the barristers with whom I used to work and whose subsequent careers proved their superiority was responsible for the very special relationship which I always enjoyed? We were co-operating on equal terms. Lines of conduct as well as points of detail were discussed and clarified by an exchange of views. It would not happen that my suggestions were not listened to or brushed aside. Frequently the authorities were looked at and analysed together. Acadamic material was consulted and it would not happen to me that a barrister whom I had decided to consult would refuse to have regard to academic writings. Nor would I ever go to so uneducated a member of the bar who, when he had become a Lord Justice – he is now a law lord would speak of "a United States textbook written by a Mr. Williston."[180] (To speak in this way of the late Professor Samuel Williston of Harvard University, the author of a text book of some 12 volumes on the law of contracts is the same as if an American were to speak about "a Mr. Blackstone".) Nor would I ever have contact with a member of the bar who, when a Lord Justice of Appeal, would say to Counsel who had referred to books on private international law by Martin Wolff or American authors: "Why should we look at what all these foreigners say?" (This was said by Lord Justice (Arthian) Davies in one of my cases, but fortunately is no longer typical. The Common Market is one of the many causes for the opening of frontiers, the diminution of insularity which in recent years has taken place.)

It was Lord Denning who has contributed more than anyone else to that development. At times his leadership seemed to be even too eager, but he is a man whose enthusiasm and fervour sometimes tempts him to propound principles which appear too widely formulated. This is frequently the characteristic of a great [190] legislator rather than a judge and does not in any way detract from his greatness. That he was and, happily still is one of England's greatest judges and, probably, the greatest judge of the 20th century cannot in my view be open to doubt. It is not only the splendid English he writes or his profound knowledge of the law, history and literature or his superb skill as a presiding judge, his unfailing politeness, his humility which makes him very willing to listen to an argument, to test it and if appropriate to change his mind. It is also and in particular his unerring sense of right and wrong, just and unjust, of good and bad that characterizes his judgments. On many occasions this sense of justice is liable to lead him astray and his battles with the House of Lords are very frequently due to the contrast between the wish to do justice and the wish to apply the law in its traditional sense. In a very large number of instances the decisions of the House of Lords reversing Lord Denning and his colleagues in the Court of Appeal have

---

180 Cia. Barca de Panama S.A. v. George Wimpey & Co. Ltd., (1980) 1 Ll. L.R. 598, at p. 609.

**232**                                                                 Paralegomena

been narrowminded and shortsighted, usually because the House of Lords preferred literalism to justice. To put one's faith in narrowly construed words should be an unacceptable process of legal reasoning. It is a process wholly alien to Lord Denning. And there are other features of his influence which deserve recognition. Few judges have done more for the creation of an effective and viable administrative law in England, for the judicial control of the Executive. Few judges have done more in fighting monopolies, including in particular trade unions abusing their immunities. Few judges have done more for a sensible reform of the law, however revolutionary the methods may have been. Look at the way in which Lord Denning achieved a change in the English law relating to foreign currency debts, – *Miliagos v. George Frank (Textiles) Ltd.*[181] If he had not ventured, by using the flimsiest of arguments, to get away from the shackles imposed by a decision of the House of Lords in which he himself had participated in 1961 we might still suffer from a legal rule which was liable not only to undermine the authority of English law in the field of commercial law, but also to expose it to ridicule. How many men have displayed similar moral courage?

It has been my good fortune to know Lord Denning personally for many years. When he was instrumental in merging the Grotius Society to whose Executive Council I used to belong, and the society of Comparative Law and to create the British Institute of International and Comparative Law. I saw him regularly at Council meetings, for he was and is the Chairman of the Institute and belonged to its Executive Council since its creation. I met him on many other semiofficial, semi-social occasions. On every single one his kindness warmed my heart. When the first F.A. Mann lecture was given in 1977 by Lord Diplock, he sat next to me and in the evening attended a dinner given by some friends. When in 1980 his book *Due Process of Law* appeared, I was not only amazed and pleased, [191] but also shocked and humiliated to read:

> "Of all my learned friends, Francis Mann is the most learned of all. Long ago, as a young man, he came from Germany, Since then he has become the head of an important firm of City solicitors: and at the same time the exponent in our literature of a wealth of legal knowledge."

Words of such generosity are, I fear, wholly undeserved and I am almost ashamed to read and repeat them. They do not characterize me. They characterize Denning's extreme kindness and benevolence.

* * *

---

181 [1976] A.C. 443

Paralegomena        **233**

Many of the men who were or became judges I met as a result of my membership of Committees and Working Parties. This work started in 1952, when the Private International Law Committee was formed at the instigation of Sir Eric Beckett. Justice Wynn-Parry was appointed Chairman. Although I have no certain knowledge; it has always been my belief that I owe my membership to him and that his eye fell on me, when in 1951 I gave evidence for six days before him in the case of *Hinrichsen v. Novello* of which I spoke earlier.[182] The Committee sat from 1952 to 1964, when it was allowed to die, without any mention and without any explanation; it was a very odd and somewhat puzzling procedure. Yet the Committee had done some considerable amount of work, – on arbitration, domicile and foreign currency in particular. Some seven of its Reports were published. Looking back on its work, it is too early to say whether its plea for the retention of the unity of husband's and wife's domicile was right. It should certainly be clear that its proposals on the reform of the conception of domicile ought to have been accepted; they failed primarily on account of wholly misconceived opposition by the American Chamber of Commerce and others led by Arthur Goodhart who, for personal reasons, was greatly interested in maintaining the outmoded English idea about domicile of origin and other peculiarities.

In addition, however, there were a number of Working Parties under the chairmanship of Lord Scarman, Mr. Justice Cooke and Michael Kerr after the Law Commission had come into existence in 1965. This was a continuous and timeconsuming activity which, I am inclined to think, was the ultimate cause for the C.B.E. being conferred upon me in 1980. The subjects were varied: the codification of the law of contracts (fortunately abandoned after a few years' work), the recognition of foreign divorces, standard conditions and terms eventually dealt with in the Unfair Contract Terms Act, the implication of the EEC's Judgment Convention of 1968 and so forth. Moreover there were many occasions when I submitted memoranda or notes on specific points or was [192] informally consulted by Government Departments and others. When the Law Reform Committee was concerned with limitation of actions, I submitted a memorandum on the international implications of the subject. The Committee suggested[183] that the subject required separate investigation and this was in fact carried out by the Law Commission[184] which I am delighted to say at last took up the right attitude and, in particular, suggested the abolition of the wholly un-

---

182 Above p.
183 Cmnd. 6923 (1977)
184 Law Commission Working Paper No. 75

**234** Paralegomena

satisfactory and unjustifiable rule established the majority of the House of Lords in *Black Clawson International v. Papierwerke Zellstoff Aschaffenbuurg.*[185]

It is easy not to write about this type of work done over a period of about thirty years. Few people can have any idea how hard the work was. The amount of paper that has to be read before any meeting is usually very large. It is necessary to think about the proposals, sometimes to carry out independent research, on other occasions to make suggestions or even to write papers for circulation. All this has to be done in one's so-called spare time. I am convinced that if one were to add up all the time, I spent on this type of work it would come to much more than a year.

\* \* \*

I mentioned just now the C.B.E. which I received in 1980 and this brings me to the subject of honours. I realise, of course, that that decoration, conferred by the Queen, was the highest honour given to me and I am truly thankful for it, for I appreciate that for one with my foreign past tne honour is greater than for a blue-blooded Englishman. Yet I confess that in many ways the academic honours I received – the honorary doctorate of the University of Kiel, one of the principal centres of research in international law, the honorary membership of the American Society of International Law, the Membership of the Institut de Droit International, the Fellowship of the British Academy – gave me even more satisfaction. The citation of the C.B.E., it is true, specifies "for services to international law" and is therefore much better than a citation such as "for services for export" or "the rights of solicitors". Yet the other honours were conferred upon me by other lawyers, by people who knew my academic work and had studied it critically. Their judgment is worth a good deal and if, as in my case, one is an outsider and does not have the full support of a chair at a University it is doubly pleasing for academics who have a full professorship are in a position to reciprocate and are therefore more likely to be at the receiving end. This applies in particular to honorary doctorates. On the Continent many of them are bought with donations. Everywhere you will probably be able to obtain an honorary degree from, say, Paris, by persuading your faculty to confer an honorary degree on a Paris professor. All this did not apply in my case. I may say, I confess with a measure of pride that whatever I achieved academically is due to what my colleagues believed to be merit.

The fact that, although the spirit of the common law was not injected into me at birth and although I am not an academic, I was in 1974 elected a fellow of the British Academy gave me very special satisfaction, – until the year 1980, when the Academy refused to expel the traitor Anthony Blunt. I was unavoidably abroad,

---

185 [1975] A.C. 591

when the Annual General Meeting took place and so resolved. Subsequently I wrote a letter of protest to the Editor of *The Times* which, very significantly, was not published. Some Fellows resigned to give striking expression to their view. I decided to stay and fight from the inside for the reversal of a decision which I considered most unfortunate, but characteristic of the moral weakness which, I greatly fear, at present pervades a large part of the English intelligentsia. My dilemma was fortunately resolved when Blunt was persuaded to resign and I as well as many others thinking like myself were thus put in a position to remain Fellows; that the foolish A.J.P. Taylor resigned on the absurd ground that "the Academy should be concerned with the qualities and qualifications by which a member was elected and not dwell on other issues", was in my view a happy solution, though characteristic of the lack of logic and moral fibre which distinguishes the left.

The terrifying lack of moral standards, of steadfastness of purpose and of a proper sense of values which this unfortunate affair brought to light was most clearly and most shockingly expressed by *The Times* in a leader of 22 August 1980 which deserves to be remernbered as a monument to England's decline:

> Mr. Taylor was right to point to the dangers of allowing any consideration other than academic distinction to influence the selection of fellows. There is no dispute about the professor's eminence in his field of art history. It is true that treason is not a matter of private conduct, nor an ordinary crime: it threatens the very liberties that the free pursuit of scholarship depends on. But treason and politics are necessarily connected, and it would be highly dangerous to create a precedent for selection on anything resembling political grounds. If the academy had wished to dissociate itself from Professor Blunt's actions, it could have passed a resolution to that effect without expelling him, as Lord Robbins suggested.

It cannot have been often that an issue of public interest has been so blurred by a responsible leader-writer. But he had supped with the devil and therefore expected the fellows of the British Academy to dine with him.

Fortunately, my opportunity of taking a public stand came in 1981, when Mr. A.J.P. Taylor and Sir Kenneth Dover were moved to write letters to *Encounter*, [194] defending the Academy's conduct. The issue for September 1981 carried my reply which I feel deserves to be repeated here, which seems to have silenced my opponents and which brought me a number of welcome letters of support, particularly one from my old friend and client F.A. Hayek:

> Mr. A.J.P. Taylor and Sir Kenneth Dover (Encounter June) disclaim any intention to revive the Blunt affair. But having done so, they must put up with a reply by a Fellow of the British Academy who unfortunately was unable to attend last year's Annual General Meeting and who ever since has considered the Academy's failure to expel Blunt as one of the most discreditable incidents of recent academic history in Britain.

First as to the law. According to Rule 11 of the Bye-laws the AGH "may remove the name of any person from the list of Fellows on the ground that he or she is not a fit and proper person to be a Fellow." The words are not subject to any qualification. They cannot be understood as limiting the power of removal to grounds appertaining to scholarship, as Rule 27 relating to elections seems, but cannot intend to do; for it is impossible to believe that it is open to the Council to nominate for election a person who has been convicted of or has confessed to a serious crime, let alone one of the most serious crimes of all, viz. treason. But, even if Rule 27, by its reference to Article 6 of the Charter, should contemplate exclusively academic achievements, the absence of any such reference in Rule 11 underlines the generality of the power of removal.

However this may be, it is distressing to learn from Mr. Taylor's letter that in voting against the expulsion of Blunt he believed he was actlng as one of "the defenders of intellectual liberty". This involves a confusion of frightening dimensions. Is it suggested that intellectual liberty implies the right to commit treason or that treason is the justifiable product of intellectual liberty? Can it seriously be thought that a spy and traitor necessarily acts in defence of intellectual liberty? Have we so completely forgotten the meaning of language as to be unable to distinguish between crime and motive (though we know nothing whatever about the true character of Blunt's motives)? Can it reasonably be believed that if Blunt's misdeeds had been known in 1955 he would have been elected or anybody would have ventured to propose him?

One of the most painful aspects of the Blunt affair (which, if he had not resigned, would have compelled me to leave so mealy-mouthed a body as the British Academy in 1980) is the lack of moral fibre which the vote at the AGM disclosed. Can we no longer recognize and condemn a crime, when it is admitted and plain to see? Must I or a foreign Corresponding Fellow or one of our Honorary Fellows at the annual dinner sit next to a self-confessed criminal? Is there, for purposes of membership, any difference between a traitor, a murderer or a thief? (There is a hint at l'affaire Dreyfus in Mr. Taylor's letter: but Dreyfus was innocent, Blunt admitted to be guilty.)

I shall defend real intellectual liberty to the last, but I deny the right of anyone to call treason an act of intellectual liberty or a man "fit and proper" for membership of the British Academy merely because he is academically distinguished. This is a matter, not of party or institutional politics, but of commonsense and very elementary moral values. It is paradoxical that by his resignation a traitor enabled the Academy to maintain them.

\* \* \*

It is the same evasion, the same refusal to face facts, the same [195] indifference which clouded the judgment of the liberals and leftists (and a good many others) in the years before the war. To commit treason in favour of the Soviet Union may be a crime, but is forgivable. To pursue a policy of appeasement vis-a-vis the Nazis may be contrary to Britain's true interest but is permitted, because it defers the evil day and buys a short time of peace. It is the same shortsightedness, the same mealy-mouthedness.

Or look at the sanctity of breaches of confidentiality which the media are propagating. If a car is stolen, no journalist would suggest that it is open to him to handle stolen goods, to become a receiver and to drive the stolen car or to use the stolen petrol. When my documents are stolen and the journalist believes them to interest his public (which is very likely to be the case), he claims to be immune from prosecution, not required to disclose the identlty of the thief, free to publish, permitted to retain the documents, or copies of them. Both as a matter of law and as a matter of morality or public interest the case is indefensible, but the media are putting it forward in all seriousness and with a ton of superior knowlea.ge that is nauseating. Again, it is the inability or unwillingness to distinguish right and wrong which precludes the media even to acknowledge the authority of elementary rules of law or the decision of three courts and nine judges. Is this the standard which the British public is now asked to observe?

Or look at the most instructive field of trade union activities. Wherever they are discussed, you have to listen or to read about rights which as everyone with the slightest degree of intelligence can recognise, are contrary to the public interest and to the law as it should be. As a result of many wrong turns taken at various stages of history English law is not what it should be and grants trade unions a unique measure of immunity. Under the protection of that immunity the public interest and the true law which protects it are being abused to an intolerable extent. Yet you will find many members of the intelligentsia on the left who defend and justify the indefensible and unjustifiable. The employer collects the trade union dues and pays them over. Yet he cannot obtain redress from a trade union for any wrong it does to him. The employer must suffer a strike and allow himself to be ruined. But the moment he applies the means open to him and embarks upon a lock-out he is in the wrong and subject to abuse. Increases in wages, unrelated to productivity, are annually obtained and must be conceded by any employer who cannot afford a ruinous strike. The consequence: inflation. If you imagine for one moment that all wage increases come to an end, – inflation would obviously be over. That end cannot be achieved by what is euphemestically called an "income policy", for experience shows that such a policy is either not observed or, where it is observed, merely defers the evil day and leads to even greater inflation. That end can only be [196] achieved by a free labour conflict and a sense of responsibility such as most German unions have displayed in recent years or by the force of economic laws such as bankruptcies, unemployment, retrenchment. As soon as you adopt this policy (as the Conservatives very rightly were compelled to do in 1979), hordes of noisy economists fill the media with their attacks upon a policy which they must know to be right and which is right unless and until a better one is put forward. This positive step has not been taken and therefore you again notice the intellectual dishonesty which I am trying to expose and which I find so deeply disturbing. This is *not* a matter of party politics (although, unfortunately, the left is so treating the problem). It is a simple matter of observation and willingness to be constructive and positive and, I am tempted to say, objective. The answer which you are liable to receive is that intellectual objectivity is an illusion, does not exist at all, cannot exist, for everything is dictated by politics and political prejudices. This is the most destructive thought you can imagine. It involves the denial of any academic and scholarly approach or judgment and reduces everything to the level of election manifestos. It may be in harmony with the teachings of one Karl Marx. But this is no proof of truth. On the contrary, it is a reason for suspicion and circumspection.

\* \* \*

I cannot help saying that the observations wnich I have just ventured to make are something of an embarassment to me. All my life I hankered after an opportunity of taking part in public affairs and trying to influence them by the spoken or written word. No such chance was ever offered to me. In particular in England I felt that it was not in line with the circumstances in which I was allowed to come and live here to intervene in public by the expression of opinions on matters of a political character. It is my belief that a great part of the position I acquired is due to the fact that I strictly confined myself to the narrow field I had made my own and for the rest kept my mouth shut.

Even in regard to the law I adhered to the confines of the law of money, the conflict of laws and public international law. This had several additional reasons. In these fields I could build up my own library which is highly specialised and enables me to work to a very large extent at home, independently of libraries. This was most important, for throughout my life it was only on Saturdays that I could go to libraries and all the scholarly work I did had to be done in the evenings and during weekends at home. This was possible only, because I had a very large, specialised library of my own. Thus my field of work was limited by my resources. In the course of years they grew very considerably, not only because I bought books, but also because very [197] many authors sent me their work, in particular offprints of articles published in periodicals, *Festschriften* etc. with the result that I now possess some thirty large boxes of offprints in alphabetical order. All this material is being kept in the office, because there would be no room for it at home. Whenever I am engaged in writing something, I have to carry the books, articles and so forth from the office to my home and back, though in recent years I have sometimes taken taxis. In order to facilitate this transportation, I left all periodicals to which I subscribe unbound, so as to enable me to carry a single issue rather than a heavy volume. So my specialisation had practical as well as academic roots. But it also meant that, for better or worse, I refrained from doing work on subjects in which I was not specialised and kept away from public affairs.

I believe that there were only two exceptions. In the 1950's I planned to write a large work, on a very broad comparative basis, about the taking of property. The starting point, of course, was the international law of confiscation in which I had become greatly interested. Very soon it became clear to me that no work on the international law of confiscation could be written without first laying a firm foundation of the standards prevailing in representative systems of municipal law. It was for these reasons that I started with the history of expropriation and in 1959 I published in the Law Quarterly Review an article on the *Outlines of a History of Expropriation*,[186] of which Arthur Goodhart always used to say that it was the best thing ever written by me. This article indicated at the very end the heading of further instalments which I then intended to study. Unfortunately I soon ascertained that it was beyond my powers and probably beyond the powers of a single scholar to continue and complete the undertaking. The research of the comparative law was too demanding for the available material was enormous, the work presupposes a knowledge of languages which I did not possess and library facilities which were not available in London. In order to illustrate my point let me mention a single example, namely the conception of the just or equitable or reasonable or "full" compensation. These are expressions which occur in public international law as well as in municipal law. I am convinced that their meaning and effect in the former is determined by their meaning and effect in the latter as determined by a process of comparative study. For a long time I looked for collaborators who would undertake the research together with me and under my direction. I never found them. Probably I lack the ability of doing and directing team work of an academic character, – this requires a special gift of organisation which I lack and which I would be loath to acquire. The net effect is that my work on the taking of property was not written and that my article of 1959 remained an isolated piece. [198] Admittedly I did write a few pieces on the international law aspects and to some extent used the comparative method in doing so, but this is far removed from the ambitious scheme I had in mind. A few years ago a professor from Cornell Law School came to see me in order to discuss the continuation of the work which my article had indicated as a program. Although I gave him every encourageuent I never heard anything further about the plan. Perhaps these lines will be read by someone who will be stimulated into taking it up.

The other exception relates to the implications of the European Convention for Human Rights and Fundamental Freedoms. Since this is included in a treaty, it does not at first sight fall outside my usual field of work. But like the EEC law

---

186  75 (1959) L.Q.R. 188

**240**  Paralegomena

which also stems from a treaty its development has taken a course which is far removed from the application and interpretation of a treaty and has, perhaps unfortunately, acquired the character of a constitutional text subject to judicial interpretation of such width and comprehensiveness that the international lawyer is stunned. However, in England the Convention on Human Rights has a very special significance, for it was never "ratified" by Parliament, never incorporated into a statute binding within the United Kingdom. All that happened was that a Conservative Government signed it and successive Governments, Labour and Conservative, without reference to Parliament, accepted Article 25 which grants the right of individual petition. The Strasbourg Commission and the Strasbourg Court of Human Rights have therefore become supreme tribunals in the United Kingdom, notwithstanding the absence of any parliamentary sanction. This astonishing situation worried me for many years. When I received the invitation to give the Blackstone Lecture in Oxford in 1978, I decided to speak about the paradox which existed in British constitutional law. The title of my lecture, later published in the Law Quarterly Review, was Britain's Bill of Rights.[187] It was an exercise in constitutional law. The subject has continued to fascinate me. Indeed, it directed me towards more general questions of English constitutional law and, in particular, to the question whether it is possible to speak about English constitutional law at all, whether England is not a country without a Constitution. The answer depends, of course, on the definition of a Constitution, but I fear must be in the negative, whatever the definition may be: as mentioned above a country in which a minority of the members of Parliament representing possibly a minority of the popular vote may with a majority of a single vote change the fundamentals of the State such as the monarchy or even the existence of Parliament itself cannot in any fruitrul sense be said to have a Constitution. So Strasbourg is at present the only real protection which the law affords and for this very reason it is such a great pity that the decisions of the Strasbourg Court are so unbelievably poor. I have written about the Sunday Times case,[188] and I [199] gave a lecture in Cambridge about a series of other decisions which seem to be quite extraordinary such as the Irish case in which it was held, in effect, that there exists a human right to legal aid! I am convinced that English judges could apply the Convention much more sensibly and this is the reason why I am strongly in favour of making it part of English law. The opposition against such a step is great. The fact that the very people who refuse to entrust the English judiciary with the application of the Convention have, without parliamentary sanction, entrusted the Strasbourg authorities with supervisory powers is, I venture to believe, one of the greatest oddities that ever occurred. It is

---

187  (1978) 94 L.Q.R. 512
188  95 (1979) L.Q.R. 348

Paralegomena                                                                **241**

a subject which, like the Strasbourg Convention and its application as a whole, is well worth while continuous and intensive study.

\* \* \*

When I said that, subject to two exceptions, I strictly confined my academic work to three subjects, I should have made it clear that even within these subjects I felt it necessary to be selective. Thus, in so far as the conflict of laws is concerned, I have for many years left family law aside, – it is a subject which is too far removed from my practical experience. As regards public international law this has become so vast a subject that no one can nowadays have a command of the whole. I decided not to do any work on what I may call political international law, that international law which is connected with the United Nations, with political conflicts, the limitation of arms, space law and so forth. In short I have tried to specialise in what I may describe as (public and private) international commercial law. In fact the seminar which for more than twenty years I held every summer at Bonn University and a course of lectures which I gave there from time to time was called "Internationales Wirtschaftsrecht", – a mixture of public and private international law comprising that large field which is on the borderline of both subjects. It is this branch of the law which has become pecularly my own and practically everything I did in recent years relates to it. My three courses at The Hague Academy (1959, 1964, 1971) belong to it: *Money in Public International Law, The Doctrine of Jurisdiction in International Law, Public Law and the Conflict of Laws.* But the same applies to many other contributions such as *The Interpretation of Uniform Laws,*[189] *The Consequence of an International Wrong,*[190] – to mention only one of the earliest and one of the latest articles on the subject. In this connection I must also mention my work on the law governing State Contracts, i. e. contracts between States and private persons. I may claim that I "invented" the subject, when my often-neglected article in the British Year Book of International Law of 1944 appeared. In particular I "invented" there the distinction between the "commercialisation" of treaty law and the "internationalisation" of contract law. I developed my views in another article in the British Year Book of International Law of 1959 (which at the same time [200] appeared in German in the *Festschrift* für Max Gutzwiller). I may claim that the enormous amount of later work which was done by numerous authors writing in many different languages is largely built on my contributions on the subject. It is, however, fascinating to observe how great the cleavage is between public and private international lawyers. When they discuss these particular questions (as

---

189  (1946) 62 L.Q.R. 278
190  British Yearbook of International Law 1976-7, 1.

# 242 Paralegomena

the elite of international lawyers did in the course of the sessions of the Institut de Droit International Law in Oslo in 1977 and Athens in 1979) it becomes apparent how difficult it is for them to understand each other. In Athens I had to intervene to save the discussion from becoming completely confused and subsequent speakers made it clear that up to my intervention they had hardly understood whether people were talking about public or private international law or about both.

The reason, of course, is that these subjects are everywhere taught and studied by different scholars, hardly ever by the same. In most continental countries public international lawyers are public lawyers who also teach constitutional and administrative law, never private interntional law. Private international lawyers are private lawyers who are usually wholly unfamiliar with public international law. This is the real cause of the enormous amount of misunderstanding which is peculiar to discussions on the borderline problems and which I have done my best to clear away. Unfortunately I cannot see any change occurring anywhere, – there are very few if any who seem able or willing to continue the work I have initiated.

There are two other examples of the interconnection between public and private international law which are worth mentioning.

The foreign Act of State is a most puzzling doctrine. In 1943 I suggested that its origin was to be found in sovereign immunity *ratione materiae* and that its scope was therefore very limited.[191] In 1975 it seemed that the Court of Appeal (and Lord Denning in particular) tended to share this view.[192] But in 1981 the House of Lords created an almost unbelievable confusion.[193] In the meantime the Supreme Court of the United States had declared that the doctrine did not belong to international law at all, but had "constitutional underpinnings" (whatever this may mean).[194] It is also said to be a concomitant of that judicial restraint which, as the House of Lords discovered in 1981, is allegedly appropriate (and permitted) in cases of an international character. These indications, I hope, are sufficient to establish the close interrelationship between public and private international law within the realm of this doctrine: the prevailing view is that it precludes the court from questioning the validity of a foreign Act of State or what are called transactions between States, – an international problem; my suggestion was and is that a court is entitled and bound to investigate the validity of a foreign Act of State to [200] the extent to which the proper law, governing it and applicable under conflict rules, would do so. It is a very esoteric problem and many aspects of it,

---

191 (1943) 59 L.Q.R. 42, 155.
192 Above p.
193 Above p.
194 Sabbatino v.

Paralegomena    **243**

such as the constitutional validity of foreign legislation, are unlikely to occur in practice.

Infinitely greater importance has to be attached to the doctrine of jurisdiction, – a doctrine which pervades the whole of a State's legislation and which, therefore, raises its head everywhere and at almost every point: to what extent is it open to a State to legislate with effect upon events or persons outside its own territory? The problem arises in many fields such as criminal law, taxation, bankruptcy, dealings in securities, but it is nowhere of more immediate interest than in connection with anti-trust legislation. The American courts have given it an unacceptably wide interpretation so as to render it applicable whenever anything done in any part of the world by persons of any nationality has substantial economic effect in the United States. It is easy to see that such a view has produced much international friction and provoked numerous and varying counter-measures. Politically, therefore, it is an unhealthy doctrine. It has been criticised by many European scholars most of whom in substance follow the views put forward by me in my Hague lectures of 1964,[195] but the problem is unsolved and is likely to remain so until the United States changes its law or an international tribunal condemns its legislation as interpreted by its courts. The latter solution does not seem likely, the former depends on economic forces: in the last resort the American practice is an emanation of the pax Americana, the idea that American power pervades the world and is entitled to assert itself and to be respected everywhere. For 25 years after the end of the war the world in fact had to obey or, to put it less crudely, to accept American wishes. Since the early 1970's this has changed and it may be, therefore, that the United States will have to restrict its attempt to regulate by the observance of American law the commercial practices of the world. In law that attempt is, I am convinced, wholly untenable, and at the same time highly dangerous to national trading interests.

* * *

I have mentioned unfulfilled hopes about certain research work such as the law of expropriation. There is one field of public international law in which I started some work, but unfortunately have so far not been able to continue it and again no-one else has taken it up in any serious way. In 1957 I published in the British Year Book of International Law an article under the title *Reflections on a Commercial Law of Nations*. My principal aim was to draw attention to the enormous amount of international law, whether customary or conventional, which relates to trade between nations and which can only be [202] found and developed by resorting to the analogy of private law or, in other words, by application of the

---

195 Above p. n.

general principles of law ascertained on a broad comparative basis. I suggested that it was sufficient to study the law of representative nations and that the object was to find an identity or similarity of result, irrespective of the methods employed to reach it. I exemplified my suggestions by reference to a number of striking cases. The article which later appeared in German in a slightly extended version was of a programmatic character. From time to time I considered continuing work on the subject. In preparation of it I have for almost thirty years collected practically all Treaties which the United Kingdom concluded about commercial relations, such as treaties of loan, sale, barter, exchange of information, agency and so forth. But there have hardly been any disputes and even fewer decisions of courts or arbitrators. Consequently one has to think up problems which may arise, but have not in fact arisen. This gives to the work a somewhat artificial connotation and is an additional reason why I have shied away from a task which in any event is daunting and requires the strength and energy of a younger man.

Another solution which I contemplated for some time was to organise a comprehensive work by a team of experts which would analyse the international law relating to the various subjects, – a treatise on world trade law. But, again, in view of my many other commitments I felt unable to undertake the organisation of so far-reaching a venture. The effect is that an interesting subject of growing importance has not been studied with the intensity it requires and deserves. I refer to it in the present context, because I hope that some scholars who may come across these lines will be stimulated into continuing what I began.

It is only fair to add that the type of work I have been describing could not have been done without Sir Hersch Lauterpacht's fundamental studies on *Private Law Analogies in Public International Law*.[196] He pointed the way more clearly than anyone else to the productive force of comparative law. At the time when I was working on the Commercial Law of Nations I gave a lecture on the subject at the Max Planck Institute of Foreign and Comparative Law in Hamburg and I remember my astonishment at the fact that among these experts in comparative law Lauterpacht's work was completely unknown. It was the work of a public international lawyer and private lawyers, so the theory goes on the Continent, are not supposed to be familiar with so strange and remote a subject.

It may be that there exists another distinction between comparative law in England and on the Continent. In England, it may be fair to say with a measure of generalisation, comparative law is recognised as a method for the solution of practical problems, one of the most significant being the general principles [203] of law which are a source of public international law. On the Continent comparative law is a branch of the law which is self-serving. I do not think that an

---

196

English student would ever be expected to write a paper or a thesis on the law of, say, compensating commercial agents for the termination of their contract of employment in German law. What is the relevance of compiling material, describing the details or pointing out the uncertainties in German law on the point? But such subjects which are of no immediate interest to German law, are very popular with many German professors who, I fear, treat comparative law as a matter of description rather than purposive exploitation or evaluation.

My academic work which I have been discussing has a feature about it which I believe is unusual: almost all of it has proceeded in a state of complete intellectual isolation.

Most academics have the support of their University behind them. They enjoy the facilities and privileges which Universities provide, such as libraries, the right to take books home, the right to research or secretarial assistance and so forth. But, above all, academics usually have their colleagues to whom they can talk, with whom they are at liberty to discuss their ideas, who are likely to make suggestions or criticism, who may be willing to read a manuscript. In the early years of my life I enjoyed intimate contact of this type with Sir Hersch Lauterpacht before he went to the Hague and with Otto Kahn-Freund until he became more and more engrossed in fields of the law which are alien to me, such as labour law, family law, comparative law as an independent subject rather than a tool. We used to read each other's manuscripts and have innumerable discussions about our respective work, but for some reason this came to an end and left me alone. No wonder that, as I have been told, students at English Universities were left under the impression that I was an old man with a long white beard who lived somewhere in the wilds of Wales and wrote esoteric articles in order to torture and annoy undergraduates!

There is another feature which in this connection I must mention and which may cause some surprise. I have never had a study of my own. All my work was done in our drawing room, frequently while the family or visitors were talking and I sat at my desk with my back towards them, immune to their talk, yet from time to time hearing snippets. While the children were at home this arrangement was inevitable, because we did not have a room which could have served as a study. Later it would have been possible to turn one room into a study, but this would have made it necessary not only to change the telephone, but also to transfer my record-player to the new study, for without listening to my records I could not do any work. Music was at all times an inspiration to me and a necessary concomitant of my working hours. Moreover, I disliked the idea of being cut off from the family, while I was working "at home". I wanted to feel that, [204] though I was reading, thinking or writing, I was part of the family and its interests. The drawing room-cum-study meant a state of untidiness and provoked many

**246** Paralegomena

discussions about possible improvements, but so far everything has remained as it has been for years.

I have mentioned music which accompanied my working hours at home, – chamber music mainly, no opera music. My large collection of records has been a continuous source of pleasure and peace. I cannot now imagine a life without almost continuous music in the house and I am pleased to say that my children have adopted the same style of life. Already while they were at school, they used to work with classical music pouring into their ears.

Although music was and is a wonderful companion, my intellectual loneliness was at all times a much more serious matter than the reader of these pages may imagine. Very often I have suffered as a result of the lack of any contact with academic lawyers. I certainly saw a lot of Mark Litmann and Michael Kerr and for many decades used to walk with them in Kensington Gardens, usually on a Sunday morning. But brilliant lawyers though they are, neither of them is really interested in theory or has the background of theoretical knowledge without which a discussion of the type so badly needed by me can be conducted. So I remained alone, – in discovering and thinking about the themes I proposed to work about in finding the material, in developing my ideas, in testing the views put forward by other scholars, in formulating my solutions. One gets used to this state of affairs, as one presumably gets used to everything, but it is always a hard and sad experience. When, perhaps somewhat unexpectedly, the work is done and one feels it to be reasonably satisfactory, the joy is great, probably greater if it had been done in more usual conditions.

\* \* \*

I have now reached the point at which, I believe, my loquacious reminiscing should come to an end.

England and Germany, practice and academic work, scholar in England and teacher in Germany as well as lecturer elsewhere, instructing solicitor in England and counsel abroad, – these were the signs which marked the double life. Had not Hitler's murderous hand and the always present memory of Auschwitz lain heavily upon it, it would have been a happy life. It certainly was a successful life if it is measured by signs of recognition by governments and academic institutions, by the development of my three children and eight grandchildren, by the friendships I formed and which in many cases survived periods of the most severe adversity. If I ask myself what is the most important lesson which my life teaches the answer, I believe, is one that will come as a surprise to many: it is that there is time for everything or, in other words, nothing will have to remain undone on the ground that there is no time for it.

I did not miss many of the usual pleasures and activities of life. We travelled a lot and had our holidays, attended international congresses, went to the theatre and concerts, read significant books, saw friends and, though we became very selective and economical with our time, we missed nothing of interest or importance. Yet I found that the evenings and weekends are long and can be usefully employed if you do not prefer running after tennis, golf or footballs and do not subscribe to the ill-founded idea that your free time should be devoted to sport or outdoor activities such as gardening, – which can much better be done by a gardener. If you organize your life intelligently: there is nothing that you cannot achieve, – lack of time usually is an excuse rather than a reality. Perhaps it is this modest lesson which my life teaches.

# Select Bibliography

Lawrence Collins, 'Dr F. A. Mann: His Work and Influence', (1993) 64 *British Year Book of International Law* 55.

Lawrence Collins, 'Francis Alexander Mann, 1907–1991', (1994) 84 *Proceedings of the British Academy* 393.

Lawrence Collins, 'F. A. Mann (1907–1991)', in: J. Beatson/R. Zimmermann (eds.), *Jurists Uprooted. German Speaking Émigré Lawyers in Twentieth-century Britain*, Oxford 2003, 382.

Gerhart Dannemann/Christoph König/Franziska Stamm, *The Correspondence of Frederick Alexander Mann (1907–1991)*, British Institute of European and Comparative Law, London 2020.

R.F.J.I., Art. 'Mann, Frederick (Francis) Alexander', in: W. Röder/ H. A. Strauss (eds.), *Biographisches Handbuch der deutschsprachigen Emigration nach 1933 / International Biographical Dictionary of Central European Emigrés 1933–1945*, vol. II, part 2, Munich/ New York/London 1983, 769.

Horst Heinrich Jakobs, 'Frederick Alexander Mann', in: J. Pietzcker et al. (eds.); 'In Memoriam Frederick Alexander Mann', (1992) 77 *Alma Mater* 9 = idem, *Gedenkreden auf Frederick Alexander Mann, Brigitte Knobbe-Keuk und Werner Flume*, Göttingen 2011 (Bonner Rechtswissenschaftliche Abhandlungen, n. F. 8), 11.

Geoffrey Lewis, *F.A. Mann. A Memoir*, London 2014.

Obituaries: The Times, 19 Sept. 1991 (anon.); The Guardian, 20.9.1991 (Sir [later Lord] Leonhard Hoffmann); The Independent, 25 September 1991 (Mark Littmann QC).

Printed in the United States
by Baker & Taylor Publisher Services